THE
UNBREAKABLE
BOY

Center Point
Large Print

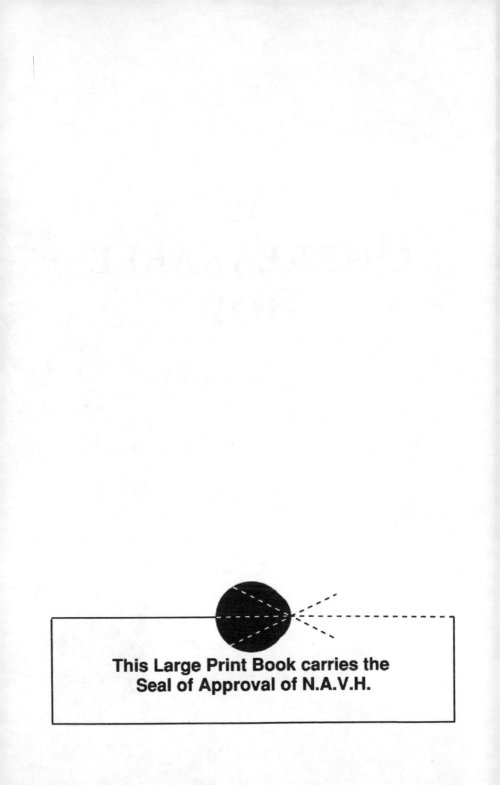

**This Large Print Book carries the
Seal of Approval of N.A.V.H.**

THE
UNBREAKABLE
BOY

A Father's Fear, a Son's Courage,
and a Story of Unconditional Love

SCOTT MICHAEL LERETTE
WITH SUSY FLORY

CENTER POINT LARGE PRINT
THORNDIKE, MAINE

This Center Point Large Print edition
is published in the year 2015 by arrangement with
Thomas Nelson.

The text of this Large Print edition is unabridged. In other aspects,
this book may vary from the original edition.
Printed in the United States of America on permanent paper.
Set in 16-point Times New Roman type.

ISBN: 978-1-62899-545-9

Library of Congress Cataloging-in-Publication Data

LeRette, Scott Michael, 1964–
  The unbreakable boy : a father's fear, a son's courage, and a story of
unconditional love / Scott Michael LeRette ; with Susy Flory. — Center
point large print edition.
  pages cm
  Originally published: Nashville, Tennessee : Nelson Books, 2014.
  Summary: "A father shares his autistic son's story and offers inspiration
and advice for families facing similar challenges"—Provided by publisher.
  ISBN 978-1-62899-545-9 (library binding : alk. paper)
  1. LeRette, Austin. 2. LeRette, Scott Michael, 1964–
    3. Osteogenesis imperfecta—Patients—United States—Biography.
    4. Autistic children—United States—Biography.
    5. Heart—Abnormalities—Patients—United States—Biography.
    6. Fathers and sons—United States. 7. Love, Paternal—United States.
    8. Large type books. I. Flory, Susy, 1965— II. Title.
RJ482.O82L47 2015
618.92´858820092—dc23
[B]
                                                              2015003351

This is for Teresa, Logan, and Austin
We are fighting the good fight
We will finish the course
And keep the faith

2 TIM. 4:7, AUTHOR'S PARAPHRASE

CONTENTS

A NOTE FROM AUSTIN LeRETTE

My name is Austin. Richard Austin LeRette. But you can call me Auz. That's a true fact. When I meet new people, I tell them everything.

I've broken so many bones. I broke my back two times. I have osteogenesis imperfecta. I am not sure what this is; all I know is that my bones break real easy.

When I was little I had something wrong with my heart too, and the surgeons had to crack my chest open, fix it, and then wire me back together.

I also have autism. Autism stinks. Some autistic kids can't talk but I can. Sometimes I make up words. It calms me down to say words over and over again. Sometimes I say bad words, and I have a hard time listening. I wish it would stop. I wish I was a better person. People don't understand how much I try. I freak out over little things and get mad a lot when feelings come.

I don't like my diseases. Logan is the lucky one because he can ride a dirt bike or skateboard. He's so lucky. No autism. Sometimes I wish Mom could just put me back in her belly so I could get born all over again and maybe my genes would change.

Dad says the odds of a person having brittle

bone disease, heart defects, and autism are 1 in a billion. "I can prove you are special," he says. But I don't want to be special. I just want to be like every other dude.

Nothing hurts right now. I don't hurt every day, only every other day. My back hurts some days. My head hurts. My legs and my feet hurt. Sometimes I can't block it out. But if I have a good day, I'm very happy. Like the day I had the best strawberry milkshake in the world. I kept trying and trying to explain how good it tasted to my dad.

Loud music makes me feel good. Eating does too. Especially when I dip things in ranch dressing. Cooking calms me down, and I want to be a chef someday. I'm going to open my own hotel with a restaurant called Auzzie's Grand Diner. I'll wear a big chef's hat and apron and have butlers serving food. My special dish will be called "Heart Attack Ravioli."

I'm a happy person with a crummy disease, but it doesn't slow me down too much.

I love everybody. By the way, want to be my Facebook friend? And then how about a sleepover at my house? We can watch Back to the Future. I love you. Do you know that? Please, thank you, you're welcome, I love you.

I have a hat collection, a music poster collection, and a shoelace collection. I take lots of showers, and I like to dress up with a jacket, shirt, tie, and hat. Wearing just the right hat makes my day. Once in a while when Dad sees how I'm dressed, he goes back upstairs and changes.

Dad says sometimes I am the one teaching and he is the one learning.

Whatever, Dad.

Right now it's time to go find him. Sometimes my dad hides from me.

Come on, Dad. I know you're in the closet. Where are you, Daddy-O?

THE
UNBREAKABLE
BOY

1

IN THE CLOSET

Your joy is your sorrow unmasked. . . .
The deeper that sorrow carves into your being,
The more joy you can contain.
—KHALIL GIBRAN

I sit cowering in my closet, the one place I find refuge. Life is hard, really, really hard, and sometimes this is the only place I can find a few minutes to ease my brain and recalibrate my soul. Go ahead and laugh. A grown man hiding in a closet like a little kid.

But even though I'm a dad and Austin is my son, I often feel like a child because I feel so helpless. Austin sees things differently, and I wish I could climb inside his brain and understand why he does the things he does. Some days it's like we're playing two different video games with two different controllers and two different sets of rules in two different virtual universes. I get frustrated. We all do.

Tonight is worse than usual. I'm scared and unsure what to do next as I sit on a kiddie chair alone in the dark, trembling and thinking and analyzing. I relive that night again. I can't get it out of my brain.

15

My stomach tightens, and I feel sick as I remember standing in the men's room at the country club, drunk as I'd ever been. I couldn't stop staring at the man in the mirror. I raised my hands and tried to touch his burning eyes.

I wanted to keep believing this was all normal and life was just fine, but the man looking back at me was someone else—lost, alone, and at the point of destruction. I didn't know who I was anymore, and I felt empty, like a lifeless cicada shell stuck on a post. I stumbled back into the dining room, the lights beating into my brain.

I have to get out of this place. Everyone is looking at me, and they just don't understand.

As the awful memory unfolds, I grab my two boys and stumble out to the parking lot, heading for the car. Then I forget how to walk. My keys go flying, and I am on the ground, staring at the rocks stuck in my palms. I have gravel in my knees too. I look up at the moon and laugh, out of my mind, hands bleeding and snot bursting from my nose.

Nothing makes sense. I laugh even harder when a random man helps me to my feet and hands over my keys.

"Be careful," he says.

"Sure. I'm fine. No problem."

I zigzag to the car. We get in.

"Dad, are you okay?" Logan asks. "Daddy?"

I work the key into the ignition, start the car,

and step on the gas. As we turn on the highway, I push the pedal all the way to the floor.

"Daddy?" Logan asks again.

I can't remember anything that happens after that. Everything is gone. Black.

Much later, alone with my memories in the closet, I rock back and forth like Austin does sometimes, the tears running down my cheeks as I remember the next morning, the thoughts screaming through my hungover brain.

What have I done?
Did I kill my boys?
Oh my God.

2

THE GIRL WITH
THE BLUE EYES

Love isn't something you find.
Love is something that finds you.
—LORETTA YOUNG

Life was good—I was twenty-nine years old, an Iowa boy living in Charlotte, North Carolina. When I first met Teresa, I thought she was pretty cute, but she thought I was gay. I was blessed with considerable self-esteem, so it didn't bother me too much. I had a great sales job, I lived in the newest and trendiest apartment complex, and I spent most afternoons exploring the awesome trails around the Piedmont on my mountain bike.

One cold winter day my friend Gary and I wandered into Structure, a trendy clothing store at Carolina Place Mall. I was sporting Bermuda shorts in multicolored stripes, a dark T-shirt with a hoodie on top, penny loafers, and round, wire-rimmed glasses. Part jock, part prep, part dork with a dash of romantic fool in the mix, I was also ex-navy and strutted a little when I walked. I've always been positive and happy-go-lucky with a streak of toughness—I never back down from a fight.

In college I could hammer out 330 pounds on the bench press, but even though I couldn't lift that much anymore and I wasn't very tall, I was in great shape. The girls seemed to like my dark blond hair and green eyes and told me I was cute and sweet and genuine. I liked my life just the way it was.

Teresa took one look at me in my funky outfit accompanied by tall, tan, and buff Gary and thought, *Gay*. She started joking around with us, picked out an awful pea-green sports coat, and kept trying to sell it to me. She was tiny, cute, and loved to laugh. And then there were those eyes. They were the color of the Atlantic, and even the whites were blue.

She wouldn't give up trying to sell me the ugly green coat, and we started talking. We discovered we both liked eating out, clubbing, and the musical *Cats*. I bragged about my new Calphalon cookware. And we both loved anything having to do with Italy. In Teresa's mind, I was her new best girlfriend.

Two days later I came back by myself, this time in more respectable Levi's 501 jeans, an L.L.Bean fleece pullover, and my killer black lizard Tony Llamas. Man, did I look good! I brought a gift—I'd made her a recording of the soundtrack for *Cats*.

Our first dinner was at the Epicurean restaurant. Teresa was still a little confused about my sexual orientation, but when I kissed her good night, it officially became a date.

I was casually interested, and we ended up seeing each other a few times over the next several weeks. I liked her, but I didn't even know her last name.

Then I got a phone call that changed my life. You know the kind? The game-changer call, the one that turns you upside down and shakes you?

I'd left work early to get some things done before heading out of town on business. I had some paperwork in hand and was lounging half out of my recliner, my leg slung over the side. The phone on my desk buzzed. I looked over at the caller ID display and liked what I saw.

Teresa. Cool.

I smiled, tossed the papers down, and punched the Talk button.

"Hello?"

"Hey, Scott. I'm having some medical things done. You know, just some routine stuff." Teresa's voice was rushed, thin, a little out of breath. "It's not that big of a deal. But, umm . . . can you run by the hospital and take a blood test?"

What?

Her voice was like a hammer to my chest, and when the shock went through my body, I flopped out of my chair and crashed to the floor. On the way down I hit my head on the edge of the desk, hard. The cordless phone bounced somewhere under the desk. I lay there, trying to understand what was happening. And I knew it couldn't be good.

Man. My life is over.

It was 1994 and AIDS was all over the news. Millions of people had this horrible blood disease, and they all died. There was no cure.

I'd grown up in the Catholic church and knew all about the dangers of sin, but Teresa was a beautiful girl and our chemistry was strong. We'd gone on several dates, some of them sleepovers. Now I was going to pay.

She must have AIDS, and I do too. Now I'm going to die.

With my bashed head throbbing and adrenaline pumping through my veins, I flailed around under the desk, trying to find the phone.

Oh, God. What have I done?

I finally located the phone, tried to stop hyperventilating, and took a deep breath.

Slow down, Scott. Maybe it's just routine. Maybe it's no big deal.

I thought I'd heard a little catch in Teresa's voice. *Is she crying?* But I was completely unprepared for what came next.

"Scott, I'm pregnant."

I turned over, threw my arms out to each side, and stared up at the underside of my desk. This time I hung on to the phone, my hand gripping it like a lifeline.

"I didn't want to bother you, and I knew this would ruin your life," Teresa said. "I know you're a good person, and you don't need to get involved. We don't even know each other." I was silent as her sweet Southern voice spiked each word into my heart.

I lifted my head a few inches off the ground and for some reason flashed back to a few weeks before. My mother had been in town, and I'd taken her to meet Teresa. I remembered Teresa had looked thinner; I told her how great she looked and asked if she'd been working out.

Ouch! My head fell back again as I realized she'd already been pregnant. With my baby.

"I just need you to do this blood work." Teresa's voice sounded stronger now. "I'm going to have this baby. Just do this and we can get on with our lives."

I must have said something to Teresa and clicked off the call, but I can't remember. When I finally rolled over and pushed myself up off the floor and onto my knees, I went into some kind of fog. My heart was pounding. I realize I should've been worrying about Teresa and the baby, but I wasn't.

This is messed up. There is no way I can be a dad. I don't even know this girl. And she's the reason my life is over.

I pulled myself up, then dropped back into my recliner. I took a deep breath, held it, and breathed out. But did I come to my senses? No. I hate to admit it now, but I was just thinking of one very important person. Me.

I am not happy about this. I have yet to sow my oats. This is not fair. I deserve better than this. And it all coalesced down into one sharp, undeniable urge.

I need a beer. Or three.

Later Teresa told me how she discovered she was pregnant. She had been getting ready for work one day when she suddenly doubled over in pain. She drove herself to the emergency room where tests showed a benign tumor in her ovaries. Her doctor recommended immediate surgery, but he said tests showed something else —Teresa was pregnant!

Teresa had no idea; she hadn't experienced any signs of pregnancy. And because of some pre-existing health issues, she didn't think she could even get pregnant. In shock, she kept the news to herself, had surgery to remove the tumor, and went home a few days later. The unborn baby, our baby, came through it all okay. Did I visit her in the hospital? No, I was out riding my bike, still blissfully unaware I was going to be a father.

Teresa felt unprepared for motherhood, and she made an appointment for an abortion. "I swore I would never have kids and here I was, twenty-seven years old, just met this guy, fell hard for him, and couldn't believe I was pregnant," she later told me. She felt alone and afraid and wasn't sure how she could make it all work. But she couldn't go through with the abortion. *I can't end the life of this baby God gave me,* she thought and canceled the appointment.

This all happened around the time my mother was visiting. Teresa didn't tell me about the baby then because she didn't want to ruin my visit with my mother. It was a few weeks later that Teresa told me she was pregnant, and I fell out of my chair and into a very different life from my carefree, before-the-phone-call life.

I had always been the black sheep of the family. I was my mama's boy, but I was also the one my three brothers called the screwup. "What'd he do this time?" was the phrase that usually followed the word Scott. I never got in real trouble; I just tended to make poor choices and didn't think enough or look too far ahead before I leapt.

I didn't really know much about this beautiful Southern belle who was about to be the mother of my child, and that needed to change. A few days later, when the shock had worn off, I bought a baby bottle, stuck a daisy in it, and took it over to Teresa's house. "I like you and want to get to know you better," I said. "I want to be a part of the baby's life."

I never did go in for the blood test, but soon Teresa was healthy again, and we started spending more time together and making some plans for the baby. One day I gathered my courage and told Teresa that I loved her.

Being in a serious relationship was uncharted territory for me, and I didn't know how to handle it. I don't think I really loved her. I wanted to love her, but I didn't know how. One day Teresa had a migraine. I didn't know about her headache, played my music too loud, and we had a disagreement. Then I got mad and took back my *I love you.*

I could have handled that better. I had a lot to learn. And now I *really* needed that beer.

I was havin' a baby.

3
TRADING JABS
WITH JOE

When a child is born, a father is born.
—FREDERICK BUECHNER

Right before I got off the plane, I started tapping my toes inside my shoes. First two taps on the left, two on the right. Then three taps on the left, three taps on the right. However many times I tap on one side, I have to tap on the other. I've always done this. It helps me stay calm, and I was about to step off the plane into the cool Omaha air and hop in a car to drive to Red Oak, Iowa. I was going to break the news to my family. I silently practiced the words *I'm going to be a father.*

Then Joe started giving me a hard time.

"You're really in a fine mess, ya big dork," Joe said.

"Dude, I'm not sure how this will go." Four taps on the left, four on the right. "I'm a dead man walking."

"Runnin' home to Mommy and Daddy?"

"Uh-huh. That's exactly what I'm doing, my man. Running home," I said. "I know what to do."

I often traded jabs with an imaginary friend I'd had since I was a kid. The first time Mom heard this running dialogue, she named my invisible friend Joe. She always gave me a lot of grief about our lively, sometimes loud conversations, but I often talked to Joe when I was trying to figure things out.

As usual, I felt pretty positive and optimistic about the future. I knew I would have to grow up, and I had always wanted to be a dad. But first I needed to go home to my own mom and dad for comfort and a shoulder to cry on. I was my mama's boy, and I knew she would put a good spin on whatever I could throw her way.

I did worry, just for a moment, that she would flip out and react like her mother, Ruth. We affectionately called my Grandma Ruthie "The Battle Axe." She was one tough lady, shepherding an enormous Catholic family and keeping the kids in line while enduring life with her hard-working and hard-drinking Irish husband, Gus. We all adored Grandpa Gus, but Grandma ruled the roost.

My mom, Marcia (or *Mawsha*, as everyone called her), was tough too. When it came to meting out punishment in our house, it was Mom, not Dad, who swung the heavy wooden spoon. She also used to twist her rings around her fingers so the stones were facing palm side and whack us boys on the head. Even though she was petite (I used to say she was four foot twelve), we had good reason to call her "The Warden."

I was the third of four boys. My father made a good living running the family appliance store where my brothers helped sell washers, dryers, refrigerators, and stoves to fill the houses of Red Oak. My brothers used to say I didn't have to work as hard as they did and I always got everything I wanted. I did work hard at school and made good grades, but I was a little ADD-ish and learned to tap my toes or hum quietly to keep myself focused.

After high school I headed off to the University of Oklahoma, graduating with a degree in business administration. I wanted an adventure so I signed with the navy and was accepted to Aviation Officer Candidate School in Pensacola, Florida. After two years in the navy, I was discharged for severe vertigo and motion sickness. You can't be too useful in a navy jet if you're dizzy, blind, and vomiting. No hard feelings, Uncle Sam. I always thought Dad and my oldest brother, Kevin, who made a career out of the navy, loved the idea of me being in the navy more than I did.

I took a job in sales for a giant pharmaceutical company called Allergan, which was how I ended up in North Carolina. *I've never been there, so why not?* I thought when I heard about the open sales territory. I kept in close touch with my family, though. The LeRettes are a tight clan.

What are they going to say about the baby? I wondered. They don't know Teresa. But then, neither do I.

When I drove up to my parents' home, a large, two-story, white frame house, I practically held my breath while my mom and dad hugged me. I followed them inside and sat down at the table with Mom for a glass of pop. Dad wandered out to his workshop in the garage. He is probably a little ADD-ish too.

I did a little toe tapping and let out a big breath. While she is tiny and cute with a friendly smile, The Warden is a staunch Catholic, and I was terrified she would judge me harshly.

"Mom." My toes were tapping furiously now. "I need to tell you something. You remember Teresa? That girl with the pretty blue eyes?"

Her eyes widened and locked onto mine.

"Well, she's pregnant. We're going to have a baby."

It's always a shock when your mom lets loose a string of expletives, but she did, calling me "stupid" and a lot of other things I can't repeat here. After that first blast of anger and disappointment, she downed her glass of Pepsi, set it down on the table with a thump, and started into the real business.

"When is the baby due?"

Okay, I can answer that one.

"What are you going to do about this?"

Umm . . . I don't know. Be a father?

"Do you love her?"

That's the one I dreaded. I didn't know if I loved Teresa. I did like her. She was beautiful and funny and smart and feisty. She was going to be the mother of my child. But did I love her? I didn't really know what that meant. I'd already tried the *I love you* thing, and it hadn't worked out too well.

I sat up straight and waited for the second wave, where Mom would grill me about *this girl,* her family, her intentions, and more. But it never happened. Instead, Mom told me she loved me, said I was going to be a good father, and she and my dad heaped encouragement on me all weekend.

When I got back on the plane, I started feeling better about being a dad. It wasn't happening the way I'd thought it would, but I was going to be a daddy and Mother Mawsha was cool with it.

When I got back home, I got a call from Mom about Grandma Ruthie. For some reason I was more scared about how Grandma would react than anyone else. But Mom said Grandma was very happy for me, knew I would be a great dad, and couldn't wait to see my baby. All was good in Red Oak, Iowa.

Back in North Carolina, my friendship with Teresa grew, along with her belly. We moved in to an apartment together, set up a room for the baby, and began to act more like a couple, doing things like taking Saturday trips to Virginia with friends for golf or going on picnics. Teresa cooked and cleaned and even made me a birthday cake. I took to calling her "T," her nickname with her friends. But I still rode my mountain bike and socialized with Gary and my other friends when I could. I still liked to hang out at clubs and drink. But some-thing was different. While my friends continued their carefree partying ways, I started to think more about the future. And that future included some very big surprises.

For one thing, I found out why Teresa had such dazzling blue eyes. One night she explained, "I have a rare bone disease. It's called osteogenesis imperfecta (OI), or brittle bone disease. My collagen doesn't work right, and my body can't make strong bones. That's why my eyes are so blue—OI causes the whites of my eyes, the sclera, to be so thin that the blue arteries show through and create the blue glow."

That is so cool, I thought. *I wonder if the baby will have those blue eyes?*

"I have Type 1 and have been able to live a pretty normal life so far," she said. "I'm not supposed to do contact sports, and I can't go skydiving."

Okay, I can handle that.

"When I was in a baby walker, before I was

one, I broke my leg. Then I kept breaking bones. My parents didn't know what was wrong. Finally, when I was thirteen, I went to the eye doctor. He noticed the whites of my eyes were blue and sent me to a specialist. I was finally diagnosed with OI. There's a fifty-fifty chance I'll pass it on to the baby, but it's not a big deal," she reassured me. "It won't be an issue."

I listened but didn't think much about it and decided to worry if and when the time came.

In the fall, about a month before the baby was due, I rolled over in the dark and asked, "Why don't we get married?"

"I love you, but I can't marry you right now," she said. "I will one day, but not right now."

I was crushed, confused, and yet a little relieved. Although I wouldn't admit it, I was petrified at the thought of getting married. But I had mixed feelings and, at the same time, I couldn't understand why Teresa didn't want to get married when we were about to have a baby and start a family. Deep down I had a feeling she was hiding something, but I had no idea what it was.

One day Teresa's Braxton Hicks contractions, the mild ones you usually don't have to worry about, grew stronger, so we grabbed our bags and I got Teresa to the hospital. After a prolonged period of labor, the contractions finally began to come stronger and faster. As Teresa began pushing, I stood by the bed, images flashing through my brain like a hyper-speed PowerPoint presentation. I thought of my family, my friends, and even the pea-green sports coat. My brain was on stimulation overload as I tried to comprehend just how much my world had changed over the past nine months and how Teresa and I were about to be connected forever as parents.

I was astonished at Teresa's strength. She crushed my hand with hers and held on tight, then looked me dead in the eyes. She didn't say anything, just stared into my eyes as she pushed. No words were necessary. I'm not exactly sure what was happening but the air between us was electric. I wept. Then I saw a tuft of blond hair. My son.

The baby's head was now in full view. More tears ran down my cheeks, the feelings overwhelming me. Delivery was slow; the umbilical cord was wrapped around the baby's throat so they tried suction, then forceps to pull him out. I could barely stand to look at the shiny metal instrument. I remember thinking, *Oh my God! Are they going to use those on my son?*

But the forceps worked and shortly after that, Baby Austin burst into the world. He was blue at first, but he quickly turned pink and started wailing. His head was pointed from the forceps. Teresa, haunted by the possibility of passing on her OI, kept asking, "Does he have any broken bones?"

But Richard Austin LeRette was perfect. He was seven pounds, eleven ounces, and loud.

I could hardly see him through the tears—I was elated, a big, bawling mess. Teresa looked peaceful and beautiful. As our son snuggled with his mommy, all I felt was joy.

I am a father.

November 10, 1994, was the most important day of my life and a day I will never forget. We'd started off on a journey that neither of us planned, and we couldn't yet know the thrill ride ahead, but at least we'd be in it together. Even if we barely knew each other.

4

THE BOX

The best thing a father can do for
his children is to love their mother.
—JOHN WOODEN

I was sitting on the end of the bed, clutching
Baby Austin tight against my chest and gently
bouncing him up and down, or *bouncy-bounce,*
as we called it. I was tired. But every time I tried
to lower him down into the bassinet, slip my
hands out, and sneak away, he'd wake up and
start wailing. It was as if he had a motion sensor
on his body and anytime he lost physical contact
with either Teresa or me, the alarm went off.

But even Austin's crying couldn't dampen my
spirits. I was floating, thrilled to be a new dad,
and couldn't take my eyes off my son. When
Teresa wasn't nursing him or changing him, we
took turns holding and rocking him. Neither of us
was sleeping much and it was rough on Teresa,
still healing up and dealing with an infection.
But I couldn't forget seeing Austin turn from
blue to pink as he took his first breath, and
nothing else seemed to matter. I was the happiest
guy on the planet.

When Austin's crying turned into a rhythmic, hungry wail, I gave up and decided to call in reinforcements. I stood up with Austin clutched tightly to my chest and looked down at Teresa. She had a pillow over her head and was trying to go to sleep.

"Your turn," I said. "He needs what *you* got!" I liked to kid her, and there wasn't much more yours truly could do to help until later, when she started pumping and freezing the baby nectar.

Teresa pulled the pillow back, blinking. "I'm up, I'm up!" she said. She pushed back the sheets and rumpled comforter and stood, grabbing a fuzzy afghan to wrap around her shoulders. Then she reached for Austin.

Austin was quiet for a minute, registering the change in location. Then he screwed up his eyes, turned red, and started crying again. Teresa whisked him away to my office, snuggled down into my famous recliner, and started nursing Austin. After a few snorts and smacks, he settled in for a late dinner.

Both of us were turning out to be night owls, up until one or two in the morning. We were used to staying up late to party, dance, and be out with friends having fun. Now the party was at home, and we didn't really have time for courtship anymore between dirty diapers, hurried meals, and baby-bouncy-bounce.

After Austin was born I started telling Teresa I

loved her, but it felt awkward coming out of my mouth. I was trying hard to make it all work, and I wanted to be in love. With other girls, it had always been a crush or puppy love. But now, each time I looked in Teresa's blue eyes, I could feel something in my heart. So I kept trying.

With Austin now busy nursing, I was wide-awake and decided to take care of some paper-work. I pulled a box out of the closet and filed some papers inside. The files were still a mess—a mix of our stuff from when we'd moved in together just a few months before.

As I ruffled through the papers, a name caught my eye—*Teresa Morrison. Who is that? Hmm. That's not her maiden name*. My eyes wandered down the form, and the word *divorce* jumped out at me.

That's strange. Then it hit me. *Teresa's been married before.*

I really don't know you that well, I thought as the questions began flooding into my tired brain. *Who are you? Have you already been a wife to someone else? What else do I not know?*

I grabbed the stack of papers and marched into the office to confront her with what I'd found. Teresa looked up, sleepy and content, with the baby at her breast, oblivious to what was running through my mind and my heart. We were so fragile still, a couple barely knit together by a little baby boy who wasn't even part of the plan.

Were we really a family? Was this going to work?

"Have you been married before?" I showed her the piece of paper. "Why does this say Teresa Morrison?"

She didn't hesitate. "Yes, I was married before." She snuggled Austin closer, then looked down. Her words tumbled out. "I was married to Joe for three months and to Rudy for a few years, and I meant to tell you. But everything happened so fast."

Two marriages? She's been married twice before?

"Why didn't you tell me?" I demanded.

"I didn't want you to get mad." Her voice grew quiet. She reached down and kissed Austin's fluffy head. He was done nursing now and asleep in her arms. "I didn't want you to get mad, then I sort of forgot about everything when we had Austin. Are you mad at me?"

"I'm mad you didn't tell me."

She looked up at me again and let out a deep breath. "I was afraid you'd be done with me." Her eyes filled up with tears, turning the bluish whites an even deeper hue.

"Is there anything else you need to tell me?" I felt hurt and betrayed, but Teresa's tears and Austin's tiny sleeping body tugged at my heart.

"No," she said. "I was just worried what you would do when you found out."

I wasn't happy, but as I looked at the two of

them, my shock and anger withered. Of course she hadn't told me everything. I hadn't told her everything about me, either. We were still getting to know each other. Even so, I had a surprising gut feeling that we were meant to be. I was probably just kidding myself, but I had a feeling deep in my heart that somehow, some way, we'd make it and become a white-picket-fence family, with Austin the glue holding us together.

We were too tired to talk much that night, but Teresa and I spent a lot of time talking the rest of the week. I found out more about her childhood. Her father had struggled with an addiction to alcohol and her parents' marriage was a mess. Teresa married the first guy who came along just to get out of the house. When that didn't work, she divorced and married again, trying to find someone to take care of her so she didn't have to go back home.

Finding the divorce papers forced a conversation that Teresa had been dreading. She told me she felt a little like the coal miner's daughter from the poor side of town who ended up falling in love with a member of the wealthy and distinguished Kennedy clan. She felt like she was in a fairy tale, and she wasn't sure if she was the princess or just one of the stepdaughters.

A few days later I got down on my knees in front of the couch where Teresa was sitting and asked her to marry me. This time she said yes.

When the truth emerged from that box in the closet, she realized I was going to stick around and that it was okay to get married again, this time for love.

"I'll never forget how you held my hand while I was lying in that hospital bed," Teresa said. "I loved the way you looked at Austin as he was taking his first breath. I love you."

I wanted us to be the parents Austin needed and to create the close and loving family Teresa always dreamed of. I wanted to tell her I loved her, and I wanted to know in my heart it was genuine. So I said it.

"I love you," I said, kissing her slowly. This time it stuck.

5

WHAT RING?

Happily ever after is not a fairy tale.
It's a choice.
—FAWN WEAVER

Teresa wore a form-fitting navy blue dress, and her beautiful, thick, wavy auburn hair was parted on the side and turned up at the ends just above her shoulders, framing her sweet face. I wore a double-breasted black suit with a gray shirt and a tie with a flashy black-and-white circular pattern. We took separate cars to meet at city hall in downtown Charlotte at high noon. It was our wedding day.

My mother flew in. My brother Kevin and his wife, Karen, decided to come down from Virginia Beach. My best friend, Andy, came, along with a couple other friends. My cousin Lynee and her toddler, Meghan, were there too. And Austin, of course.

As Kevin, Andy, and I got in the car to drive downtown, Kevin spoke up. "Where's the ring?"

Huh? What ring?

Getting a ring hadn't just slipped my mind—it had never even crossed my mind.

41

He looked at me with piercing eyes, freezing me in my tracks as only a big brother can. "What about flowers? Do you have any flowers?"

Um, no. Negatory on both counts.

"I don't have a ring or flowers," I said.

This is embarrassing.

We took a hard right and made a quick stop at Sears in the South Park Mall. I found two generic gold bands for a grand total of fifty dollars. I guessed at Teresa's ring size. We grabbed a fistful of red roses at Flowerama on the way out of the mall and ran to the car.

I stole a glance at Kevin as we drove. He looked so calm and collected, but I thought I saw tears in the corners of his eyes. My mind was racing with a gazillion thoughts and feelings. And the excitement of Austin's birth was fading away.

What in the world am I doing? A baby and marriage all within the same breath? Why don't I ever have it all together like Kevin . . . or any of my brothers, for that matter?

I felt alone. Completely out of my league.

The minute I walked in the door of city hall, I really felt out of place. We waited in a big, horseshoe-shaped, echo-y room among assorted criminals there to file papers or talk to a judge. Austin slept soundly, and we passed him from person to person; everyone wanted a chance to hold him.

Little Meghan lightened the atmosphere by

skipping around the room, singing and dancing. Every other lap or so she slammed her hand on a heavy metal door labeled Mecklenburg County Magistrate.

Then noise filled the room . . . *BAM! Bam, bam, bam, BAM!*

Loud footsteps. The metal door flew open and out stomped a tangle of jack-booted police officers in full SWAT gear, complete with automatic weapons, body armor, and bulging biceps.

"Whoever is banging on these doors will immediately refrain from doing so," barked the commander. "If you do not or will not, we will place you under arrest. Thank you!"

"You're about to arrest a four-year-old," I said. The SWAT team wheeled around and marched back inside, the last commando throwing me a quick smile over his shoulder.

A moment later a haggard-looking middle-aged man poked his head out the same door. It was like the Wizard of Oz appearing from behind the curtain, but he was the justice of the peace. "Come on in," he said. "Let me take care of this one other thing and I'll be ready."

We followed him back through the door and into a small room with ten plastic chairs mounted to the floor in a row, the commandos nowhere in sight. The justice sat on his diminutive throne behind three inches of bulletproof glass with a perforated section at eye level so you could hear his voice.

The "one other thing" he had to take care of turned out to be a tiny little man in the front row next to a rather large woman who must have outweighed him by at least two hundred pounds. The man looked scared to death. His wife had been beating the tar out of him every night, and he wanted a restraining order. As they argued, I wondered if the SWAT team was nearby because they might be needed at any second. The justice's lips twitched into a small, crooked smile as he brought down the gavel.

"Restraining order granted! Next?"

Teresa and I stepped up to the glass.

"Would you like the long, short, or in-between ceremony?"

Before we could answer, the justice broke back in. "You know what? Let's go outside and do this. I know just the spot. Plus, I gotta get outta this cage for a while."

The justice led us back through the busy hall and across the street to the most beautiful secret garden I'd ever seen. It was a perfect little slice of Eden.

As the ceremony began, I looked over and saw Kevin's eyes full of tears. Mine filled up too as I looked down at my bride. By the time we said those famous words "to love and to cherish, in good times and bad, in sickness and in health, as long as we both shall live," I felt as though we really were meant to be together. Our bond was beginning to grow, and now we weren't just Austin's parents, we were also husband and wife. *God, thank you,* I thought.

After we signed on the dotted line, we caravanned back to the apartment where Teresa's mom and sister, along with some other friends, were gathered around a most unusual wedding cake. Mother Mawsha had ordered some trays of food and a white wedding cake with red piping, but somehow it came out a blood-red cake with white trim. It looked like something from a horror movie, but we laughed and ate it anyway.

My single friends had a grand time drinking well into the night. When Teresa, Austin, and I got tired, we stayed behind while they headed out to the bars. I sat in the new glider rocking chair, beer in hand, and thought, *I am no longer the cool partier I once was.* Just like that, my whole life was different. I couldn't charm my way out of this one, nor could Mother Mawsha fix it. *I am now a daddy and a husband.* I sat in the quiet and let the weight of my new responsibilities sink in.

Monday I went back to my job as a medical rep. The real world beckoned, and the honeymoon would have to wait. Teresa was still home with Austin but looking forward to going back to her new job as a loan officer. My natural optimism kicked in; we had all the time in the world to get to know each other and settle in to being a family. So yeah, we had it goin' on—good friends, good money, cool toys, and a healthy baby boy—everything I needed. What could go wrong?

6

STITCHED TOGETHER

I love being married. It's so great to
find that one special person you want
to annoy for the rest of your life.
—RITA RUDNER

We soon discovered Austin had three gears:
crying, vomiting, and sleeping (in that order).
When Austin was awake, he cried. "He's just
colicky," everyone said. Then came the advice.
We tried everything—we rocked him, talked to
him, walked with him, snuggled him, swaddled
him, sang to him, burped him, and bouncy-
bounced him. Both grandmothers suggested we
dissolve peppermints in his bottle to soothe his
stomach. It seemed to work . . . for a few minutes.
Occasionally everything worked right and he
slept. And once Austin went to sleep, he was out
for a while.

At first I thought it was normal baby stuff.
Every baby cries, correct? Every baby wants to
be held and rocked. Every baby spits up. But
Austin was extreme in every way. He seemed to
cry louder and longer, vomit more, and sleep
more deeply than any other baby I'd heard of.

When he was just a few weeks old, Austin had a bad cold. At first we didn't think much of it, but it lasted for more than a month. It settled in his lungs, and he couldn't seem to shake it. More crying. More vomiting. His doctor didn't seem to worry, but we did.

But in between the worries were moments of joy. I sometimes poured myself a glass of wine or beer and talked to Joe while I sat, staring at Austin. "Can you believe I'm a father?" I'd say, the words sounding strange to me. "I have a son."

My new status was still sinking in, and I was in awe of what Teresa and I had created. But while we were both in love with our precious little boy, it was obvious we still had quite a way to go in our relationship.

Sometimes when we wanted to do something fun together, Teresa and I would take advantage of Austin's periods of deep sleep and sneak off to the movies. If we were lucky, Austin would sleep through the movie and no one would ever know we had a newborn along.

On one of those rare baby-asleep movie dates, we were zooming to the theater in my white Ford Taurus, Austin snoozing in his car seat. Teresa and I were talking and laughing when *sploosh!* Something warm hit the back of my head and trickled slowly down the inside of the flipped-up collar of my polo shirt.

What is that? Austin? Nooo!

The loud cries from the backseat confirmed my fears. Austin was awake. And he'd projectile vomited his entire last meal toward the back of my neck. The thick, goopy curdled milk splattered everywhere. And now he was screaming at the top of his lungs. Date over.

It was hard for Teresa and me to settle in to a routine because everything was so new and foreign and awkward and unknown. The events of the last year had come fast and furious, and I was still trying to catch up to my new responsibilities as a husband and a father. Most of the time I felt alone, missing my single friends and my single life. At my core, I mostly cared about myself.

Teresa still wasn't feeling great. She didn't seem to be healing up from Austin's birth, and her doctor decided to do exploratory surgery, which turned into reconstructive surgery. Then two reconstructive surgeries. He finally found the cause of the infection—a misplaced sponge, left over from surgical repairs after Austin's birth.

Meanwhile, I worked and tried to sleep and eat in between helping Teresa care for Austin. We tried a battery-powered baby swing, and we ended up wearing out several swings since the motion seemed to soothe him.

When Austin was about five months old, Teresa started looking for day care so she could go back to work. She found a small in-home day care center recommended by a friend who'd sent her children there. We checked it out, and it seemed clean and cozy. The owner's teenage daughter helped with the children, and we felt good about it, even though we wondered if Austin would adjust. *As long as they have a sturdy baby swing,* I thought.

It was springtime and starting to warm up a bit. With the days getting longer, I went golfing whenever I could steal away for a few hours. My worries about Austin's constant crying or Teresa not feeling well went away when I was out with my friends, drinking beer and hitting golf balls on that beautiful, lush North Carolina grass. Every time I hit a great shot, I felt like I was hitting away my problems and enjoying a brief moment of my carefree, pre-baby, and pre-wife life.

When I couldn't get a foursome together, I unlocked my mountain bike and hopped on, pedaling furiously down the street and out onto the trails around Charlotte. Working up a sweat helped, and I loved the wind on my face. Riding soothed something deep inside, and sometimes if I was alone I'd talk to Joe while I rode. I've always had lots of energy and four or five thoughts bouncing around at the same time inside my head, but with mountain biking you have to concentrate or you'll crash. The danger helped me focus and kept my ADD tendencies trailing along in the dust as I skidded around corners, pedaled hard up hills, and coasted down narrow trails, ducking under branches, dodging big rocks, and hopping over the small ones.

One weekend I was mountain biking with a friend and got carried away on a jump. I lost control and crashed, catapulting over the handle-bars and landing on my right shoulder. My friend loaded up the bikes and drove me home, and Teresa took one look at me, packed up the baby, and drove me to the emergency room in Pineville. The ER doc said it was just a bruise, and I would be able to work out the intense pain by lifting my arm up and down using those colorful stretchy bands.

Great—no cast. And okay. I can do my own therapy. Cool.

I started lifting my arm up and down the next day. And the next. Since I never seem to do anything halfway, I raised my arm over and over and over. But my arm got worse, not better. Within a few days the pain was excruciating, and it became clear the injury was more than a bruise. I saw an orthopedic doctor, and he found the break. I didn't have much experience with broken bones but Teresa did, and she likes to use the proper terms. So to be precise, I'd broken my humerus and had a tuberosity fracture. Because of the severity of the break, and the delay in proper treatment, the doctor decided to do surgery. So much for fixing it by lifting my arm up and down.

51

I came home with my upper torso wrapped in bandages. Teresa was a saint; not only did she face a constant and demanding routine of caring for a fussy baby, but now I was out of action and needed help with eating, dressing, and bathing. Even combing my hair was a major chore.

As soon as I could, I peeled off the bandages so I could do things for myself. As usual when you peel off bandages, I was covered in sticky tape residue, orange blotches from the surgical disinfectant, pink scars with black spidery stitches on my arm, and . . .

Wait, what the heck is this?

I was running my good hand across my chest, the skin tingling from peeling off layers of bandages, when I felt something strange. Something that didn't belong. I looked down and could see a speck along the top of one pectoral but couldn't quite see what it was. I leaned over close to the bathroom mirror and tried to see.

Is it . . . ? No. It can't be. Wait. Yes, it is! I have a staple.

In my chest.

It's just not something you see every day of the week. I freaked out.

"Teresa!" I yelled. "Come look at this. I have a *staple* in my chest!"

No answer. So I got louder. *"Teresa! I have a staple in my chest!"*

Now that I look back on it, I wonder if Austin inherited some of his intensity from me.

Maybe.

I was screaming in the bathroom and Teresa ran in, thinking something must be seriously wrong. I was surprised she had any adrenaline left after everything we'd been through over the last six months. She burst into the bathroom, worried, and I showed her the metal staple in my chest. She took a good look and did what any normal, sane, loving wife would do. She laughed. Loud and long. At first I was a little hurt—after all, I'd been wronged here. The doctor had injured me.

"That doctor's going to hear about this! Don't you realize I have metal hardware embedded in my chest?"

But her laughter, as always, was infectious, and I started laughing too. We laughed about the staple. We laughed about the misplaced sponge. We laughed about our crying, vomiting, demanding baby and our beautiful, weird wedding and our crazy courtship. We laughed until we cried, and then we laughed some more.

I found out later that during my surgery, the doctor had grabbed the surgical stapler in the operating room and stapled the sheet to my chest because it kept falling off.

So far our life together was no fairy tale but at least we could laugh. And now we had something in common—we'd both been on the wrong side of a scalpel. But these wounds were temporary and fixable. Maybe our stitched-together bodies were like our relationship—a little broken, a little raggedy, but holding together with our son, Austin, at the center.

7

THE RIB

Endure and persist;
this pain will turn to good by and by.
—OVID

One day after Teresa went back to work, she
pulled up to Austin's day care, and one of the
employees came running out with Austin's baby
carrier.

*Maybe she's in a hurry, thought Teresa. She's
got something important to do, and she's running Austin out to the car so she can go take
care of it.*

But the carrier was empty. The woman's face
was pale, like she was in shock.

"Where's Austin?" Teresa almost shouted.
"Where's my baby?" She looked into the carrier
as if he might actually be inside, hidden down in
the cracks somewhere.

"There's been an accident," the worker said.
She thrust the carrier toward Teresa. "Austin's
okay, but he's at the hospital."

"What kind of accident? What happened?"
Teresa was shouting now. When she's worried
about Austin, she morphs immediately from a

sweet, Southern girl to a ferocious, don't-you-dare-get-between-me-and-my-cub mama bear.

"He fell but he's okay," the woman said.

"If he's okay, then why is he at the hospital?" Teresa spit out, grabbing the carrier and throwing it in the backseat before jumping back into the front seat and speeding off. The hospital was just a few blocks away, but there was commuter traffic and it was slow going. Teresa was in an adrenaline-induced haze, and the cars seemed to be creeping along. Finally, she made it to the emergency room and found someone to lead her to Austin. He was whimpering, and he had a softball-sized knot on the left side of his head. Not a baseball. A softball.

"He has skull fractures, but he's going to be okay," said the nurse. This news would have comforted most parents, but not Teresa. She knew he was definitely not okay. Unfortunately, this was the same hospital where Teresa's doctor had botched her post-childbirth surgical repairs. It was also the hospital where a sheet had been stapled to my chest.

"No! I want him moved to a different hospital, right now!" she said. "I want you to call Austin's pediatrician and tell him to meet us at Presbyterian." Then she took a breath and began to cry.

Does he have OI? Teresa thought for the millionth time. *Is this the start?*

She wanted to pick him up and comfort him but was afraid. Her baby was so small lying in that bassinet. She knew he needed some tests, so all she could do for now was stroke his arms and legs gently. "It's going to be okay, Austin. Your mama's here."

The hospital put Austin into another ambulance, and while Teresa drove to the new hospital, she remembered hearing about her first break in the walker. That early accident started a string of broken bones. Every break was painful, and Teresa hated the restrictions on her activity, but her grandparents spoiled her whenever she got hurt. Her Grandma Rosalie let her watch lots of TV and gave her little gifts and treats.

At home was a different story, though. Her father drank up the family money, and Teresa felt as though her bone injuries cost her parents money they didn't have. "I felt like everything would be better if they didn't have a daughter who was always sickly," Teresa told me once. Her parents took to calling her "an accident waiting to happen."

After that, Teresa wasn't allowed to take PE or be part of the cross-country running team. As she got older, the breaks lessened, and when she passed the awkwardness of adolescence, she learned how to be careful and avoid situations that could injure her fragile bones. Most people didn't know she had OI, but she always felt self-conscious; she had some family members with mild OI, but she didn't know anyone else who suffered from the disease, and she kept it to herself through marriages one and two.

But she couldn't ignore OI any longer. Her first sight of the huge lump on Austin's head kept replaying in her mind. Teresa knew he had it. She just knew. Later, diagnostic tests and a full body scan showed that Austin had suffered severe blunt trauma to the head at the day care facility, resulting in two separate plate fractures on the lower back and side of his head, along with splinter fractures around the upper back of his skull. But as horrible as he looked with the giant lump on the side of his head, doctors gave us a hopeful prognosis. Though it was possible Austin could experience learning difficulties or seizures as a result of the accident, it was unlikely.

The full body scan showed something else, though. Austin's tenth rib had been severely broken at some point and subsequently healed over. By this time I'd arrived at the hospital, and Teresa and I puzzled over the test results with the doctor. Because of his fussiness and crying, we'd practically been holding Austin on our chests for the entire six months he'd been on the planet. When we weren't cradling him, he was in his car seat, his swing, or snuggled safely in bed. There wasn't a moment he'd been in a situation where he could have possibly broken a rib.

Then the doctor solved the mystery. "It most likely happened in childbirth," he said. "If Austin has OI, his rib probably broke during the birth process." We couldn't be sure yet—the test involved DNA analysis in a lab across the country and would take months. (It eventually validated what we already knew in our hearts.) But the broken rib explained why Austin hadn't stopped crying and vomiting since the day he was born. Our baby had been in excruciating pain for the first few months of his life.

I thought back to how he'd cried during his bath or when he was being dressed or changed. Or, and this thought almost made me sick, when we'd burped him. Can you imagine how that must have felt to a newborn? Your chest on fire with pain, held tight, and thumped on the back? Tears sprang to my eyes.

Austin, I'm so sorry. I didn't know.

I felt bad for all the times I'd been angry at his crying, wondering what was wrong with him and why our baby couldn't be like other babies. I went by his hospital bed, my hand lightly on his chest.

Then it got worse. We found out what really happened to Austin at the day care center.

The owner of the day care had gone on an errand, leaving Austin in the care of a sixteen-year-old. Since it was almost time for Austin to be picked up by Teresa, the teen started changing

Austin's diaper. Midway through, she left him alone on the changing table. I'm not sure why. To grab a diaper or some wipes? To answer the phone? Check her makeup? Who knows. Austin wasn't strapped down, and he rolled off and fell to the floor.

The girl heard and ran over to him. He cried a little, threw up, turned blue, and momentarily stopped breathing. A lump began to form on the left side of his head.

Some time passed—we're not sure how long—and the owner returned. We do know that 911 was never called. Instead, the owner picked up Austin, carried him to her car, and drove him to the hospital.

Minutes later Teresa arrived at the day care and was met by the teenager and the empty baby carrier.

The day care disaster made the evening news across the region. The day care people told us they would not help with medical expenses and had already retained legal counsel. They informed the hospital that Austin's injury happened before Teresa had dropped him off at day care that morning, so they lawyered up and tried turning us into the bad guys. I still can't believe it, even after all these years.

Eventually the truth came out. The day care log of feedings and diaper changes was found to have been altered. The teen left in charge of

Austin wasn't properly trained. And several months later, the state of North Carolina cited the day care for more than seventy violations and levied a fine.

When we took Austin home from the hospital after the day care disaster, we must have been a sight. Teresa was still healing and moving slowly from her surgeries. My arm was still bandaged and in a sling from my bike accident and surgery. And Austin, our sweet little baby boy, was coming home with a broken skull and a healed rib. He was just six months old.

The three of us were broken, but not apart. We were broken together.

8

MORE GLUE

There is a thin line that separates laughter and
pain, comedy and tragedy, humor and hurt.
—ERMA BOMBECK

Austin's accident haunted my dreams for several
years. I'd wake up with images of him on the floor
of the day care, alone, cold, and unconscious. A
thin stream of blood from his nose to his lip.
And his longing, distant eyes. His skin gray, then
blue, the opposite of what I saw when he was
born and took his first breath.

*I hate them. I hate these people. Look what they
did to our boy.*

The more I thought about the day care disaster,
the more I realized Austin could've died that
afternoon. He was in a dire situation with a group
of people we trusted to take care of him. We
had assumed Austin was being treated like a
treasured guest for eight hours a day.

But the reality of what could have happened
shook me. As my dreams spawned those horrible
images of the accident, I sunk into a nightmarish
fog of anger and bitterness. I felt jaded, cynical,
and angry. Some of that anger I directed inward.

I felt guilty that instead of caring for him ourselves, we had left him alone with relative strangers so we could maintain the two-income lifestyle we enjoyed.

But most of my anger was reserved for the day care people. The director had treated a shopping errand as more important than my son's life and safety. We were shocked to learn later that the doctors and staff at the first emergency room were told that Austin had bumped his head while sitting on the floor. They lied to the people who were trying to save our son's life.

When the day care finally admitted to the fall from the changing table, I wondered if they were telling the whole truth. Would they ever truly account for what they did? I didn't know, and I struggled to forgive them. And as a consequence of the accident, Teresa and I both became very protective of our fragile little baby boy. As he began to heal, we searched for a high-quality day care with closed-circuit televisions.

As Austin started into his second year, he began to exert his will. When he acted up or had outbursts, neither of us knew how to handle him. "We can't spank him," Teresa said. "We might break him."

Austin was a typical active toddler and very quick to run and fall and get hurt and break things. Teresa started really worrying about Austin and his OI. "It's almost like being held captive," she said. "I'm panicked all the time, and I never know what's going to happen next."

Playing with other kids was a potential nightmare too. Out on the sidewalk or at the park I watched him like a hawk, especially when other kids were around. I didn't trust the kids, and I didn't trust the parents either. Austin's skull fractures healed, and he loved to be outside, running more often than not. I too wanted to keep him inside or wrap him up in bubble wrap with a motorcycle helmet protecting his recently knit-together skull, but I couldn't.

Eventually we found a day care we liked; it cost a fortune, but we were willing to pay to make sure he would be safe. Teresa went back to work, and we began to think about growing our family. Before long, Teresa was feeling nauseated, and we discovered she was pregnant again. We were excited, but this time I was determined to do everything the right way.

When Teresa was about three months along Mother's Day rolled around. Her morning sickness was wearing her out, and since it was a special morning, I decided to get Austin up, fed, and dressed so she could sleep in.

After breakfast I sat at my desk to do some paperwork. Austin wandered around, playing with *Star Wars* figures and looking at his books. One of his favorites was *Curious George*; he loved the famous hyperactive monkey that always got himself into trouble and was rescued by the Man in the Yellow Hat.

I was working, in the zone and completely focused on filling out a form, when Austin got tired of looking at his book and sprang to his feet. He scampered up behind me and put one foot on the plastic wheeled crossbar at the base of my desk chair. Then he grabbed the arm of the chair and lifted his other leg to climb up the back.

"Daddy . . . Daddy . . . Daddy," he chanted.

"Austin, please get down." I tensed up my body and used my feet to give the chair a sharp little shake to shrug him off and discourage his climbing. But the sudden movement was too much for his unsteady eighteen-month-old grip, and he lost his footing and fell straight down. He fell hard, his leg striking the crossbar underneath. I heard a popping noise and a loud scream.

I looked down and saw something I'll never forget. Austin's lower leg was broken, his shin bent at a ninety-degree angle. He was lying in a crumpled little heap, hyperventilating with pain.

Teresa heard the screams and came running, rubbing her eyes. "What's going on?" she yelled.

I couldn't talk. I looked around and the yellow cover of the *Curious George* book caught my eye. I grabbed it and opened it up, then slowly slid it under Austin's leg. I had some packing tape in a drawer, and I used it to wrap around the outside to improvise a splint. I wanted to cover up and immobilize his leg so we could get him to the hospital without hurting him further.

As I worked, Austin's cries quieted, and he looked up at me through huge tears in his now-liquid blue eyes. There was a light in his eyes, almost like he knew something I didn't. His look touched something deep inside me and I felt a strong connection to him. But I also felt terrible, like the accident was my fault. It seemed like every time I felt like I was getting the hang of being a dad, I did something to wreck it.

"What happened? How did he get hurt?" Teresa demanded.

"I don't know," I said. "He just fell down." I was really afraid to tell her about my shrug-him-off move. I didn't know what she'd do if she knew the truth. I felt horrible, guilty, and like a terrible father.

It got worse at the hospital. The intake staff asked question after question, and slowly it became clear that they were suspicious. It was such a bad break they weren't buying my story, and I began to feel like a suspect in a child-abuse case. Now I *really* felt bad. Finally, our pediatrician arrived. He explained Austin's OI diagnosis to the staff, and the questions stopped. They removed my *Curious George* book–splint, set the bone (more screams), and put a cast on his leg.

On our way home from the hospital, I felt like

I'd failed Austin. I was supposed to protect his fragile bones, not cause them to break. And it wasn't much of a Mother's Day for Teresa. I decided never to tell anyone what had really happened. And I began to wonder, *Is this how it's supposed to be? Is our life going to be one extreme moment after another? When is it going to stop?*

Austin had a harder time than usual settling down to sleep that night so we brought him into bed with us. It was heartbreaking because every few minutes his leg would jerk—almost like a muscle spasm. He'd jump in pain, wake up, and start screaming. We'd get him calmed down, then he'd jump and scream again. As his leg healed, we fell into a pattern of letting him sleep with us, not always a comfortable arrangement as Teresa's belly grew with the new baby.

For this delivery, Teresa arrived at the hospital for a scheduled C-section in full makeup. She looked gorgeous. And I was overwhelmed by feelings, but not the wonderful, becoming-a-dad high I wanted again. I was overwhelmed by the C-section. I didn't realize it was hard-core surgery and I would be watching a cold steel scalpel slice through Teresa's layers of skin and muscle. During the surgery I broke into a cold, prickly sweat and almost passed out. Teresa and baby Logan came through it great, though. It was an easy birth, Logan was perfect and healthy, and everything that was so complicated and difficult and drawn-out with Austin's birth was easy, quick, and simple with Logan.

I was now the father of two boys.

After Teresa was out of surgery, recovery, and back in her room resting, I sat by her side and held Logan for a long time.

"Hey, little man." I touched the top of his head, his ear, the tip of his nose. "I love you."

Baby Logan was more glue. Our family now had two big reasons to stay together and make this work.

I reluctantly handed Logan back to the nurse. She tucked him in to his warm bassinet, and I headed home to pick up Austin from our neighbor Lonnie's house. I wanted both of us to get some sleep so I could take Austin to the hospital the next day to meet his baby brother.

The next morning I was in the bedroom getting ready while Austin ran up and down the hallway. He was two years old, his leg was healed up, and he was getting faster all the time. After a few warm-up laps, he took the corner fast and zoomed into the master bedroom. I was by the side of the bed, facing the other way, and just as Austin ran full bore toward me, I took a step to the side to grab something off the dresser and unknowingly dodged him. At the same time, he launched himself toward me, and when I moved, he ran face-first into the nightstand. The resulting sequence of events was becoming familiar—a popping sound, then a loud scream. And another.

I crouched down to see how bad it was. *Please don't let it be his leg again.*

It wasn't—Austin's nose had taken the full impact. He bled, his face red and white and covered with tears. I saw that strange light in his eyes again, winding its way straight into my heart. I picked him up and held him against my chest.

"Austin. I'm so sorry, sweetie. Are you okay? You're going to be okay."

I hoped nothing was broken.

Then the thought struck me. *Teresa just had a beautiful baby boy. And I just broke the nose of her other beautiful baby boy. How on earth am I going to explain this to her?* Another father failure.

When we arrived at the hospital, Teresa took one look at Austin's swollen face and black-and-blue eyes and ordered, "Take him to the emergency room. I think his nose is broken." I did, and it was (the first of several broken noses), but it wasn't displaced, and the doctor said he'd be okay.

There was that word again. Okay.

But would he really be okay? His nose will heal up like his rib, his skull, and his leg did. But will he really be okay?

I held Logan again. He was quiet, sleepy, and so sweet.

What about Logan's bones? Does he have any broken ribs? He seems healthy and perfect, but could he have OI too?

Being a father wasn't turning out as I'd planned. It was way more emotional, more complicated, and more painful than I had ever imagined. I'd always heard that God wouldn't give you more than you can handle. But for some reason God was giving us plenty.

9

THE RUN

When my heart is overwhelmed;
lead me to the rock that is higher than I.
—PSALM 61:2

It was summer, and bees buzzed around our heads every time we opened the French doors at the back of our house. Austin was two and a half and Logan was just one, and with Austin's fractured skull and broken bones healed, I was taking every precaution to keep the boys safe and healthy. Remember that John Travolta movie *The Boy in the Plastic Bubble*? That was Austin's life. He was our bubble boy, and we were fierce about his safety. So the bees had to go.

But maybe not just yet. I still had some coffee to drink.

It was a glorious Saturday morning, the kind of day where the sun is so bright you have to shield your eyes. And even better, it was humidity-free, a rare treat in North Carolina. Teresa had bounced out of bed at o'dark-thirty to hit the garage sales; she didn't get out much on her own, and she was excited. I was excited too, happy to be on Dad duty with the Auzman by my side and Logan safely stashed in the playpen. I poured a cup of coffee and smiled, knowing I could do everything my way for the next few hours.

Then I heard a knock on the door. Two repairmen stood there, work order in hand. I wasn't aware that Teresa had called the builder a few days before. We'd noticed the French doors at the back of the house had been improperly installed with the hinges facing out. Any knucklehead with a screwdriver could pop the pins and be inside our house in five minutes. The workers were here to reinstall the doors with the hinges inside.

Hey, maybe they'll help me get rid of the bees.

"Why don't you go around the side?" I said. "There's a bee nest under the eaves we need to get rid of before you work on the doors." They nodded. "I'll go get a broom."

As I walked by, I saw Austin on the floor watching *Star Wars* and holding his Luke Skywalker and Hans Solo action figures. Logan was playing in his playpen. I went out the front door and knocked down the small hive while the two men sprayed the bees. In a few moments, we vanquished the swarm and the men could do their job.

Every time I opened the door to demonstrate the hinge problem to the workers, an electronic chime sounded, courtesy of our alarm system. Every door and window was wired, and it wasn't just for intruders. With an active toddler in the house and no fence around the yard, we wanted to be alerted if Austin decided to head outside. Behind our grassy backyard was a row of small trees and thick bushes bordering a creek, and we didn't want him exploring the area and deciding to go for a swim.

The alarm continued to go off as the men opened and closed the doors, discussed the problem, and tried to figure out how to fix it. It seemed simple enough. But no, it was more complicated than that. I caught snatches of their discussion, and it sounded like they were going to reverse the doors and flush-mount them inside the house.

Meanwhile, the door chimes were driving me insane as the door opened and closed. I finally got up and disabled the alarm. My quiet, relaxing Saturday morning date with the paper and the boys was not going according to plan.

I settled back down and then fifteen minutes later I realized I hadn't heard a peep out of the boys. Man, they were being so good.

Wait. Maybe that's not good. It's too quiet. Better check.

I headed back to the front of the house. It seemed a little too bright. Then I peeked around the corner and what I saw was every parent's worst nightmare. The front door was wide open.

Oh my God.

Logan was in the playpen, busily sucking on a

frozen teething ring with little plastic fish inside. Good to go. But where was Austin?

Maybe he just opened the front door and then came back in.

I ran upstairs but I already knew. Austin was not in the house. Just the night before Teresa had taken the boys on a walk with Doreen, a neighbor who lived three doors down. Doreen had two kids, Audrey (eight) and Vince (five). After the walk, we'd grilled burgers and eaten out on the back patio. Logan was in his high chair and all was well, when suddenly Austin climbed down from his chair and bolted. I took off running after him, grabbed him, and carried him back home. He was fast for a two-year-old.

But this time I had missed Austin's takeoff, and he could be anywhere. As I feared, the upper floor was silent, and I ran back down.

As I vaulted down the stairs, I realized that when I had turned off the annoying beeping door alarm, I had also disabled the chime on the front door. Somehow Austin had unlocked and opened the front door, and now he was gone. Probably running. I just hoped he hadn't gotten too far.

On my way out of the house, I stopped by the playpen and grabbed Logan, teething ring and all, and ran out the door, screaming for my two-year-old.

"Austin. Austin!" I looked down the sidewalk, both ways. Nothing. I ran out to the middle of the street, Logan wailing as he clutched my neck. I was in a full-blown panic. It just couldn't be. The boy had escaped the bubble.

Neighbors started emerging, wondering what was going on with the screaming madman in the middle of their quiet Mr. Rogers neighborhood on a sunny Saturday morning.

"Aussttiinn! Auz. Where are you?"

No way. This has to be a dream.

Our neighbor Lonnie approached, and I almost threw Logan at her in an adrenaline-fueled panic. "What happened?" she asked, calm and collected. She peppered me with questions, trying to figure out what was going on. I tried to listen, but I was breathing hard and fighting panic.

"How long has he been outside? When did you turn off the alarm? Where is Teresa?"

Teresa. Uh-oh. I am in rock-star trouble here.

"Neil is calling the police," she said. Neil was her husband. When I heard the word *police*, I felt like I'd been hit upside the head. This was the type of sad story you see on the nightly news or in the Sunday paper. A child goes missing. His dad was watching him. My whole body went hot, then cold, and I really thought I was going to pass out again.

I ran back inside the house and into the garage. I thought maybe I could cover more ground on my bike so I took off riding down the street. I kept screaming, "Auusstiiin! Auz!"

People were walking around, looking behind bushes and garbage cans, combing backyards, searching for any sign of my little boy. I dropped my bike in someone's yard and ran down to the creek. I forced my way through the brush, branches and thorns tearing at my skin and clothes, and then ran up and down the banks.

Nothing.

I headed back out to the street. No one was finding any sign of Austin. It was as if he'd vanished into thin air. I rode around awhile longer and then turned back toward the house. Maybe it was all a dream and I would find him standing by the front door in his diaper, wondering what in the heck his crazy dad was doing.

Swarms of police cars screeched down the street. A K-9 unit arrived. Officers fanned out across the neighborhood.

God, please get me out of this.

10
FACING THE
QUEEN BEE

There are shortcuts to happiness
and dancing is one of them.
—VICKI BAUM

When I skidded to a stop in front of the house,
panting, Lonnie approached with Logan in her
arms. She looked straight into my eyes.

"Have you called Teresa?" she asked again.

"Uhhhhhh . . ."

That was it, the only sound I could make. No,
I hadn't called her, but I couldn't tell Lonnie
because my mouth didn't seem to be working. I
couldn't talk, and I couldn't think. So I decided to
do the manly thing and let Lonnie handle it.

I listened in terror as she called Teresa and told
her she needed to come home. Teresa pressed for
details, and Lonnie finally told her Austin had run
out the front door and we couldn't find him. She
left out the part about the police and the dogs.

I could hear Teresa screaming over the phone.

"What the &%!# was Scott doing? Why wasn't
he watching Austin?!" Teresa is the queen bee
of our house, and in difficult situations she

sometimes lapses into salty language. This was one of those situations.

The police approached with endless questions. "What kind of lock do you have on the door? Tell me about your alarm system."

I didn't care about the alarm or the locks. My son was missing! Then they asked for a pillow-case for the K-9 units. "The dogs really like pillows to get a good scent."

A good scent for what? Oh, God.

An officer noticed my bleeding scratches, and I told him how I'd searched the creek. He tried to reassure me that a missing child is very common and happens more than you think. "It usually turns out fine," he said. He radioed a request for a chopper on standby, ASAP.

Right. This happens every day?

Then Teresa arrived. I waited, my heart on standby as her car pulled in to the driveway. Police cars, people milling around, dogs and officers down the street. My head felt like it was full of a million bees, buzzing and angry. She got out of the car and marched in my direction. Right before she got to me, she turned and ran down to the creek, frantic. She'd always been afraid of Austin falling into the creek.

Then a shout went up. "Here he is!"

Oh no. Tell me he's okay. Please let him be okay.

Someone was pointing up to a house. It was the

back of Doreen's place. Everyone who heard, ran. There, framed in the second-story window, was a little boy, dancing and laughing like he was onstage. He waved at us all, a big, joyful smile plastered across his face. It was Austin. And he was naked.

I started laughing too, sucking in big gulps of air for the first time since he'd disappeared. I felt the terror melting away, and my body felt lighter.

Thank God. Auz is okay.

We knocked on the back door but no one answered. Then we ran around to the front door but no answer there either. No one was home.

How on earth did Austin get into that house?

We banged on the door, and Austin came down the stairs. Teresa told him to open the door and, being the master locksmith we now knew he was, he figured out the locks and opened it up. We smothered him in hugs and kisses, our naked little runaway. Teresa hugged him over and over, crying, while I checked for broken bones.

Then Teresa did a quick search of the house for his clothes and finally found them upstairs, next to the toilet in the bathroom. We'd been potty training him, and for some reason he always insisted on taking off every stitch of clothing to use the potty. This time was no exception. Teresa retrieved his clothes and noticed he had, indeed, used the potty. Teresa cleaned up, and we headed back home after leaving a note of explanation.

Back home, the police finished their paperwork and left. Teresa showered Austin with hugs and kisses and me with scowls. And we pondered the mystery.

How did Austin get into Doreen's house? Did he find a key? Did he even know how to use a key? Or was a door left open by accident? We could only wonder.

Later that day, when Doreen and her family got home from the Saturday soccer games, her husband and kids ran upstairs before anyone saw Teresa's explanatory note. Vince's room was a mess. All his Lego creations were torn apart, Legos thrown everywhere. Audrey found her previously carefully posed Barbies strewn about. The kids ran downstairs, shouting to their dad.

"Someone broke into our house! Someone tried to rob us!"

Doreen's husband shrugged them off, told them to quit lying, go to their rooms, and clean up. He didn't know Austin had been there, doing some rearranging and filling the toilet with a little gift.

Teresa talked to Doreen later that day, and we reconstructed what probably happened. Austin ran down the street to Doreen's house, just as he'd done the night before. The garage door was open, and Doreen was inside getting the kids ready to go. Austin must've slipped into the garage during those few moments. When Doreen's family was ready, they went out the front door to the car parked in the driveway, climbed in the car, and used the remote to shut the garage door. Somehow they never spotted Austin. They pulled out of the driveway and went on their way. Meanwhile, Austin opened the door from the garage into the house.

Once inside, he climbed the stairs and had a field day playing, with no one to bother him. When nature called, he listened (after shedding his clothes and Huggies, of course). My Saturday had turned into a horror story, while my intrepid two-and-a-half-year-old had a pleasant morning with the neighbor's house all to himself.

Running away just to dance naked in the neighbor's window was typical Austin. He never misses an opportunity to dance like no one is watching.

11
PARENT TRAINING

Find out where joy resides,
and give it a voice far beyond singing.
For to miss the joy is to miss all.
—ROBERT LOUIS STEVENSON

Eight o'clock Sunday morning. Time for church. Oh joy.

I hadn't been a regular churchgoer since my early teens, so church wasn't a habit, nor did I like getting up early on the weekends. Teresa scouted out a nice church with a good preschool program and started taking Austin and Logan, now five and three, to Trinity United Methodist's pre-K program. The three of them also went to Sunday services and sometimes Wednesdays too. She kept after me to go along.

Teresa's faith seemed to factor into just about everything she did. I can see now that she was fierce about building a strong foundation for our family. Her priorities were her faith, her kids, her husband, and *then* herself. Teresa was, and will always be, a person who loves to give and to please the Lord. Of course, at this stage of the game I never really noticed.

Sometimes when I was sitting down, relaxing with a drink, and talking to Joe, I'd catch myself laughing at T.

How can this woman actually love me? I'd chuckle. *She doesn't know a lick about me. Not really.*

Two things were wrong with this picture. I was laughing at the fact that I was closed off and not fully investing myself in my marriage with the mother of my two boys. And second, I was talking to my imaginary friend a whole lot more than I ever thought about talking to God.

Teresa kept trying. She was way ahead of me on the love-and-faith meter, and when it came to our relationship, Teresa steered the ship. I did feel I was growing as a father. But I was having problems understanding what it meant to be a full partner in life and love.

But Teresa can be relentless, so I ended up being dragged along to church on the occasional Sunday. I wasn't kicking and screaming, but I often had other plans, usually involving sitting in a golf cart rather than a wooden pew. When I did make it to church, I tolerated it, at best. I knew going to church was the right thing to do, but another part of me pushed those feelings aside. I preferred to remain aloof and alone with my own thoughts.

I did really like Preacher Rick, though. He was one cool cat. I couldn't seem to embrace the whole idea of organized religion, but listening to him was pretty easy. The man could get up in front of a packed house with just a Bible, and from the first word, I was hooked. He was charismatic, engaging, and believable.

Even though I wasn't thumping any Bibles or planning my social calendar around church events, I appreciated Preacher Rick's genuine interest in me and my family. He hounded me to take part in more things in the church, such as Methodist Men or Sunday school, but deep down I knew he pursued me because he cared. So I would occasionally relent, tag along with Teresa and the boys, and grace the congregation with my presence.

One fine Carolina Sunday morning, Teresa talked me into helping her in the church nursery.

Stinky diapers and cranky babies instead of Preacher Rick? Humph.

Teresa kept Austin in the nursery with us. At five years old, he had way more energy than the average kid, and he was extreme—excited and hyper, or exhausted, quiet, and withdrawn. We were both worried about Austin's development: he talked later than normal, and when he did talk, he couldn't seem to look us in the eyes. Sometimes Austin's words came out in gibberish, almost as if he remembered chunks of his thoughts and then spit them out quickly, like he needed to get a rhythm going. If we tried to make him wait and not interrupt, when he finally got the chance to say something, he often forgot what he wanted to say. We also noticed he spoke in a strange, flat monotone.

Austin didn't socialize well with other kids his age and preferred to be around adults or younger children. Since he was due to start kindergarten soon, we worried and visited doctors who led us through an alphabet soup of childhood syndromes, diseases, and disorders. Doctors had suggested several possible diagnoses: oppositional defiant disorder (ODD), obsessive-compulsive disorder (OCD), attention deficit disorder (ADD), attention deficit hyperactivity disorder (ADHD), and on and on. So far the professionals were leaning toward ADHD and ODD, with a little RLS (or restless legs syndrome) thrown in as a bonus.

I looked up the word *disorder* and found it meant a random abnormal disturbance. I wasn't about to argue with that definition. Random abnormal disturbance pretty much characterized my whole stint so far as a husband and a father.

Teresa and I were always second-guessing ourselves as parents and wondering if we were doing something to cause Austin's peculiarities. Health-care workers we encountered often lectured us about spoiling Austin and recommended we use firmer discipline. I still mostly felt like a failure. Teresa was a terrific mom, but even she felt inadequate as we struggled to get a handle on Austin's behavior.

In any case, this morning Trinity United Methodist Church was about to get a full-blown lesson on the neurological alphabet soup our son was blessed with.

I was busy helping Teresa corral another wiggly toddler when *Bam!* The lower half of the Dutch door to the children's nursery slammed. I turned toward the noise in time to witness the upper half of the door shaking and rattling on its hinges. My eye caught a shock of light wispy hair sticking above the bottom half of the door. Then it di-appeared, and I heard quick footsteps fading away down the hall.

Uh-oh. Austin is on the move.

"Your turn, Big Boy," drawled Teresa from the rocking chair where she cradled a baby on each shoulder. "Go get him!"

I dropped my head and let out a slow, deep breath.

Of course, sweetheart.

I opened the door, turned right, and trotted down the hall. I had a feeling I knew exactly where he was headed.

Please, God, don't do this to me.

But even though I was in God's house, I knew my prayer was for naught. In fact, I bet He was probably laughing at me and cheering on the boy.

I sped up, running down the hall and power

sliding around that first corner only to come up empty. No Austin. *Argh!*

I catapulted down the second hall and spotted Austin, close to a sanctuary door.

Don't touch that door, Austin. Don't you dare.

I stopped, held my breath, and watched. Austin bounced back and forth off the walls like a pinball, and just as he grabbed the knob to the sanctuary door, he turned to me with a thousand-watt smile and a look of, *Game on, Dad! See if you can catch me.*

As Austin slipped through the door, I ran. I saw Preacher Rick leading the opening prayer, the congregation quiet. Then the door closed.

I took another deep breath, stood up tall, and approached the door.

What do I do?

I had two choices: go the embarrassing route and just let him go, or go the really embarrassing route and follow him into the sanctuary.

Oh man.

I eased the door open a crack and slid into the pew where my family usually sat. Austin was familiar with the spot—maybe he'd end up there.

But no. I spied the rebel dashing up the center aisle toward the exit doors leading to outside, and freedom. Right before he ran outside, he turned again and shot me a smile. Austin was having a blast.

I got up and walked toward the altar on

Preacher Rick's left. I nodded to him as if we were neighbors passing on a walk around the block. "Good morning, Preacher Rick," I said. "Make it a great day." He smiled and nodded back.

As I strolled up the center aisle with every eye on me, Rick said, "This is perfect. Let's take a moment and observe how Scott handles this situation."

His words didn't quite make sense. *Why did he say this is perfect?* But I didn't have time to wonder. I needed to capture my elusive prey.

I sped up and made it through the front doors just as they slammed shut. I blinked in the blazing sunshine. Nothing. Austin was gone. As I hurried down the steps I heard scattered laughter and hoots from within the sanctuary. *Well, at least we gave everyone a story for the day.*

I slowed down a bit, figuring Austin had made his way back to the nursery and the safety of his mother. I was wrong.

Twenty feet from the front doors of the church was a massive old oak tree. Austin's little face popped out from one side.

Aha! He's waiting for me. I got him now.

I lunged around the left side of the tree where I'd just seen him, but he juked to the right and shot past my outstretched hands.

Another slow breath and I turned to see him back at the top of the sanctuary steps, just inside the front doors. I stared at my son. He smiled that same big smile and his eyes looked directly into mine. I swear, this time the light in his eyes looked more like a twinkle.

Then something strange happened. I'm not quite sure what it was, but those eyes bathed in blue, just like his mother's, froze me, and in that instant I felt something deep—an emotion a thousand times stronger than anything I've ever known. This little boy, my son, made me think hard, and in that moment I took stock of my life, my heart, and my soul.

What am I doing with my life, God?

Then the feeling was gone. And I still had to get him.

I gave up any pretense of subtlety as I burst back into the sanctuary. Several hundred eyes met me, then turned away. Then back to me. And then I saw. Austin was on the floor, crawling under the pews through the tangle of legs and feet and purses. He'd almost made it back to our pew— home turf and closer to the nursery and safety with Mom.

I looked up at the preacher, and he had the same Austin-style smile across his face. Preacher Rick and the congregation were enjoying every single minute and couldn't wait to see what was next.

I stood up straight, then did the only logical thing I could do.

I gave up, turned tail, and headed toward the side door. I opened it and shuffled back toward the nursery a defeated man. I'd been taken down by a five-year-old boy. And not just any boy, but Austin, the dad-slayer.

I peered over the Dutch door into the nursery and there stood Auz, arms wrapped firmly around Mommy's leg with his head tilted and eyes locked onto mine. That same cherubic grin, just like at the oak tree, and again, it stopped me in my tracks.

What a beautiful little boy I have. I am truly blessed.

I turned my ear toward the speaker and listened as the church choir burst into song just before the end of the morning service. And I heard Preacher Rick say this: "That was a fine example of parenting in action."

What?

Teresa cleared her throat much too loudly. I waited for her usual jibe and her laughter. She handed me the church bulletin. "Take a look, Scottie." Then she started laughing. Austin joined in.

I looked down at the piece of paper she held out and read the title of Preacher Rick's sermon: "Parenting and Discipline in the Home."

I'm not sure what the congregation learned, but that Sunday I learned a little bit more about being a dad and the hard work, patience, and love it was going to take. I was beginning to understand that life with Austin was going to be a journey—perhaps a difficult one. I also learned I didn't need to make that journey all alone. I had Teresa. A church family, if I wanted it. And maybe even a God who cared and sometimes laughed with me more than He laughed at me.

When I went to bed that night I didn't get on my hands and knees, but I did lie on my side for a long time, listening to Teresa's soft breathing on the other side of the bed. As I stared out the window up at the moon, I said a few quiet words to God.

"I don't know what to say, but, God, I really do not know what I am doing here. How am I going to be a good father? Two sons and a woman I'm still getting to know . . . If You're really there, please think of me and my little family. Amen."

I fell asleep hoping my prayer would work, at least a little bit. But even though I was, in the smallest of ways, trying to reach out, I was still a brat stuck in yesteryear.

12

MY OWN LITTLE RAIN MAN

RAYMOND: 97X, bam! The future of rock 'n' roll. 97X, bam! The future of rock 'n' roll. 97X, bam! The future of rock 'n' roll.

CHARLIE: Ray, enough already! Change the channel.

RAYMOND: 97X, bam! The future of rock 'n' roll. 97X, bam! The future of rock 'n' roll.

—FROM THE MOVIE RAIN MAN

At first, it was a small motion. I didn't think much of it. Austin would stroke his right palm over his left eyebrow. Then his left palm over his right eyebrow. Next he started adding a brush of his right hand down the left side of his face, over his cheek. Then the left hand down the right side of his face.

"Austin, what are you doing?"

"I don't know, Dad."

Again and again he repeated the motions until his skin was pink and irritated. Was something itching? Or hurting?

Again and again. Then he began to follow up the face-stroking routine with a vigorous rub under each eye. Over and over and over. Not only was his skin irritated, but his eyes began to get red from the friction and the pressure. It had to hurt but his eyes were vacant, and he didn't seem like he really knew what he was doing.

Rub, rub, scratch, brush, rub, rub, rub. Both hands side to side, back and forth. *Rub, rub, rub.* Faster and faster, almost like something bothered him from the inside out. I watched him, again and again, as he struggled to scratch the unstoppable itch. *Faster. Harder. Rub. Scratch.* It was as if an unseen force grabbed his hand and forced it through a ridiculous choreography over his face.

Eventually he added his upper lip to the routine. Back and forth he rubbed, alternating his hands. Faster and faster and faster until the skin above his top lip was raw, crusty, and bleeding.

He kept at it. Back up to the eyebrows, cheeks, underneath the eyes, then the lips. A cycle, mechanical, unstoppable.

"Can I help you, Auz?" I felt helpless. "Can I make it any better for you?"

He shook his hands, then pumped his arms in a circular motion, like the wheels spinning on a steam locomotive. "Chugga-chugga-choo-choo!" His voice was loud, excited, agitated.

"I want it out of my head, Dad. Please make it go away."

I wondered what was going on in his head to cause this fierce itch-rub battle. Finally, after his cheeks were flushed red with bruises rising to the surface, he sighed, long and hard. "Ahhhh . . ." His breath rushed out, and I could almost hear the tension leaving his body.

Why now? What released him from the cycle?

Patterns and cycles and habits have always been a huge part of Austin's life since he was young. From the first moment he could grip a toy, he loved to sort and arrange following some internal system I couldn't understand. And he wouldn't let me help. If he was arranging his Star Wars action figures, a process that could take hours, we needed to leave him alone until he was done. If Austin was interrupted from a repetitive movement or process, whether it was rubbing his face or arranging his toys, a frenzied temper tantrum ensued. He needed to do things his way but he couldn't always explain his way. He just needed to get through it.

During his first year of school, we couldn't help but compare Austin to his classmates, and we noticed he didn't talk as much. At recess and lunch he always stayed inside with his teacher or other adults instead of running around with the other kids. He didn't like to be touched and he seemed a little bit off. But there was no huge flashing neon shouting out, *"Hey! Your kid has autism!"* Two decades ago, not much was known about autism. So I ignored his quirks. There was no way anything was wrong with my son.

When Austin was six years old, we had some testing done at a behavioral clinic in Charlotte. He spent several hours on various tests, exercises, brainteaser problems, and puzzles. I already knew he could spend hours immersed in a puzzle, and he's still the only kid I know who starts in the middle of a puzzle instead of the edges.

Then he tried tangrams. A tangram is a puzzle consisting of seven different flat plastic pieces that fit together to form shapes. The object is to copy a shape printed on a card by putting the pieces together properly. The tangram has been called the earliest psychological test in the world, and in ancient China they were used to evaluate a person's intelligence. And Austin rocked it. Those early tests showed he was nearly off the charts for these types of complex puzzles and creative-thinking exercises.

I was fascinated as I watched Austin work on the tests; he was a boy totally driven and engaged in a test of his own internal will. When he was trying to solve the given puzzle, it was as if we didn't exist and nothing else mattered. Austin was in a separate world, temporarily on a different plane of existence.

Test results showed high artistic and creative scores. Austin also had highly developed skills for visual deduction. He could see, remember, and reconstruct patterns and cycles.

One night Teresa came across a *Time* magazine article about the alarming rise in the number of children with autism. She yelled to me from the living room, "This fits Austin. I think he might have autism or Asperger's syndrome."

What little I knew about autism made it seem like a form of mental retardation. And all I knew was that my son was not retarded.

"What?" I looked at Teresa, my eyes hard. I did not want to hear this. And I certainly didn't want to discuss it. "Autism? No way." I turned around and almost ran out of the living room. I knew he was exhibiting some quirky behaviors, but they were just goofy little-kid things he would outgrow. Then he would mature and develop like all the other kids.

But whether I acknowledged Austin's quirky behaviors or not, they continued and increased, with nervous tapping and rubbing and random gibberish coming out of his mouth. As his dad, I wanted to have all the answers, but I didn't. I couldn't understand what he was feeling, and I didn't know what to do to make it better. He would just have to grow up and grow out of it. He *had* to.

But Teresa, sweet and stubborn as ever, wouldn't let it go. She thought there was something serious going on with Austin even though we had no clear consensus from an army of doctors. We saw specialists. We filed away box loads of opinions and diagnoses. The acronyms changed and rearranged and changed again with no clear diagnosis. It was a painfully slow discovery process of dribs and drabs.

One day I walked into Austin's room and saw him on the floor. I watched in horror as his eyes rolled up in his head. A moment later his eyes relaxed, and he looked up at me, staring, with a little smile. His lips twitched a tiny bit. Then he fell into a deep, deep sleep. Doctors called it a petit mal seizure. He never convulsed or contorted on the ground; he just seemed to let go of consciousness simply and quietly and float downward into himself for a twelve- to fifteen-hour period of deep sleep.

Austin soon settled into a pattern of several petit mal seizures a month. They looked painless, innocuous, and simple, but they did seem to take a toll on him because the strange shutting-down process was always followed by a long, deep period of sleep, as if his body was trying to recover or reset. He suffered the seizures in the classroom, on the playground, at church, and out playing in the yard.

As much as I wanted to ignore my son's quirks, I couldn't. His strange behaviors began to assemble themselves into the tangram for autism, although it was still unclear what variety he had.

It was time I listened to Teresa. These weren't growing pains. Something was wrong with Austin. Besides the brittle bone disease, that is.

I still fantasized, as I covered miles upon miles for my sales job, that I would walk in the front door after one of my business trips and Austin would be okay, all the strange behaviors and patterns and cycles magically dissolved away. I wanted the routine, typical American family, like the kind I'd grown up with. Not perfect, just ordinary.

But each time I walked in the front door, Teresa's eyes told me everything I needed to know. *Good week? Or bad week?* She didn't need to say a word.

I had some big arguments with Joe about it.

"Hey, your son is autistic!" he said. "You need to read the signs. They're right in front of you."

"I don't want my baby to be a special-needs kid," I said.

"You're wasting time, Scott. Man up and do the right thing."

I finally gave in. Joe was right, and I started learning as much as I could about the terms the doctors were using. I figured the more information I had, the better I could know and help my son.

People always seemed to have opinions about what was going on with Austin. I mostly took it in stride, but there is one question that still drives me insane: "What can Austin do?" When I hear that question, I know what comes next.

"Does Austin have any cool abilities? Can he do anything like Dustin Hoffman in *Rain Man*?"

No, Austin didn't seem to have any extraordinary powers or psychic abilities. He wasn't a human calculator or a player piano who could reproduce any song he heard. He couldn't count toothpicks or tell you the day of the week for April 24, 1935, or the lineup for the 1978 Boston Red Sox.

But as I began to accept the strangeness and uniqueness of my firstborn, with his broken bones and face rubbing, his gibberish and seizures and long, deep sleeps, I settled in for the long haul. I wasn't in control of this puzzle. I could only sit back and try to see how it all went together and hope that it would make some sort of sense. And maybe I'd learn something along the way.

13

THE DOOR

Becoming a father is easy enough,
but being one can be very rough.
—WILHELM BUSCH

We have a long history of gaming in our house. Most families with boys can relate. But in our house, the mom is the primary gamer. Because she suffers from OI too, Teresa can't go out and play volleyball or take a Zumba class like her friends. So she goes online and plays games. Over the years she's made friends and connected to a whole community of like-minded women who love video games and are social and competitive.

Teresa has always played video games alongside the boys and she often hears, "You're the coolest mom!" from the boys' friends. She's been a member of several competitive online gaming teams, and her favorite at the moment is a very popular zombie game. That's right, zombies. My lovely bride destroys zombies for fun. Well, at least in the virtual world.

So video games are a big part of our lives, and we've had fun as a family playing together in games like *Crash Bandicoot Racing*, where your bandicoot, who looks like a red furry rat crossed with a coyote, zooms around an island on motorbikes and jet skis when he's not running and jumping to collect Wumpa fruit.

But there was a moment when it all almost ended, when an incident involving a video game led to a near disaster in our house, and our family was nearly destroyed. I almost can't even bear to talk about it, but life with Austin is not always bright and warm-fuzzy and Hallmark card–worthy. Sometimes, many times, our lives don't make any sense and we've broken under the weight of it. This was one of those times.

We were still trying to get a diagnosis for Austin's strange behaviors, which continued to evolve. At seven years old, his compulsive behaviors along with the ups and downs of his moods drove us to try one wonder drug after another. Did Austin have ADD, ADHD, or OCD? We kept trying, hoping for a breakthrough medication or treatment, but nothing worked and Austin only seemed to be getting worse. Teresa and I did our best. We wanted health and happiness for our firstborn child, but neither of us had signed up to be parents of a child with special needs, and we relied on the experts. I sometimes think the doctors dealing with the kinds of behavioral issues Austin exhibits might just be winging it, trying new therapies to see what does and doesn't work. I know they have science and precedent to draw from, but after experiencing less than stellar results from the efforts to fix what ails Austin, I wonder how much is science and how much is a crap shoot.

A neurologist we'd been seeing for some time decided to change some of Austin's medications to offset side effects. We are generally cautious about starting medications or changing dosages because Teresa has always been sensitive to medications. Even though her OI causes tremendous pain, she can't even take Advil; her body can't tolerate it. Austin seems to have inherited some of these sensitivities, and this time the new medication hit him hard. Within twenty-four hours, he became very anxious and agitated. As luck would have it, I was out of town on business and Teresa was home alone with the boys.

Austin grew violent and enraged and started throwing toys around the house. He grabbed his weighted plastic sippy cup and flung it at Teresa, hitting her right between the eyes. She battled him for thirty-six hours, trying to calm him down and ride out the side effects. She thought it was just a passing reaction and happy, sweet Austin would soon reemerge. But he got worse. There were moments when he seemed unable to control his body, drooling and jerking.

At one point, she was trying to restrain him during a temper tantrum when he grabbed her hair and wouldn't let go. As she wrestled with him, holding him by the arms, he bit her arm in rage. She was afraid and screamed, "Logan! Run next door to the neighbor's house." Logan obeyed and stayed safely over there for a few hours.

Finally, the battle became too much and Teresa gave up, calling me to come home and help. "Austin's eyes look strange and black. He's almost acting like he's possessed," she said. I cut my trip short and drove home. When I got there, Teresa fell into my arms, crying. We talked about what to do, but we both hoped the side effects had run their course and Austin's body would adjust to the new meds.

Teresa, Austin, and Logan were all exhausted, but the worst seemed to have passed, and it turned into a quiet evening. The boys decided to play in their room. Then I heard a sound I never want to hear again: Logan screaming.

Then quiet.

I bolted up the stairs and turned the corner to the boys' room. The door was shut. I grabbed the knob but it was locked. Still quiet. I pounded on the door. "Austin, open the door!"

Nothing.

"Open the door right now. Austin! *Open this door!*"

I couldn't wait any longer. I lifted up my foot and kicked the door open. It shattered around the doorknob and popped inward.

It worked. Just like Bruce Willis in the movies, I thought for a brief second. Then I saw.

Oh my God. Logan was on the floor with a cord from the Sony PlayStation wrapped around his neck. His face was turning white. I got between the boys and grabbed Logan, yanked him up, and untangled the cord from around his neck. Austin was crying, bellowing over and over, "Logan doesn't know how to play the way I play."

I screamed for Teresa, and we didn't stop to think. We just acted. Logan seemed fine, no bruises, just a little frightened. I think we were more scared than he was so we put the boys in the car and dropped Logan off at a friend's house. Next, we hustled Austin to the emergency room at Presbyterian Hospital. Something was very, very wrong.

After an examination, doctors not only noticed the obvious behavioral symptoms, but also determined the right side of his body wasn't functioning correctly and seemed partially paralyzed. Blood work showed that his liver wasn't properly metabolizing the new meds. They wanted to keep him in the hospital until the medication flushed out and his body detoxified, then start over with a reassessment and a new course of treatment. We agreed. I felt weary and knew he needed help. But then the doctors explained they were going to admit him to the psychiatric ward.

What? My seven-year-old son in the psych ward?

My mind started reeling, but I was numb. Teresa was too—I could see it in her eyes. In a few minutes we found ourselves on the seventh-floor wing for children and teenagers with severe behavioral and psychiatric health problems, in front of a big, heavy slab of a door like a bank vault. A big guy with a gun was guarding the locks. This entry was by invitation only. Both white-faced, we signed some papers and pushed them back through a locking window. Then a loud ka chunk and a slight grinding noise as the massive door yawned open. This was the end of the road for Teresa and me. We could go no farther.

I knew he had to be there, but I have never felt so alone and undone.

There was a feeling in the air, palpable, so thick you could almost grab it. It was resignation, defeat, failure. I was a failure. As a dad, as a husband, as a leader of my family. *I let Austin down. Somehow we missed something. We're not good parents, and we're not even good people.*

He was jabbering and agitated, so they gave him a shot of Ativan and he quieted. Then we stood at the door and watched as orderlies escorted Austin inside. He looked back over his shoulder and turned toward us. He reached out like he was trying to pull us in. His look told me everything—he didn't understand why we weren't walking with him. His face crumpled up into abject terror, and he burst into tears.

The door slowly swung shut, sealing us off from our boy. Teresa turned around and backed up to the door, crying to herself. Then she slowly slid down into a sitting position, her back jammed up against the massive door. It was as close as she could get to her child. She refused to leave. Earlier that day she'd almost lost one son and now she'd lost the other. "Please take care of him, God," she sobbed.

I wasn't crying. I wasn't doing much of anything. All I knew was the sun was going down and I had to go get Logan. I needed to be with him and be sure he was okay, and I knew he needed me after what had happened. I got into the elevator and watched another door close. As the elevator slowly hummed down seven floors, I felt lost and ashamed.

When will we see him? How long will Auz be in there?

What did we just do?

I am the worst parent there ever could be.

Then I realized I was only thinking about myself and about Teresa. *What about Austin? What was he going through?* I was so hung up on feeling bad that I wasn't even thinking about his feelings. *Austin doesn't have a clue what's happening. He's locked up in restraints behind a door guarded by a man with a gun. Will he survive?*

14

DAD, CAN I HAVE SOME RANCH DRESSING?

Often we look so long at the closed door
that we do not see the one which
has been opened for us.
—HELEN KELLER

The next four days were hell. I was in shock. The only emotion that broke through the numbness was anger. I was angry at God. I wondered what He was really like—this God I barely knew. Did He know what was going on? Did He care? Was He going to do anything about it?

Hey, we're in trouble down here, I wanted to shout, banging on the doors of heaven. I pictured them in my mind. Huge. Solid. Locked.

When I wasn't fuming at the unfairness in this particular game, I decided to try throwing out some prayers. I began to beg God for help. At first I was polite about it.

God, we need some help here. Austin is in trouble. What if his body can't handle the medication and he gets really sick? Or what if he goes insane? What if he's locked up for the rest of his life? God, he's just a little kid!

The more I prayed, the more desperate I felt. It was as if God were off duty, not available that particular moment. We heard nothing from the hospital, no hint that Austin was going to be okay. I resorted to bargaining.

God, if You're really there, You'll help Austin.

If You help him, heal his body, and give him back his mind, I'll believe in You.

God, if everything turns out all right, I will be so thankful.

I'll never forget You or what You did for us.

I'll stop drinking so much.

And . . . I'll start going to church more often.

Wait. Church? Where did that come from?

I still rarely joined Teresa and the boys at church; I had too many important things to do, like ride my mountain bike. My relationship with God was fragile and volatile. Most of the time I wondered where He was.

But now, in these desperate and confusing moments, I could see that I was missing something—my mountain-bike buddies weren't coming by to comfort me; Teresa's church friends were. They came to our house, held Teresa's hands, and prayed for strength and for Austin to be safe and not afraid. I noticed that Teresa seemed to know God in a whole different way, and she acted as though He was listening. That He cared. And she found a deep comfort in that. I wished I felt so sure.

I felt alone, with no one to turn to. For some reason I couldn't see Teresa right in front of me, and instead I turned away. We'd been acting more like brother and sister than husband and wife, with the boys as our lynchpin.

Back at the hospital, we had to wait for what seemed like ages to see our son; the doctors wanted to get all the meds out of his system and down to a stable baseline level. After four days of trying hard to pretend everything was okay for Logan while wondering if we'd done the right thing and if our lives would ever be okay again, we were permitted a twenty-minute visit with Austin. That's it. Twenty minutes.

On the elevator ride, the floors ticked up as I tried to stop the silent tears. *What will Austin say to us? How will he feel about us?* I felt sure Austin would look at us like traitors who'd abandoned him. *Wasn't that exactly what we'd done?*

We signed in, the guard nodded, the vault door swung open, and this time we walked inside. Someone guided us to a community room and then brought in Austin. The first thing I noticed was that he looked calmer, happier, and his eyes were clear. Teresa bombarded him with hugs.

Don't be a wuss, I warned myself. But the tears welled up anyway. I watched Teresa and Auz and felt paralyzed with joy.

"Mom! Dad!" Austin said, "There are some really, really, really messed up people in here, and they need help just like me. Do you want to meet them?"

Yes. We do.

And as we met Austin's new friends, both patients and staff, my grieving heart and my spirit, coiled and bound up like a tortured spring since I'd kicked in that door, finally began to let go and unwind. I could tell that Austin was on his way back to us. His innate sense of love and compassion was surfacing as he showed us around the common areas, happy and smiling.

I had been so worried about Austin, but it turns out I didn't need to be. While I'd been completely lost, he was meeting this new challenge with lightness and joy, almost as if it was an adventure. He didn't really understand why he was there, but he was making the best of it, and he'd already made fast friends. It still doesn't make sense to me, but somehow Austin was the strong soul in this trying time. Who else would see a psych ward lockdown as a chance to make new friends?

Austin's stay at Presbyterian Hospital was ten long days. After that first visit, we returned every day and were buzzed in through the vault door at 4:20 p.m. We learned that our visits were dependent on Austin's behavior and progress, and since he was doing well, we were always able to see him. He seemed pretty happy, and he told us he liked the food, although he'd made a few suggestions to the staff about how to improve some of the entrees. By the last day, though, he was ready to come home. We arrived, excited, and signed the papers for his release. When he came out we wept, hugged him, stroked his head, looked in his all-blue eyes. He came with us and didn't say much until we got in the car.

On the way home, we stopped for lunch at Showmars, our favorite Greek food stop. Austin ordered Calabash shrimp, hush puppies, fries, coleslaw, and a strawberry shake. And then he said the only thing he has ever said about his lockdown: "I am not going back there. Can I have some ranch dressing, please?"

I didn't know what to say.

He got louder, as he always does. He can be relentless. "Dad? Can I have some ranch dressing?"

I couldn't believe it. Austin had just been through the kind of trauma no kid should ever have to experience, but he was able to go on as if nothing much had happened. Even now, he wasn't afraid to ask for what he wanted. And keep asking.

Then something clicked. If I wanted to know what God was all about, I'd have to walk up to His door, no matter how big or scary it was, and knock on it. And keep knocking on it, raising my voice and asking for what I needed. If it worked for Auz, it just might work for me.

The next Sunday I was in church with Teresa and my two boys. For the moment, I was resolved to make God a bigger part of my life.

15

THE EARWORM

He who sings scares away his woes.
—CERVANTES

Have you ever seen those family portraits where everyone in a big family wears a matching red Hawaiian shirt or a blue denim shirt? When we were still on the chase for a firm diagnosis, a specialist showed Austin a picture like this. Everyone in the large family photo wore blue jeans and an untucked, white button-down shirt.

"What is special about this picture?" she asked Austin after she covered the picture. "Tell me what you saw."

"There was a picture of water, with a green sailboat, white clouds, and a big sun at the top," said Austin.

The specialist looked confused. That wasn't the picture she'd shown him.

She looked carefully at Austin. He seemed okay. Fidgety, talking about the cool paper clips on her desk, his usual intense Austin-self. Then she looked back at the picture. There it was! On the wall behind the white-shirted family was a small, framed picture. And if she squinted her eyes and looked really hard, she saw water, a sailboat, and some white clouds. It was so tiny she couldn't see if the sailboat was green or not, but she was going to trust Austin on this one.

Austin just sees things differently, and he often sees things no one else does. Then he tries to talk about it, and half the time we have *no* idea what he's talking about. When I don't get what he's saying, he repeats it. Again and again. He gets louder, more animated, and focused on making me understand. The louder and more excited he gets, the less I understand. Most of our waking hours consist of Austin trying to explain something, me not getting it, and both of us getting frustrated. And he never gives up. I mean, never.

Eventually, when I've had enough and I get annoyed or angry and I'm about to lock myself in my closet because he won't stop talking about that thing I don't understand, I threaten him with taking away a favorite toy or I bribe him with a trip to get his favorite fast-food and he will get distracted. Sometimes I never figure out what he is trying to tell me. But other times it will all become clear, and I will realize, just like Austin saw the picture of the sailboat behind the family, that he's seen something in his unique, Austin kind of way.

Once he was going on and on about a bear.

"Isn't it cool? The bear was climbing the wall. Do bears climb? Could a bear climb our house?

Could a bear climb my school? Dad, the bear was climbing the wall. He was black with big claws and teeth. Dad, did you see the bear? He was climbing the wall."

Austin was just getting warmed up. He was about to leave the bullpen and really get into the game.

"Dad, have you ever seen a bear? I saw a bear. He was black, and he was big. He was climbing the wall. Why was he climbing the wall, Dad?" His voice was getting louder.

I had no idea what he was talking about, and it sounded like he was making up a story.

"Austin, I don't know. Please give it a rest." I used my deepest, sternest voice.

He moved closer, chest to chest, and shouted up at me in case I didn't understand.

"Dad, do bears climb? It was so cool. The bear was climbing a big wall."

Time for a distraction. I was an accomplished father, and I was pulling out the big guns.

"Austin, you want to watch *Back to the Future*? I haven't seen it in a while. Isn't that silver DeLorean the best car ever?"

It didn't work. For days we heard about the bear climbing the wall. Then weeks. The bear climbing the wall haunted my dreams.

Then one day we were in the car and drove past a big zoo. I glanced at the sign, then stopped and stared, Austin's bear obsession for the last few weeks reverberating in my head. There, on a full-color billboard in all its black furry glory, was an enormous, two-story gorilla climbing up the side of a fence. Okay, it wasn't a bear, but close.

"There he is!" Austin screamed.

Of course he is. I should never have doubted you, Auz.

I'm learning to be a better listener and realizing that Austin may never see things like the average bear. He seems to experience the world differently than Teresa, Logan, and I do. But then again, who wants to be average?

Not only do we often misunderstand Austin, but we have often felt misunderstood because it's difficult to explain how hard it is to live with our son. Sometimes I feel like I'm trying to describe the bear climbing the wall and no one gets it. Most often the really tough stuff, the meltdowns, seizures, migraines, bad days, and hurting hearts, happen at home. When it comes to life with Austin, we've been lectured, laughed at, and ignored. We're used to being told to "get tough" or "show him who's boss." Others have accused us of spoiling him or letting him get away with too much. Sometimes I've even sensed that people think we're dramatizing Austin's problems or even making things up. I've often berated myself too. *How can I let a hyperactive kid rule the house?*

As we struggled to navigate the plateaus and

peaks of raising Austin, the questions and accusations from people close to us amplified our indecision. Maybe the naysayers were right. Maybe we *did* let our hyper kid rule the house. The accusations hit hard, and we second-guessed almost every decision.

Friends and family tried to give us an occasional break, but we found when we needed a babysitter, the sitter would usually make it through one session and after that, he or she was always too busy to come again. I understood. It stinks, but I got it. Babysitting Austin is hard. Living with him is even harder. *Hard* doesn't even do justice to the strain, but I can't think of a better word to describe how all-encompassing, exhausting, and in-your-face our boy with autism can be. Austin's special needs and autism consume not only time but energy, financial resources, strength, patience, and sanity. So when Teresa and I get the chance to get away for a day or even just an evening, it's a rare treat. We love our boys more than life, but a weekend away? Priceless.

Respite care for Austin was almost a foreign word to us. We had a near-impossible time affording, appreciating, understanding, or enjoying a break from Austin. So much of our family's existence revolves around his needs. And when we do get a break, we spend time wondering how the boys are doing and crossing our fingers for no emergency phone calls. We're not paranoid, just realistic.

But we know it's important to spend time away, just the two of us. So several years ago we decided to try for a quick weekend getaway. Our longtime friends Bob and Mary volunteered to keep Austin. When I think back, I'm not quite sure where Logan was for those two days. Probably at his cousin's. Logan was different, God bless him. Easy, uncomplicated, sweet-natured. And low maintenance. I always tell people you could dump a bag of Oreos in the corner of his room, throw in a case of Gatorade, and Logan would be good to go for an entire weekend.

Before our weekend away, we had Bob and Mary over for dinner to go through a dry run of a one-on-one with Auz. On the menu: turkey burgers, fries, and, of course, ranch dressing. We were going through cases of that stuff. Austin uses it to dip almost all his food.

We weren't sure which Austin would show up for dinner—the one who throws nonstop curve-balls or the peach. Usually, if it was anyone other than Teresa or me, he would be easy to take care of. We went over his medicines and regimen step by step. He has strict, self-imposed routines for before dinner, after dinner, bedtime, and the morning. I was pretty confident that Bob, a marine, could appreciate the precision and regimental drumbeat Austin marches to. And honestly, the walk-through was as much for us and our peace of mind.

But still I worried. *Will they have met their match with Austin? Will he break something? Would they be shocked by Austin waking them up in the middle of the night and asking for an omelet? Or will he shine and they'll laugh?*

Thus began our rare and magical weekend away. T and I drove off, and when we pulled in to the hotel driveway, I felt a little lost.

Wow. We are alone. What do we do? Who should we call? Should we check in with Bob and Mary? Does Logan need a quick call? What are we supposed to do now?

We were frozen, standing beside our car with our luggage in hand, not sure what to do next.

As we looked at each other, we burst into screaming laughter.

"We're alone! We're alone! Yippee!"

Then we stopped. I breathed out a very long and slow breath. I realized I'd been holding my breath. For just that moment, I felt the stress, tension, worries, and concern slip right out of my mind. I felt good, peaceful.

Then I noticed the two people standing a few cars down. They were staring at us. I looked, and we locked eyes. *Kris and Bob!* They were from our hometown, and Kris had been Austin's special ed teacher. We said hello, and Kris asked about the boys. Then she told me a story about Austin.

Austin came into my classroom one day. I could tell he was in a "highly motivated" mood. I'd gotten pretty good at telling what kind of day Austin was going to have.

As soon as he crossed through the doorway, he started singing a song. He had on a hat, and I could only stop and watch for a minute before I motioned for him to get a move on and get seated. He kept singing.

"Dahhh, da-da, dahhh da-da, dah da-da . . . dahhh da-da dahhh da-da, dah da-da!" He sang it again. It sounded familiar. At first I thought it was the theme song from the old TV show The Munsters. But then it hit me. It was that repetitive, crazy-fast tune we called the "Mexican Wedding Song." It's the kind of song you can't get out of your head. I said, "Austin, please stop singing and let's get to work."

About forty-five minutes later, I couldn't help myself and I started singing, *"Dahhh da-da dahhh da-da, dah da-da,"* and then the entire class joined in. I thought, *Austin, look what you started. You made me do this.* And I couldn't wipe the smile off my face. I thought about what he brings to my classroom, and probing a little deeper, I realized that Austin brings good to everyone he encounters. It made me happy.

Later that day I arrived home and informed Bob that I can never hear the "Mexican Wedding Song" again because it was now forever etched in the back of my mind. Another word for it is an earworm, a jingle that gets stuck in your mind and you can't shake it. That silly song kept a constant drumbeat going in my mind for my entire day. But I still had to smile.

T and I went on to have a wonderful weekend away. We slept in on that Saturday morning, which doesn't happen often in our house. Logan had fun with his cousin. And Austin? After a dinner of hot dogs, potato chips, and lots of ranch dressing, he discovered Bob and Mary's hot tub and proceeded to spend the rest of the evening soaking like a king. He did try crawling in bed with Bob and Mary at about three in the morning just to see how they were doing, but Bob wasn't alarmed in the least. Instead, Austin and Bob ended up enjoying some more hot dogs, chips, and ranch dressing in the kitchen together at 3:00 a.m. You can't ruffle a marine. Ever. *Semper Fi.*

Looking back, I was so caught up and engaged with trying to survive my life that I didn't take seriously the idea of respite. But that weekend I learned that we needed to take ourselves just a little bit less seriously. I worried and fretted so much over what crazy thing Austin was going to do next, or what injury would take us back to the ER, that I was missing the amazing things he was trying to tell me or show me. I realized that joy lurks in unexpected, everyday places, and I needed to try extra hard to see the green sailboat or the bear climbing the wall, or take time to sing a little song.

16

SAND ANGELS

To myself I am only a child playing on the
beach, while vast oceans of truth lie
undiscovered before me.
—ISAAC NEWTON

I don't know if it's the fresh salty air or being
kissed by the sun or just the beautiful waves
flowing onto the beach, but wherever the magic
comes from, the beach has a powerful effect on
Austin. He runs up and down, crashes through
the waves (the waves are pretty gentle in South
Carolina), hums along with the foamy surf, and
lies in mounds of white, wet sand buried up to
his eyeballs.

One glorious July Fourth we were at the ocean.
As we waited to watch the local fireworks show
from the beach, Austin, Logan, and two cousins
crawled around on hands and knees as they
worked on an enormous sand castle. This wasn't
just any ordinary sand castle. This architectural
wonder measured twenty feet across. It was late
afternoon, and the sand engineers had been
working hard for about an hour. Austin was right
in the middle, but I knew the kind of help he was

providing—the last time I'd looked over he had covered himself in about two feet of sand and was trying to make sand angels with his hands and feet, just like you do in the snow. He was in his element, completely and utterly blissful with the cool sand cradling his body and the warm sun on his face.

After Austin finished his sand angels, he started working on his own construction project. I watched out of the corner of my eye as he crawled around on his knees, working with a little sand shovel. But he didn't seem to be building a castle. Instead, he slowly dug a trench. He didn't say a word or even look at his sand castle competitors. He was silent, completely and utterly focused on the task at hand. Before long, Austin had dug a deep circular ditch and he was in the middle. Instead of a sand castle, he'd created a moat.

I was sitting in a nearby beach chair, the sweet smell of Banana Boat SPF 50 in my nose as I tipped my Jimmy Buffet hat lower and sank down into my chair. The kids were busy, Austin was safe, and I could relax, for once. My eyelids grew heavy and I think I was dozing. Then, from out of nowhere, a hail of sand, shells, and driftwood twigs showered over me.

"What?!" I sat up, pushed back my hat, and blinked my eyes, trying to wake up.

All I saw was the blur of Austin brushing past

me, and I heard his hurried mumble, "Bye. I'm done. Let's go." Then he was already twenty feet past me and running down the beach, making a beeline straight for the condo at breakneck speed.

What should I do? Should I chase him?

I was still half asleep, my brain fuzzy, and I didn't really want to get up.

Come on, Auz!

My anticipation of the Fourth of July festivities was at war with my responsibilities as a dad. I knew I should go get him, but I didn't want to. *It's almost time for the fireworks, I argued with myself. That's why we're here.*

Just then, even though it wasn't quite dark, the first crackles and pops started across the water, the bright colors exploding in bursts over our heads.

Why now? Why do I always have to chase him? Why does he have to ruin everything?

But of course Austin wasn't trying to ruin anything, and he didn't realize the dangers of a boy running down the beach and heading back to the vacation condo by himself. And I knew I had to get up and go after him. I also knew I wouldn't be bringing him back to the beach and the fire-works show. I was going to follow him back to the condo to make sure he was safe. Then I'd sit there alone while he shut down and descended into a deep, deep sleep. Some days those shut-downs are a relief, but not this day. I wanted desperately to stay on the beach with the others. But I couldn't, and I walked down the beach, fireworks sending bolts of color through the warm Carolina skies.

When Austin is done, I'm done. Sometimes when he's in shutdown mode there's no creative solution to apply or profound philosophy to implement. You just give in and go with it and follow your kid down the beach. There aren't any warnings. You never know when you'll get a meltdown. There is no seizure schedule. You can't predict when he's going to check out, withdraw, and shut down.

One of the ways Teresa and I have learned to cope is by taking turns. We've learned to divide and conquer. Teresa chases after him one time and the next time I'm up. Believe me, we had many moments when we lost our minds and our cool, and we still do sometimes when family get-togethers, parties, picnics, or nights on the beach or at the movies are canceled or cut short.

There is no road map, and what Teresa and I try at home pretty much amounts to a whole lot of trial and error—mostly error—but at least we try. Sometimes our journey as parents of a son with autism is like that run down the beach—it's getting dark, there's a lot of noise and confusion, and you're moving slowly as your feet sink into the sand, but you're working really hard to get there. You rekindle hope, beat down the fear, look into the future. And it's really, really murky. So you freeze, like I did in my beach chair.

But Austin doesn't spend much time worrying or agonizing over the future. He starts and stops quickly and effortlessly, making me guess what in the world he's thinking. Maybe I'm not meant to understand after all, but only to have faith, accept, and embrace this terrific kid.

Back at home on a different summer day it was just me, Austin, a lumpy bench, some cold popcorn, and an empty hallway. The rest of the family was inside enjoying the movie. Me? Not so much. The walls were shaking and trembling from the on-screen crashes and roars, a rising crescendo of swords clanging, creatures shrieking, and distant cries for Frodo to save Middle Earth from the evils of Mordor and the vile Gollum.

Our family is fanatical about all things pertaining to *The Lord of the Rings*, so we were excited to be able to see the most recent installment of the LOTR trilogy on the day it premiered at our favorite movie theater in Pineville, North Carolina. Teresa, Austin, Logan, and I had been eagerly awaiting the film's release, and the excitement of the audience in the movie house was tangible. We bought our tickets and loaded up on popcorn, pop, nachos, candy, and hot dogs and settled in for an epic three hours of fantasy at its best.

But thirty minutes in, we were done.

Or, I should say, Austin and I were done because he got up and left. I don't mean got up and left to go to the bathroom or get a drink at the water fountain. I mean stood up, ran out, and ain't coming back.

I ended up experiencing the blockbuster smash movie with my eight-year-old in my arms on a worn-out vinyl bench in the hall outside the theater. I couldn't see anything; I just listened to the battle raging inside as I clutched my son, now asleep. I found myself gently rocking Austin back and forth, holding him tight.

Maybe the booming sounds and vivid colors were just too much for him and he checked out. And once that happens, there's no going back.

So when we decide to go somewhere and do something as a family, there's a very good chance that at some point, and probably when I least expect it, Austin's done, boom, I'm outta' here. He'll stop whatever he's doing and take off. Why? I don't know. Maybe it's like when he ran away and pulled that dancing-naked-in-the-window stunt as a toddler. Is he bored? Tired? Overwhelmed? Or does he suddenly get a burst of energy, some sort of electrical turbo boost in his autistic brain and nervous system that gets his feet moving and going? I don't know why he does it. I only know that whenever life gets the tiniest bit predictable, Auz flips it upside down and around and flees on his brittle-boned feet, smack into unpredictable.

As his dad I've tried and tried to figure him out. I've read all the recommended autism books, scoured the websites, talked to other parents, and stayed up many a night munching on my goldfish crackers and thinking about neurodiversity and the issue of "Would I fix him if I could?" But most of the time I'm still clueless as to why Austin does what he does. Trying to understand Austin is like trying to capture a shadow. You see it, you think you can grab it, you reach out, and it's gone. Am I supposed to figure him out? Is that my job as his dad? Because if it is, I'm not doing so good. Austin's behavior is often just a mystery.

In fact, as I write this, Austin is sitting on the floor next to my chair, eating goldfish crackers. Most people make a little noise when they eat. You might hear a smack here or there, crunching sounds, a slight echo of a swallow. But not Austin. No one will ever wonder if he is enjoying his food. He moans. He grunts. He yells to everyone in hearing distance that it's the best thing he's ever tasted as he throws whatever he's eating down the hatch. Give him a sausage biscuit and he'll scream his joy out the window. He'd make a great spokesman for his favorite foods, and his enthusiasm would be 1,000 percent genuine.

Today I'm curious, so I lean over the arm of my

chair and ask him, "Austin, why do you grunt while you eat?"

"It's just the way I eat, Dad."

The more I research and study autism and try to uncover the secrets behind Austin's behaviors, the more I'm coming to see him as someone who doesn't necessarily need fixing. I'm beginning to see my son as someone I need to better understand and accept instead of continually trying to change him as if something is broken and wrong.

I'm fascinated with the idea of *neurodiversity,* a new word being batted around the special-needs community. My own interpretation is the idea of simply accepting differences in how people function and appreciating people for who they are, not what disorder or diagnosis they've been labeled with. My son is not abnormal, broken, or disabled, just different. Who is to say that what my son is seeing, feeling, experiencing, and saying is wrong or abnormal? Maybe Austin is doing everything in just the right way, the way he is supposed to. Why should I be angry, frustrated, ashamed, or afraid to shout it from the rooftops?

If the legions of experts and clinicians are having such a hard time figuring out this thing called autism, maybe they never will, and maybe they aren't supposed to. Maybe God made Austin and every other person like him exactly the way they were meant to be.

And me, I'm learning how to not only accept my son but to embrace Austin for all that he is. What was once a chase after a runaway toddler is becoming a journey where sometimes Austin takes the lead and I follow, gleaning a little more wisdom with each step.

17

THE DEVIL'S GRIP

If I can stop one heart from breaking,
I shall not live in vain.
—EMILY DICKINSON

Brittle bone disease and autism aren't the only things Austin has to deal with. Besides being born with broken bones, Austin was born with a broken heart.

I've struggled with how much to tell people about my family. I don't want sympathy, although it is nice when people care. I don't want to over-whelm people, because everyone has their own problems. And I don't want to brand or label Austin as disabled or dysfunctional—my son is so much more than the sum of his current diagnoses.

So just like Austin dug that moat around himself in the sand, sometimes I've created my own moat using my mountain bike, my golf clubs, my work, or even my drinking, a moat that cut me off from Teresa and my boys—the people I've needed most. I've kept my worries to myself and rarely, if ever, told anyone the whole of it; it all seems too complex and overwhelming.

That's why I've hesitated going into detail about yet another Austin problem. But for you to understand how I felt when Austin struggled with the devil's grip, you need to know about his heart. When he was a toddler and struggling with lung infections, his doctor thought she heard a murmur. When he was four years old, doctors discovered Austin had an atrial septal defect, a hole in the wall between the two upper chambers of his heart. He also had a ventricular septal defect, a hole in the wall between the two lower chambers of his heart. He had a leaky heart.

Teresa and I were still trying to figure out how to make our marriage work while dealing with Austin's fragile bones and challenging behavior. And now we had to watch as orderlies whisked him away to an operating room on a gurney far too big for his little body.

I still marvel that they could fix his heart when it was just the size of a plum. They hooked him up to the heart/lung machine, and he was on the table for five hours while they patched up the holes and transposed two major arteries. They rebuilt Austin's heart, and he has the scars to prove it—and I'm sure he'll volunteer to show them to you if you ever meet him in person.

Now that I look back on it, I'm amazed that it all worked like it should. With Austin's brittle bones, how did he withstand such a major surgery? How did his heart and his bones and his chest heal up and allow him to get up out of bed and be a regular kid? (Well, a regular kid, Auz-style!) But he did heal, and even though the open-heart surgery was a major ordeal at the time, we came through it and now it's just a bump in the road on our journey with Austin.

But one summer night after a beach trip, when Austin was twelve, he started complaining about chest pain. Austin is used to pain; he deals with it every day and tolerates more than most people could stand. Pain is part of his life. So when he complains, we listen. And when he said his chest hurt, my mind immediately replayed the memory of his heart surgery years before.

"Mom, I really hurt. Please stop this," Austin screeched through tear-soaked sobs. "Oh my God. What is wrong with me, Dad? Please make it stop. I'm so sorry I hurt, Mom, but it won't stop."

We tried unsuccessfully to comfort him while figuring out what to do next. This was no tummy ache. Something was very wrong.

Teresa had developed an uncanny sixth sense when it came to Austin. Because of her own OI, she usually knew when Austin had a break that needed to be seen by a doctor or when it was something minor that could be fixed with a rest on the couch, a movie, and a milkshake. But tonight we were all stumped as Austin's chest, stomach, and torso wracked in convulsions. He writhed in pain, crying and complaining about his chest. "It's really tight! It feels like something is pinching me!"

Acting on Teresa's instincts, we rushed Austin to the emergency room just five miles away. But the doctors couldn't figure out what was causing the pain. They decided to keep him overnight for observation and dosed him with strong pain medication. We sat up with him until he fell asleep. He was quiet for a few hours, but when morning came, the pain was back and it was fierce.

Within hours we were in an ambulance with Austin as he was transferred to Children's Hospital. They still didn't know what was wrong. The paramedics in the ambulance said they'd overheard something about pneumonia or an upper respiratory issue—that was news to us. I felt a little relief.

I can live with that diagnosis. Put him on an IV drip of antibiotics and he'll be good as new.

No worries. Or so I thought.

At Children's Hospital, Austin developed a headache and chills. It was torture watching the wrenching contortions of his chest and upper body. He was wracked by burst after burst of excruciating jolts of pain and then, just as fast, they would abate. Even though he looked like he was in a living hell, in between the waves of pain he smiled and told us he was going to be fine.

Somehow he was in agony one minute and then comforting us the next. Maybe hospital admissions had become almost a comfortable routine for Austin.

After another night of tests, poking and prodding, a cardiologist walked into the room. I was still clinging to the pneumonia idea, so seeing a heart doctor kind of threw me off. "It's called the devil's grip," he said. He thought Austin had a rare condition, most often associated with a virus first reported in Australia many years ago. "Because of Austin's heart issues and his bone disease, we want to do an MRI. Tonight. We need to see what's going on."

When the results came back, it wasn't pretty. The MRI showed a large, unknown mass behind Austin's pericardium (the bag-like lining around the heart). My anxiety level ratcheted up several notches as I thought about his rebuilt heart. Meanwhile, the news didn't seem to bother Austin, and he was having a great time smiling and joking with the nurses in between the pain.

Concerned about the mass, the cardiologist scheduled Austin for open-heart surgery the following morning. I was shocked and staggered on my feet. All I could do was pray. I tried, *Lord, please heal Austin. Touch Your hands upon our son and his surgeons. And give us strength.* I prayed repeatedly, pleading with God.

I was amazed at Austin's strength throughout

the ordeal. His positive attitude and his faith seemed to be at levels I could only hope to reach someday. I was starting to realize he was stronger than I knew.

Later that day, the doctors decided to run a few last tests to rule out any unforeseen issues or obstacles they might encounter during the heart surgery. Then an unexpected reprieve. Teresa and I sat in stunned silence as the cardiologist delivered more news, this time good: the last test showed the mass behind Austin's heart was blood leakage into his pericardium, not a tumor or devil's grip, and surgery would *not* be needed.

This was one of those roller-coaster moments, highs and lows coming so quickly I couldn't catch my breath. I shook my head to clear it and tried to listen to what the doctor was saying. The new tests showed that Austin's sternum, the large breastplate of bone in front of his heart, had a crack. The cracked bone had pricked the pericardium sack. Blood had been slowly leaking into the pericardium, and the pooling blood created tremendous pressure, causing the extreme pain and inflammation. It was still serious, but not having the open-heart surgery was a relief—a minor victory and an answered prayer.

Doctors prescribed rest, along with antibiotics and anti-inflammatory medications. Nothing further. We decided to trust the doctors, and after a few days of treatment, the pain and spasms lessened and finally went away completely. It worked.

While the mystery of what caused the pain had been solved, we had no idea what had caused the break in Austin's sternum. It could have been anything as Austin can suffer bone breaks from even the subtlest of insults. Was it a rogue wave on our beach vacation? A joking, playful punch from one of his cousins? Maybe someone had hugged him just a little too hard? As Austin recovered, we speculated. Finally, Austin himself provided the answer.

"I jumped off the high dive." Austin smiled at the memory, then saw our faces and quickly apologized in his quirky way. "Please, thank you, you're welcome, I'm sorry. I jumped off the high dive."

What? I couldn't believe it. Then I remembered. The day before the chest pain started, we'd attended a birthday party at the local swimming pool. I was on duty, watching Austin. I had turned away in a brief moment of distraction, and at that moment Austin had scampered up the ladder of the high dive and taken the plunge. The impact alone could have killed him. But I couldn't get mad—I knew how much he wanted to play and be like the other kids, and so in his mind, the danger was worth the risk. Now we've made it abundantly clear that diving boards of any kind are a no-fly zone for him. Until he tries again, and I'm sure he will.

Austin is not afraid of the high dive, and he doesn't seem to be afraid of anything life throws at him, including unimaginable pain. I will never forget him laughing and joking with the nurses when we thought there was a tumor behind his heart and they were about to crack him open again. He laughed, dug in, persevered, and vanquished that dragon with joy.

I wanted my heart to be warm and open like Austin's. All along I'd been wishing I could climb inside his brain, see what was going on, and maybe help him. But I was starting to understand it was me—I was the one who needed help and Austin was seeing what I had been missing. I knew I needed to pay better attention. But when I learned, would I be capable of changing?

18

THE JESTER

A hat is a flag, a shield, a bit of armor . . .
A piece of magic is a hat.
—MARTHA SLITER

Behold the power of the hat.

The hat was acquired a few years ago while we were visiting relatives back in New England. We spent a few weeks in my mom's hometown of Scituate, Massachusetts, on the coast halfway between Boston and Plymouth. We had a great time going to see the Red Sox play and catching up with family and old friends.

One day my cousin Wendy took Austin and Logan down to the harbor to eat lunch and do a little shopping on the pier. As they strolled along, Wendy and Austin spotted a hat. It wasn't just any hat. This was the hat of all hats—a magnificent, towering creation of huge bright green, yellow, blue, and red horn-shaped thinga-majigs made of felt with tassels and prickly pompoms dangling off the ends. It was crazy and sparkly, about three feet high by three feet wide. Austin had to have it and Wendy bought it for him. Five minutes later the hat was on his head, where it remained for the rest of the trip.

Austin's interests often veer into obsessions and when he was old enough to make his wishes known about what he would or wouldn't wear, he developed a burning passion for hats. Nothing tops his quest for the ultimate hat. He doesn't wear a hat to keep the sun out of his eyes or support his favorite team. Austin wears hats because they mean something. I'm just not sure what that something is, and I don't always see the beauty in a particular hat the same way Austin seems to. He falls in love with certain hats, each one like the elusive lost piece of a puzzle. When he selects his hat of the day, he wears it with reverence and pride; the hat is now part of him. Never plain baseball caps or run-of-the-mill beanies, Auz hats are sometimes loud but always off-the-wall unique, and the jester hat is the crown jewel of his collection.

On our way home from Massachusetts, we decided to stop off in New York City. I'd booked a reservation for us near Times Square, front row and center at the crossroads of humanity in all its chaotic and colorful glory. When we hit the streets and took in the insane neon and in-your-face flashing lights and overall hubbub, I worried that it might set off one of Austin's seizures. But when I looked over, Auz was beaming from ear to ear under the jester hat.

I had a pretty good idea why—his eyes were

fixed on the mass of video screens covered in bright, flashing, dancing graphics that wrap around the Toys-R-Us store. It's the biggest toy store in the world, 110,000 square feet of childhood dreams come to life.

Austin and Logan headed for the toy store like twin starships being sucked in by a tractor beam while Teresa and I stumbled along behind trying to keep our eyes on them as we pushed through the crowds. When we finally stepped inside, my senses were assaulted and I didn't know where to look first. The sixty-foot Ferris wheel? The life-size *Tyrannosaurus rex*? The four-thousand-square-foot Barbie dollhouse?

How about my own boys?

Wait! Teresa's right by me, but where's Austin? Where's Logan?

I spun around, looking for a blond head and a crazy hat through the crowd.

How did they disappear so fast?

Teresa and I split up and did a quick search of the immediate area. Nothing. The boys were gone. While Teresa and I had been gawking at the sights, Auz and Logan had ditched us and taken off for parts unknown. By themselves. In the world's largest toy store in the middle of a massive, unfamiliar city.

My feelings of awe and wonder vanished, instantly replaced by fear, worry, and anger. I can't even describe what went through my mind in those first few minutes. Teresa and I needed to find them immediately, or we could be facing a situation of epic proportions. With Austin, anything was possible and he was fast—he could be anywhere. And hopefully he'd keep his clothes on this time.

We split up again and took off, riding up and down the escalators, searching the stacks and looking through the crowds. I was about to go into a full-blown panic when, like a shining beacon of the Scituate Lighthouse cutting through the fog, I saw the hat. I was in a lobby area looking up when I spotted the sparkly peaks and dangling tassels of Austin's hat bobbing around a couple floors above me. I hopped on the escalator, my eyes focused on the hat. As I got closer, I saw Austin and Logan talking to a store employee. All three looked calm and deep in conversation. They didn't see me yet.

Okay, no worries. Austin and Logan are telling him they're lost and asking for help. Whew. Glad they remembered. At least we've done some-thing right.

But no. As I approached, I realized they were engaged in an animated discussion with the store employee over which toy was cooler—the new Toy Story Buzz Lightyear plush figure or his buddy, Rex the green dinosaur. After Teresa caught up with me and we'd showered the boys with hugs and kisses, we realized they had no clue what had happened. It turned out they hadn't even noticed. Austin and Logan weren't lost— they were just fine. It was Teresa and I who'd been lost.

A little later we launched back out into the sea of humanity flowing in and around Times Square. I kept a firm grip on my family this time as we pushed through the throng of tourists, sidewalk vendors, and street entertainers. We saw the Naked Cowboy (not really naked), the Hulk, and a six-foot-tall guy dressed in a furry red Elmo suit.

But now something else seemed to be getting more attention—people began to stop and stare at Austin. Several pointed, whooped, and gave him high fives and "Boo yahs!" After the first three or four, we gave in and stopped to enjoy the phenomenon. Everybody in Times Square, it seemed, wanted to know where Austin got his awesomely cool hat. Auz was a sensation, and his jester hat ruled the night.

When Austin first wore the jester hat home from the outing with Wendy, I didn't realize it would become a permanent fixture on his head. He went everywhere with it. He wore it to school and church, to go shopping, and some-times even to bed. He wore it with his finest dress-up threads, his jeans, his sweats, and even his pajamas. After a while I got tired of it, the loudness and the size and the color, and I'd catch myself getting irritated and begging him to stop.

"Man! Austin! Please! Leave. It. In. The. Car."

But the hat stayed on. Others more readily understood his passion and embraced the hat. Our preacher donned the hat for a Sunday sermon. The school principal wore it in the homecoming parade. And slowly I began to realize the jester hat was a missing part of him that he had recovered. I was the one with the hat issues, not Austin.

After that moment of clarity, I was freed of my hat issues and Auz was welcome, even encouraged, to wear the hat regardless of the time, place, or occasion. Austin and his hat are one.

I once asked him why he likes the hat so much.

"It makes me happy," he said. "I feel good when I wear it. It's the Austin hat, Dad. The colors, the way it moves and jiggles. The chicks dig it, and it's cool. My jester hat just rocks. I like the way it makes me feel."

After the Times Square incident, I started to pay more attention to Austin's hats, and I began to understand the joy and the calm they provide. Austin looks and acts more comfortable and secure when he wears the jester or any other favorite hat, as if a profound and soothing force takes over and guides him. When he puts on his jester hat, he seems to be more fully alive and present.

The jester hat and the toy-store adventure remind me of a scripture a pastor showed me one day. "I tell you the truth, unless you turn from your sins and become like little children, you will never get into the Kingdom of Heaven" (Matt. 18:3 NLT). This verse helps me remember how real and meaningful and beautiful my two boys are and how much that silly hat stands for. Maybe if I could see the world more through Austin's eyes, I could better embrace the passion he has for pure beauty and simple pleasures, like picking out just the right hat.

Austin is his jester hat—bright and loud and colorful. I'm learning to believe in the power of the hat . . . and the power of my son. He's comfortable in his own skin. I want to be too.

19

ESCAPE

I was an accomplice in my own frustration.
—SIR PETER SHAFFER

I was sleeping off the alcohol I'd consumed at
the Super Bowl party when I heard a noise in the
middle of the night. I lifted my head and cracked
open one eye.

There's someone in the hallway.

I forced open the other eye and turned my head,
trying hard to see who it was. There was a dim
light coming from the laundry room down the
hall, enough for me to see the silhouette, right
outside my bedroom door. As I shook my head to
clear the fuzziness, the figure slowly came into
focus, like the turning of a lens on a heavy old
camera. It was Teresa. She was clutching a big
butcher knife.

"You gonna kill me?" I lay there, waiting. Then
she smiled an odd little smile and hid the knife
behind her back.

I'm alive and still married and writing this
book so you know she didn't kill me. But let me
back up and tell you more about that crazy day.
Yes, I know we have a lot of crazy days, but

this day seemed to kick off the craziest time of all, when it felt like my life was going to blow apart into a million pieces so tiny and jagged no one could ever put them together again.

Teresa is a fantastic mom. She was so strong, keeping all the balls in the air. I loved being a dad, but Teresa and I were still far apart in our marriage. We existed like college roommates, far apart in priorities—Teresa's were in the right order and mine were not. She was in charge of maintaining the house, supervising the boys, keeping them in school and doing homework (except for math—my forte), getting us all to church, and coordinating the endless visits to doctors and specialists for Austin's various medical needs. I was more concerned about traveling for my sales job and making sure I had the right kind of beer in the fridge for the upcoming weekend.

Even though I had a steady job blessed with really nice bonuses, money was becoming a problem, the red ink threatening to drown out the black ink in our checkbook. Part of it was my fault—I'm a gearhead and like to have the right equipment for whatever new hobby I take on, so I not only kept myself outfitted with mountain bikes and golf clubs but I also took up fly fishing and model airplanes and helicopters. Then there were the watches. I loved my Swiss Army watch. I moved up to a Tag Heuer. After a good bonus, I graduated to a Rolex. As you can imagine, Teresa became very resentful over my spending and would have rather used the money to pay bills or take a vacation. But I worked hard and felt like I deserved something for it. It didn't sink in that I had a Rolex before Teresa had a diamond wedding ring. After all those years, she was still wearing the Sears ring I'd picked up on the way to the courthouse.

We didn't talk much about money or anything else important. Teresa's anger and resentment built up, and she retaliated by doing her own share of shopping. She loved buying for the boys and would go to Target for every single Star Wars figurine so Austin could have a complete collection. When Beanie Babies were popular she loaded up on hundreds of the stuffed collectibles, buying, selling, and swapping with other collectors. And her impoverished childhood, when she sometimes had nothing but peanut butter sandwiches for a week, prompted her to stock up on way too much food for our family of four. She purchased huge amounts of canned and boxed food and stockpiled it all in the basement.

But now my income wasn't enough to cover the bills anymore. Teresa did her best to manage, paying bills late or sometimes not paying them at all while her spending continued to increase. I was too busy working and playing to really notice, although occasionally we had noisy arguments. I made her take a box load of forty Hallmark Christmas ornaments back to the store and get a refund. And she once sold a Beanie Baby (Spot the puppy dog, made in Korea, not China, no spots) for an incredible $1,500. Spot had been a present for Austin from his aunt and uncle. But it was too little, too late.

One day Teresa came home and the trash cans were gone. She ran next door and knocked on the neighbor's door. "Did you see someone take our trash cans?"

No one saw anything so she called the trash service to report them stolen. "They weren't stolen," said the customer service rep. "We picked them up because you haven't paid the bill." We'd never heard of anyone getting his or her trash cans repossessed before.

The mailbox was always stuffed with bills. We had good medical insurance, but our out-of-pocket expenses were daunting. With co-pays, doctor bills, surgery costs, and even pharmacy bills, we were drowning in debt. Eventually we also started getting behind on our mortgage.

At the same time, Austin's quirks and behaviors were increasing and school wasn't going well for him. One fall day I'd made sales calls in the Smoky Mountains and was driving hard to get back to Charlotte for a very important meeting about Austin's Individualized Education Plan (IEP) at his new school. Teresa and I were excited—this was one of North Carolina's best magnet schools, and we'd managed to get Austin enrolled. But out of nowhere, a very freaky October snowstorm descended on the area. I couldn't get through the blizzard and down the mountain, so I ended up stranded in my Asheville hotel while Teresa braved the IEP all by herself.

No big deal, I thought. But it was. What Teresa heard at the meeting turned her inside out and upside down. She left in tears and called to tell me what happened. The school had put Austin through various tests, and the results showed he was so low on the IQ scale that the test categorized him as retarded. They called my son *retarded!* There was no educational plan. School officials wanted him immediately transferred to a different school better suited for his needs.

Teresa was blindsided by the findings, and the principal's words felt more like an irreversible order than a concerned recommendation. She ended up agreeing to the transfer but on the phone, she said, "I think I just made the worst decision of my life." It seemed the school's priority was test results and GPAs. In other words, Austin's presence there would have been a big drag in the school's overall ranking. His low test scores had pushed him right out the back door. Teresa was devastated. She felt alone and I wasn't much of a support. I was emotionally unavailable, devoted to my own selfish pursuits.

The new school plunked Austin into a prefab hut at the back of the property with other kids who didn't fit in to the regular program. It turned out to be a catchall room for kids with behavior and discipline problems and Austin hated it. He started acting out at home and using foul language. One night at dinner he cried, "Please don't make me go back to that room."

Teresa did the paperwork to switch Austin back to the magnet school. She was running the show, and I didn't mind. I was lost on so many different levels and was proud of being married to such a strong and driven woman. I didn't understand she was being strong because I wasn't.

We fell further behind in our mortgage payments, and foreclosure was a distinct possibility. Worried about losing the house, Teresa and I pulled together and found a guy who specialized in mortgage and debt relief. We handed over several thousand dollars to him with the assurance that he would fix everything. He promised our house would be safe, with all legal proceedings halted and rectified.

And then everything fell apart. The school denied our request to transfer Austin back, and when it started to look as if we really were going to lose our house, the mortgage fixer guy went missing. He stopped returning calls so we went to his office several times, trying to catch him at work. We knew he was inside but he wouldn't unlock the doors. Once we actually saw him sneak out the back door and run for his Lincoln Town Car. Teresa and I jumped in our car and followed him onto the freeway. But after chasing him for a few miles, I gave up. If we caught him, what could we have done anyway?

We held on through fall, and then, right after Christmas break, we were invited to a Super Bowl party at a friend's house. The whole gang was there. I was looking forward to blowing off some steam and forgetting our problems. I enjoyed myself for a while and drank a lot of beer and wine. At some point during the game, Austin came and stood in front of me. "I hate my school," he said. "Please don't make me go back."

At first I ignored him. Then he turned it into a chant. "I hate my school. Please don't make me go back there. The teachers and the students scare me." He said it over and over, getting louder and more intense each time. Then he fell to his knees, still chanting, and began to sob. He crawled under the large, wall-mounted TV showing the game and into the cubbyhole directly beneath. He curled into a fetal position and rocked himself back and forth, shaking and chanting. I finally realized something was definitely wrong. How's that for denial?

Teresa phoned the on-call ER doctor at Presbyterian Hospital and he told us to bring Austin in on Monday. We left the party with

Austin exhausted but still mumbling and crying about his school. Logan was quiet as usual. I was drunk and angry at everything and everyone. And Teresa? I'm not sure how she was feeling because I wasn't thinking much about her.

When we got home I fell into bed to sleep off both the alcohol and the emotional intensity of Austin's pleas. After a few hours of dreamless sleep, I woke up to see Teresa in the hallway with the butcher knife. When I asked her what she was doing with the knife she grinned, a mischievous twinkle in her eye. Then I heard the stairs creaking as she walked down to the kitchen, and I must have felt safe enough to fall back asleep because next thing I knew it was morning and I woke up with a headache. I stumbled into the kitchen and saw the butcher knife in the knife block. I found out later she'd been hiding the knife up in the laundry room in case an intruder ever got into the house. But now that the boys were older she was afraid they or their friends would find it, so she had chosen that night to carry it down to the kitchen where it belonged.

Okay, my life is safe for now.

Then I noticed something strange—there were dozens of empty beer and wine bottles in the recycling can.

Did I miss a party last night?

"I poured it all out," said Teresa. She'd walked into the kitchen and was standing by the stove, watching me. "Every bottle. I'm tired of your drinking."

I was mad, but between my hangover and knowing we had to get Austin to Presby to deal with his Super Bowl breakdown, I don't remember what else I said. Like a good soldier, I got dressed, and we took Austin to the hospital. The doctors felt he'd experienced a psychological breakdown due to the extreme stress he was experiencing in the problem-kid hut at the new school and recommended that he spend a few days in the hospital. Instead of feeling like a failure and that my son was being ripped away, like I did when he'd been checked in to the psych ward a few years before, I felt relief. I knew Austin needed more help than Teresa or I could give him. We were struggling on so many fronts.

With Austin safely in the hospital for a few days, I had a little space and time to think, and I started to become more aware of the pressure Teresa was under. But it wasn't until she told me something that had happened before Christmas break that I really understood how much she was struggling.

She'd been driving the Mustang home from a meeting with school officials. She'd known Austin was in trouble there and asked to withdraw him. She didn't know where he'd be going to school, but she knew he couldn't go back. She became overwhelmed with emotion and pulled to the side of the road where she cried and cried. Between the school situation, our never-ending bills, the crooked mortgage fixer, Austin's health, and my lack of support, she couldn't take it any longer. She had been strong for so long but she'd finally broken. She put the Mustang in gear and floored it, closing her eyes and aiming for the ditch on the side of the road. She wanted it all to end.

As she veered off the road at high speed, the rumble strips on the road chattered under her tires. The noise broke the spell, and she pulled hard on the wheel, yanking the car back onto the road while slamming on the brakes. She skidded, fighting the wheel to keep the car on the road, and finally slid to a stop. She ended up crying by the side of the road. I didn't find out until much later, and when I did, I realized how alone and isolated we both felt. The bond that held us was fraying.

When Austin came home from the hospital, all of our problems overwhelmed me, and Austin's plight was the hardest to bear. That night I cried and called out to God, *Why him? I am not worthy, so let it be me. I deserve anything You want to give me. Anything. But my little boy does not deserve this.*

Our life seemed to be turning into one of those weepy, emotional TV movies where a poor, beleaguered family can't ever catch a break. It was becoming clear, although I was having quite a time coming to grips with it, that we needed help. We couldn't do this alone. Our overwhelming problems and crises meant I had to do something different. My idea? Pack up and leave.

So we ran back home. Together.

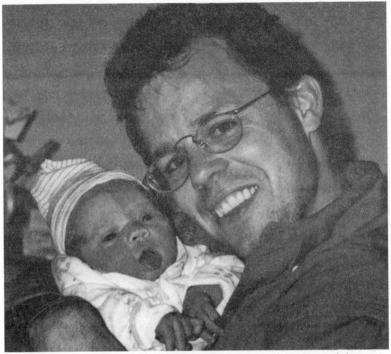

Austin, probably about twenty minutes old—
a moment I will never, ever forget.

Austin, age 7. Another trip to another specialist—
this particular setting was quite routine.

A self-inflicted broken nose.

Austin, age 10.
The eyes of a truly unbreakable boy.

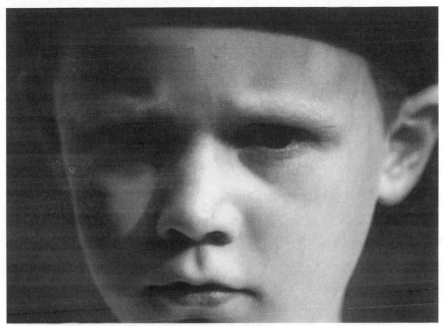

Austin, age 8. I still look into these eyes today and realize how much I know and don't know about what makes my son who he is.

This beautiful picture of Teresa still hits me right in the heart.

Teresa and I in a rare moment of downtime
hanging out with Sammy, my first dog.
Early 1995.

Logan and Austin, ages 6 and 8, growing up in
Charlotte about eleven years ago.

Logan and Austin, ages 5 and 7, on the first day of school in 2000. Austin sporting another designer cast.

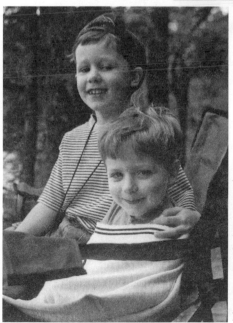

Camping at Lake Norman, North Carolina, right before Austin threw the walkie-talkies and fishing rods in the lake. He decided we needed to go home.

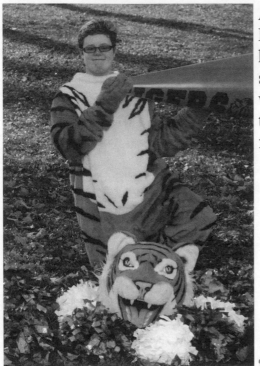

Austin, age 19, as the Red Oak Tiger. There has always been something magical when Auz puts on the tiger head or any hat for that matter.

Austin, age 18, and I just goofing around.

Logan, age 11, whom we have
always called Boo or Boobear.

Logan, age 16, doing
one of the many
things he does well.

Logan, age 17, getting ready to do another thing he does well— surfing.

Austin, age 18, heading off to his junior prom with me as his personal chauffeur.

Father and son.

More goofing around. Auz's favorite hat.

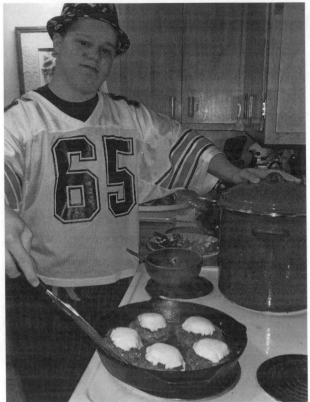

Austin, age 16, cooking up a one-of-a-kind creation. He'll be going to culinary school.

Austin walking across the stage, ready to embark on the next chapter in his (and our) life. The ceremony is something he cherished as with anything from school.

20

FULL RETREAT

Children, you are very little,
And your bones are very brittle;
If you would grow great and stately,
You must try and walk sedately.
—ROBERT LOUIS STEVENSON

Hurting, worn down, and defeated, we left North Carolina and moved back to my hometown of Red Oak, Iowa. My parents still lived in the same neighborhood I grew up in. My brothers Kent and Brian lived nearby with their wives and families. I knew we'd be bumping into childhood friends and neighbors and teachers all the time. I hoped moving back to Iowa meant moving into a built-in community that would welcome us with open arms and a cookout or two featuring that awesome Iowa beef.

Red Oak is a nice little railroad town of five thousand people with stately redbrick buildings and large Victorian homes with wraparound porches. The hilly, tree-lined streets are full of neighbors mowing and kids playing. Drive outside the city limits and you're into rolling fields covered in densely packed bean- and cornfields with cattle and pigs on every acre. On the surface, it's a picture-perfect town. Underneath, everyone has all of the problems and challenges people anywhere struggle with, and we were no exception. Teresa and I were the furthest apart we'd ever been, resentment over each other's spending a prickly barrier between us. Would my rash decision to uproot us and flee back home work?

After we moved to Iowa, Teresa immediately started looking for a new church. More and more, I noticed how she relied on God to get through each difficult day. When she'd almost driven off the road in desperation in North Carolina, her church friends had rushed to the house to pray with her. I watched her growing in her relationship with God. But that's all I did—watch. Instead of trusting in God to help me through our money and marriage and Austin problems, I trusted in what I could drink out of a glass or cold bottle. When Teresa joined a local church, I joined the country club and spent my time hanging out with friends on the golf course.

I had more time than usual because my work situation had changed. I had a chance to leave the company I'd been with for many years and take an early out package, so I quit to become a stay-at-home dad while Teresa built a home-based business. We both thought our new arrangement would be good for our marriage and our family—

a reset from the money problems and school issues we'd left behind, and an opportunity to get to know each other better and spend time with the boys. But deep down, I knew I might be fooling myself that the early out was a good idea. Did I really need more time to indulge myself? Maybe Teresa's way of coping was better, but I wasn't ready to find out. I watched as Teresa put her faith and trust in God, while I thought the move itself would make everything all better. I only flirted with God, using Him as a resource when convenient.

One overcast day when we'd been in Iowa for about a year, I decided to get the boys out of the house. It was gray and cool but not raining yet so we headed up to the park a few minutes away. Logan plodded along beside me while Austin pedaled his bike up the sidewalk just ahead. I walked my usual OCD way, taking exactly two steps between every single sidewalk square. I was in a pensive mood, thinking about the move and my job change. My brain was foggy and my heart felt lost and empty.

What have we done? Is this change going to be all we, or all I, *thought it would be?*

At the park were ten swings, some of them the little kiddie kind with cutouts for a child's legs. But most were the usual kind—a big rubber rectangle to sit on, dangling from thick chains. The swings hung down from a gargantuan steel-tube frame that looked like it could withstand a hurricane.

Immediately the boys jumped on side by side. While they started to swing, I gazed across the street through several backyards to a small corner of my backyard I could see through the trees. I was so unsure of everything. I'd grown up an extremely confident young man, with what I would call high self-esteem, but today I felt none of it. And I didn't know what that meant.

I sat down on a swing, preoccupied.

Ka-bump! Two small hands pushed at me from behind. I craned my head around to see Logan heave-ho and push me with all his might. I hadn't heard him get off his swing and sneak up on me. He continued pushing hard with a gleam in his eyes and giggles to match.

"Push!" I yelled.

Logan kept pushing, and we got into a rhythm. Soon I was soaring.

"Okay, Dad! Now I'm going to run under," he shouted. "Are you ready? Keep your legs going, Dad."

As I swung back, he pushed harder than before and I saw him shoot out underneath me as I swung forward. Logan squealed as he ran, then circled around behind me to do it again. After about the third run under my swing, I stole a look at Auz lounging, swaying in lazy arcs, in a world of his own as he communed with his swing.

Logan continued his quest to push me even higher, then run under. I was laughing now because he had carved a trail into the sand and his laughter and determination captured me. He was having so much fun it was intoxicating and I drank it in.

That's how I missed seeing Austin get out of his swing.

Ka-bump! Another push from Logan, and as I swung forward, another quick glance over to Austin. And . . . not there.

Where's Austin?!

Like before, Logan ran screeching underneath and at that moment everything slowed to a mind-numbing crawl. I remember turning my head to the right, down, and backward. Somehow I knew exactly what was happening, and there wasn't a thing I could do.

As I reached the end of my forward swing and was free-falling back to earth, I saw a blond head underneath me at the same moment I heard Austin's voice scream in joy.

Oh my God. He followed Logan under.

Austin was still screaming as I crashed into his little body. I saw Logan off to the side with his mouth wide open. I knew he was trying to say something, to warn me, but it was too late, and he watched as my speeding-freight-train body slammed into his brother.

In a split second we were on the ground, me on

top of Austin. He was already bawling, mouth open but no words or sounds coming out. I knew it was bad. No, it was a nightmare.

Then he shrieked in a voice soft and high, "Daddy? Why did you do that to me? I hurt really bad. Dad, I can't move. You're on top of me!"

Logan stood stock-still with his mouth still agape. I told him to run as fast as he could to tell his mom Austin was hurt.

I didn't know what to do. Any other kid would probably have just had the wind knocked out of him. But Austin? This could kill him.

There's no way this turns out good, and it's my fault. How did this happen? Why wasn't I paying attention to Auz?

And then, *What should I do?*

I knew Austin could be, and probably was, seriously hurt, but as I lay there, now holding myself up on hands and knees, all I could think about was getting him home to Teresa. I picked him up, sat him on his bike, and with my arms around him I pushed us both home as fast as my legs would carry us.

We glided to a stop in the driveway just as Teresa came running out of the garage. I quickly told her what had happened as I laid Austin down in the backseat of the car. He was whimpering.

"Let's go!" I screamed. I didn't need to tell her where. She and Logan jumped in.

I slammed the car into gear, and from the

backseat, Austin said between sobs, "I only wanted to be like Logan."

At the hospital, I got the hard truth. I had broken Austin's back.

The local hospital put Austin into an ambulance and sent him to Omaha because of his injuries, compounded by the OI. Teresa rode with him. I dropped Logan off at his cousin's house and then drove to Omaha to meet them at the hospital.

As I drove, I prayed, but I wasn't sure who it was I prayed for—me or Austin. I felt horrible about what happened and started berating myself.

Why should my son be enduring all of this while I live my life the way I do?

I am a fool.

I am a horrible person.

I am the worst father.

I . . . I . . . I . . .

Who in the world am I praying for?

I was so conflicted, and I was beginning to realize I was a mess. I was lost, like one of my model helicopters careening around with the controls no longer working.

My feelings were all about me. I was scared and alone. Yet I was only thinking about how bad I felt, while I followed behind an ambulance carrying my boy to the hospital with a broken spine.

That ride in the car left me confused. I knew

my life needed to go in a new direction, but I had no idea which way to go.

Auz spent the next three days in Children's Hospital. He was plastered into a full-torso, custom-made carbon fiber cast to wear for the next six months to allow the two broken vertebrae in his lower back to heal properly. As usual, Austin bounced back full of life and energy and smiles. The body cast didn't slow him down a bit. For me, it was another front-row seat in how to get back up and face adversity with grace, Auz-style.

I was also learning that maybe it was okay to be unsure. Maybe part of my problem was I was too sure of myself. Ego or confidence? I don't know. Either way, I was part of a family, but I didn't act like it. I didn't really appreciate the strong, beautiful, and driven woman I was married to. I thought I had all the answers. I relied on myself and did what I wanted to do.

But now I was scared, and I didn't know what to do anymore. My life was approaching total meltdown.

21

THE SHROUD

Not until we are lost do we begin
to understand ourselves.
—HENRY DAVID THOREAU

The bed was drenched.

I am in big trouble.

My head was thumping, as if I could hear
and feel and touch every beat of my heart right
there in my skull. I hurt so badly, the thought of
moving sent my nerve endings into panic mode.
Welcome to my hangover.

My attention shifted away from my pounding
head and back to the cold, clammy sheets.

*Did I wet the bed? I'm forty-one years old, and
I wet the bed. Wow.*

I slowly moved my legs, stretching out my feet
to see if I could find a dry spot. Teresa wasn't
there. My alcohol-soaked brain tried to figure out
why, and I came up with two possibilities: One,
she got up early. Unheard of. Two, she never went
to bed last night. Strange, because she'd stayed
home from the party with a migraine.

I closed my eyes against the light and felt the
pain in my head reaching down my spine and

pulling at my neck muscles. Then I heard a rustle and felt someone standing by the bed.

Teresa.

And then those five words reverberated again around the inside of my skull. *I am in big trouble.*

Did I kill my boys? Oh my God.

No. I wouldn't be lying here in bed if something like that had happened. They must be okay. But I knew I wasn't. And I couldn't bear to open my eyes.

"Do you remember anything?" Teresa asked. "Do you have any idea what you did last night?"

I rubbed my hand over my face and opened my eyes. I knew I was pathetic—sprawled out on wet sheets, hung over, and in a thick fog.

"Right now you are going to go to your sons and apologize. You are going to tell them you love them and that you are sorry. And then you are going to come back to me and tell me why you almost killed them last night."

What? I was no stranger to hard wake-ups after a night of partying . . . . *But what?!?*

Then it slowly started to come back. I'd been driving home when I decided to stop and grab a six-pack of Bud. Back in the car, I cracked open a beer and emptied it into my Starbucks commuter mug. Then I shoved the rest of the cans through the hidey-hole into my trunk and headed back onto the highway. No one was the wiser. I reached back and fished out another can as I pulled into town. I deserved it—I had worked hard, made money, and there wasn't much I could do without Teresa knowing about it or directing me how to do it. It wasn't like I had ever done this before. Maybe, just maybe, I thought, I was pulling one over on the queen bee. I had her fooled.

I'm just getting a little head start on the party.

We had a big event to go to at the country club that night. Some good friends of Mom and Dad were celebrating their fiftieth wedding anniversary. They were wonderful people who'd been in Red Oak for a long time, so it would be packed.

I loved the country club. For me it was proof that I had friends, I knew how to have fun, and I knew there was more to life than just work, work, work. Plus, I was excited to play golf again!

Teresa wasn't going to the party. She'd been struck with a migraine and was feeling crummy, so when I walked in she told me to take the boys and have a good time.

I got dressed, then headed to the kitchen for a cold bottle of Newcastle Brown. It tasted good after the Budweiser. I gulped down another, called the boys, and tossed the bottles in the trash on my way to the car. *Clink.* I loved that sound. It was going to be a great night.

And it was a blast, the light spilling out through the windows onto the velvety green grass, music going, people mingling. Austin and Logan were dancing and goofing around with their friends. I was talking and laughing with my friends, staying near the bar. Later I danced with the boys. And I was a fool.

At one point I slid over to where my folks were sitting with their best friends. Dad looked at me but didn't say anything. Mom asked if I was all right.

"Of course," I said. "Just peachy."

Back in my bed, as I lay there in the damp sheets, the memories flicked along like an old-fashioned slide show, snapshots of the night. Next slide, I was in the men's bathroom by myself, staring into the mirror. I'm pretty sure I stood there for several minutes. Then I reached up and touched my eyes in the glass, then rested my hands on the mirror. I had a big grin on my face. It was strange, though. I was looking at myself grinning, but the face smirking back at me didn't reflect what was going on inside. I was not happy. After a few moments, I started talking to the guy in the mirror.

"You think you are so cool . . . like you got it goin' on. But you don't. What are you doing? What am I doing?" My voice echoed, bouncing off the tiles.

"I am failing as a dad. I have no idea of my station in life. My moral compass is broken, and my internal constitution in life is smashed."

I loved saying those big words. In my stupor I thought it was clever, even if it was true.

"Get out there," I said louder. "Sober up and keep your cool. Everything is fine, and I am still in control." I laughed, realizing I was giving myself a pep talk in a mirror and, at the same time, recognizing my drunkenness. I was delusional. I made no sense, but I thought I did.

I went back outside where the celebration was now in full swing. I sat down next to a familiar face, a woman from an established Red Oak family and a matriarch of our town. I tried having a coherent conversation with her, but when she smiled at me, I realized I was doing all the talking. She'd known me as a child, and I knew she wasn't seeing the same little boy she used to know.

As I type these words, I feel nauseated. That moment, and every moment at the country club that night, makes me sick. But I cannot forget it. It is part of who I am, so I need to finish.

I must have been starting to lose control because several friends hinted that I might want to call it a night. In a flash I grabbed the boys, one in each arm. I felt a quick wave of paranoia. *I have to get out of this place. I have to get out of this place. Everyone is looking at me and they just don't understand.*

I burst out the front door, half dragging the boys down a wheelchair ramp. I laughed, stumbling and mumbling. The boys shook loose and stood nearby. I laughed harder.

We headed for the car and I tried to hold their hands. *We're going to be just fine. Me and the boys. I know they had a great time. Maybe I had a little too much fun, but it's okay. It's not that late, so I made the right decision in getting outta there and heading home.*

We walked across the parking lot and then I took a wrong step. My right foot did not come down and meet the ground straight, almost like I'd forgotten how to walk.

Wham! I found myself flat on my face, my cheeks and forehead pressed into the gravel. I burst out in laughter. I lifted my head and laughed so hard tears came to my eyes. At the same time I had snot running out of my nose. I laughed harder, almost cackling. I pushed myself up to my knees and looked in wonder at my palms, laced with countless tiny pieces of gravel stuck in my skin. I was bleeding. This, too, seemed funny.

I looked up. The sky was brilliant with stars.

I knelt there, rocks embedded in my hands and knees, and the laughter froze in my throat. For a brief second, my heart cried out, *Where are You now, God? This is seriously messed up. I am a train wreck, and I don't know what to do. I don't know why I am the way I am.*

I squeezed my eyes shut as tears pushed out the corners.

I might be ready for something. Give me a sign or throw me a line. I need help. Someone, anyone, please help me.

A man crunched over the gravel, and I looked down as two feet stopped in front of me. "Hey, guys, what's up?" said a voice somewhere above me. "You okay?"

No. But no words came out.

"Here are your keys," he said. "When you fell, they flew all the way over there. Hey, be careful."

"I'm fine." My words were slurred. "I'm heading home as we speak." I stood up, grabbed my keys, and we got in the SUV. It was big so I figured we were invincible. *What could go wrong?*

"Dad, are you okay?" asked Logan. "Daddy?"

Somehow I got the key into the ignition, started the car, and stepped on the gas.

"Daddy?" Logan asked again. "What's wrong with you?"

I blasted out of the parking lot and down the steep driveway to the country highway. It was a curvy, dangerous road.

"Dad?" Logan again. I stomped on the gas pedal, shooting onto the highway.

"Dad!?"

I don't remember anything after that until I woke up in the wet bed. There had been no accident. The boys were safe. But the more I remembered about the night before, the more my stomach hurt. I was ready to throw up from the hangover, but I was even sicker about the person I'd become and what I'd done. God must have been watching over my boys and protecting them because we had made it home, but I still don't know how.

I felt more than heard Teresa's words, their sharp, dried edges battering against my withered and scarred heart. The truth was I had almost killed my sons and myself. A strange sort of calm settled over me, wet sheets and all. This was my reckoning, and her words pierced my heart.

"I feel like I've married my father, and I'm not going to live this way. It's time for you to make a decision and it's really very simple, Scott. If you don't make the right choice, you are done. Unless you fix this, the boys and I are gone. You can pack a bag and go live with your mother. No decision? We're history."

I was quiet for a minute, then we talked. There were no raised voices. It really was very simple. I had a choice. Still sitting in the wet sheets, I called a friend I hadn't talked to in many years. I talked and he listened. Then he told me I had a decision to make. I could continue living this way, or I could make a turn and do something different. I saw myself again, mumbling into the mirror, then on my hands and knees in the gravel, then Logan crying in the backseat and Austin in his own world while I rocketed down the highway. I felt ashamed. I was nothing more than a sinner, and I was falling apart. I felt it—I was a broken man. And I wanted to be whole.

As soon as I made the decision, I felt a little flicker of hope. I knew Teresa would be there to help. Perhaps I *could* change. Something made sense in my brain; I had missed it all along, but something tiny clicked, and I saw a brief flash of what could be. By some miracle I was still alive, the boys were still alive, and we were still a family, at least for the moment. Teresa. Austin. Logan. My family was my life.

Then Teresa told me I hadn't really wet the bed. Instead, she'd poured an entire pitcher of cold water over me the night before after I'd barged in, stumbling by her on my way to bed. I passed out and slept wrapped up in wet sheets all night long. I'd been so wasted I didn't even notice. It was a strange baptism.

To this day, I think of that last drink. It was a fancy bottle of Grolsch beer—the kind with the really cool metal and rubber stopper on top. While I remember only pieces and parts of that night, one of the strongest memories is the silly bottle I almost traded for my sons' lives.

I was in big trouble and I'd been offered a last chance. I got up out of that bed, unwrapped the wet, clingy shroud, and took my first step into the light.

22

A REAL LIFE

Wherever my story takes me, however dark and
difficult the theme, there is always some hope
and redemption, not because readers like happy
endings, but because I am an optimist at heart.
I know the sun will rise in the morning, that
there is a light at the end of every tunnel.
—MICHAEL MORPURGO

My journey is so similar to everyone else's
journey, because we are all human. We all have
been defeated by the powers of darkness, and we
all find redemption in the light of Christ.
—TED DEKKER

As much as I would like to forget that night at
the country club, I know that I can't. I distinctly
remember, in my inebriated condition, talking
with an old friend that night who'd been sober
for some time. He must have thought I was quite
a sight as I told him how proud I was of him.
"How did you do it?" I asked, swaying. I do not
recall what he said.

When I got up out of that slimy bed, I knew my
first steps needed to be sure and right in order for

me to start living again. I called the sober friend from the party, and he shared his story again. I listened, and I reached out to others for help. I never checked in to a facility or had any type of intervention, although years later Teresa told me that option was on the table and close to being implemented.

I knew I had a singular opportunity. I thanked God I'd never hurt anybody—I'm so fortunate I didn't end up in jail or dead. Then I made the decision to admit that I had a problem and that I would change. I was scared, but I knew my next few decisions would affect everything—my health, sanity, family, and marriage. I spent time in my closet thinking about the close call, weeping, and agonizing over the future.

But within a week, I knew. I just *knew* what I had to do. It was a clear and powerful moment, as if the veil had been lifted and my vision was no longer clouded by alcohol or false self-esteem and confidence. I saw how for many years I had been projecting a brave front, hiding my fear, pain, insecurity, and resentment. I also knew it took beer upon beer, for many years, to build up that cloud inside my brain on that horrible night. And I accepted that I could never, ever have another drink of alcohol. Ever.

In my quest to heal and become the father, the husband, and the man I should have been, I can never forget who I was—it pains me to relive the past, but remembering and owning my past enables me to understand how real consequences are determined by my actions. It is easy to say I can never do *this* or *that* again, but the reality is I work hard every day and I always remember.

After I decided to quit drinking, the first thing I did was apologize to my family. To this day I still feel the need to apologize, and apologize more. Next, a really crazy thing happened—as I began to see things more clearly, I understood what I most needed was to restore my relationships to those closest to me and to God. Just maybe, hitting bottom enabled me to see what I should have seen before—that God was there all along. He was there whenever I talked to Joe. He was there through the surprises and the disasters and the surgeries and the broken bones. He was there when I'd looked into Austin's eyes and seen a strange sort of light. He was there in my closet. He was there when I faced the guy in the mirror at the country club. He was always there.

And Austin, my unbreakable boy, was always there too. Our lives were forever woven together, and his birth completely changed my life. It's still changing my life.

My first few weeks of sobriety, I barely recognized the raw feelings and messy thoughts I'd numbed for so many years. But as I persevered, I started to get to know myself, my real self again, and as I changed, so did all my relationships.

Facing life without the bottle made everything more vivid, and now I was overwhelmed by a colorful kaleidoscope of emotions and feelings and thoughts crashing around in my toxin-free brain.

While trying to sort out and understand my feelings, I recognized a new one—the feeling of grace. I had never really understood the meaning of grace. I learned it means "the love and mercy given to us by God because God desires us to have it, not because we have done anything to earn it . . . a gift from God, spontaneous, generous, free, totally unexpected and absolutely undeserved."*

I needed it, I wanted it, and I gratefully embraced it. Grace changes everything, and it changed me. But I still had to figure out what that change meant. Who was I? How was I going to live my life going forward? I knew I'd changed inside, but could I change all the messy stuff I'd built up around me like an impenetrable cocoon? Could I break through and become the loving, wise father I had always yearned to be? Or was it too late for me? And could Teresa and I finally get to know and love each other after all those years when the only thing holding us together

---

* "Our Wesleyan Theological Heritage." United Methodist Church, February 10, 2014, http://www.umc.org/sitc/c.lwL4KnN1LtH/b.

had been a broken, blue-eyed boy and his little brother, Boo?

I was ready to find out. For me, sobriety and church went hand in hand. I started attending regularly, and Teresa and I were asked to lead the high school Sunday school class. I felt honored and took it as a sign that we could make a difference, no matter how big or small, in a kid's life. I started a praise band at church where I played the acoustic guitar, and I fell in love with performing.

Each Sunday I carried my Bible to church, wondering why so few people do. I read my King James Version I'd had for years, but later I found a study Bible that was actually interesting and exciting (yes, exciting!) to read and learn from. I was a sponge, looking to be a part of something bigger than me. I committed myself to my new life and to the God who had extended me grace.

I could see and feel my new life. God's grace quickly enveloped me and shook me to the core. It affected every cell in my body. Something was set free inside me, and it was, simply, grace.

And the more I practiced my sobriety, the clearer my mind and heart seemed to become, and finally, my spirit began to come alive. The more I embraced God, the stronger and surer I became at accepting and living in sobriety. I did not flout my sobriety, but I also felt no shame or worry if people found out. My family deserved me, the faith-filled me, and I, them. For the first time life felt right and I began to settle in. My resistance was gone, left in the gravel in the country-club parking lot. I knew I was in the right place.

I learned early in my sobriety that I might begin to feel pangs of guilt for my past or hunger for my old ways. I was shaky, a little timid on my new legs as the euphoria and excitement wore off. But I fought back by reaching out to Teresa and drawing on her strength and her friendship with God.

I'd been sober for almost a year, and my faith had grown stronger than ever before, when I was challenged by church elders to go on a weekend retreat called Walk to Emmaus. More than just a retreat, Walk to Emmaus is a seventy-two-hour spiritual renewal program. Learning how to go deeper in my faith? It was an intriguing promise and potentially a powerful salve for my soul, so I signed up.

The first day didn't really have much of an impact. *No big deal,* I thought. Second day, about the same. But on that third day, my heart or my soul seemed to open up and tune in and God somehow allowed me to see inside myself. I can't really explain what those three days meant to me and my faith. I saw how far off I really was from where I thought I was, but at the same time I grew. I gained hope for the future and a passion for knowing I could be a better Christian, a better leader, father, and husband, and a more alive human being. The Walk to Emmaus turned out to be a life-changing weekend.

When my soul opened up that weekend, what I saw wasn't the inner truth and beauty that many religions promise; instead I saw all my flaws and sins. They were abundant. The Walk didn't give me a to-do list or a set of steps to take; it showed me the type of person I could be if I simply accepted the grace of God fully and totally with my whole heart.

What's crazy is that as I got sober, I felt as if I had been given completely new eyes and I was able to clearly see the right path to a deeper faith. And as my faith grew, I was stronger in my struggles with sobriety. So the two elements— faith and sobriety—were inexorably linked, and surrendering myself to a walk with God empowered me to stay sober and walk this new path of freedom and forgiveness. I felt I could maybe even fulfill the roles I'd been failing at, although I knew I would never be perfect. I found my true self and good and bad, it's who I am. At least now I can see it all with my eyes wide open.

Finally, Teresa and I became a real couple. We have a long way to go and we're learning more every day, but we embarked on a new life together. No longer were we just roommates. I hoped Teresa was happy that the friend she met in the mall that day was back, and now she could learn to really love me, and I, her. Like it should have been. Our marriage went from almost dead to fully alive, like Austin turning pink when he took his first breaths all those years ago in the delivery room.

Logan seems to understand what happened that night. A few years ago he said, "Dad, I am so proud of you. I love you." We weren't having a deep conversation at the time, but I knew exactly what he meant. I looked back at him and smiled. And then I hugged him. We both knew what my walk with God was doing.

I still go on those walks, but now they happen every day. Some walks don't go so well but others are profound. And now I know when I walk, I am not alone. He is my Sword and my Protector and my own personal Rock. My God, and He alone, has enabled mc to return to my family.

And so I walk.

23
HELPING HANDS

I am coping. Not triumphing.
Not overcoming. Just coping. Which is a lot,
and really all any of us need to do.
—ELLEN PAINTER DOLLAR,
A WRITER AND BLOGGER WITH OI

While I was discovering a faith-filled, sober life
was a far better way to live, we still had to cope
with the many challenges of life with Austin.
We'd been overprotective, but as Austin got
older, he wanted to go to parties and movies and
dances without us.

When he was about twelve years old, Austin
wanted to attend a youth dance at the local
YMCA. I had never heard of grade school
dances, but after going as a chaperone the year
before, I understood. The boys on one side tried
to act cool and talked to all the other little guys
being cool. The girls danced with each other and
sang silly Britney Spears songs. It was harmless
and fun.

So I took a leap of faith and this time I let
Austin go to the dance without me while I stayed
home to hang out with Teresa. I was learning how

to relax and enjoy time with my wife. But of course it didn't last.

Ring. Ring.

There it was. The phone call. Always, the phone call, causing dinners half eaten, movies half watched, and parties cut short.

This phone call came at about nine o'clock, and apparently Austin's feet were hurting. His right ankle seemed to be the worst and he was asking for pain medicine. We told the chaperone who called that it was fine to give him some Tylenol or whatever kind of painkiller they had on hand.

Then the phone rang again. It was a different chaperone, a friend of ours. "The people at the Y won't allow us to give Austin anything. He asked for ice to put on his feet but was told to just go and sit down. They told Austin to suck it up and deal with it."

Suck it up and deal with it. Right.

By this time Mama Bear Teresa had already flown out the door and was headed over to the dance. And yes, T had a few choice words, delivered in her sweet Southern accent, for the man who was giving Austin a hard time.

Austin told his mom the pain was sharp. We listened, because his right leg is about two inches shorter than his left. And I've learned the hard way to listen when Austin or Teresa says something is wrong. They are always right. They know their bodies and their bones.

The next day at the hospital X-rays showed a small fracture in his ankle. We had been told years before that because of his fragile bones, as he grew he would suffer micro-fractures in both his lower legs and ankles. And they were right—Austin still has back and lower leg pain every day. Sometimes he limps. He also has a curved spine—early signs of scoliosis. There's not much doctors can do for the micro-fractures. Just rest and pain meds along with shoe inserts and the occasional leg brace.

A few months later at McDonald's, we ran into the gentleman from the YMCA dance who had denied Austin the painkiller and the ice. Austin jumped up from his Big Mac, walked right up to the guy in line, and said, "Hi. It's okay. My mom didn't really mean to call you a &#%@."

The man's eyes grew wide. Auz smiled at him with total sincerity and compassion. "My legs feel better. I had a broken foot. And I like you."

I'm not sure what the man was thinking, but I like to think he learned something that day.

One person who does seem to understand Austin is Donna Mae, an older woman who lives next door. She has a special bond with our son, who doesn't often talk about his feelings or fears. She is one of Austin's favorite people (out of his 3,549 other favorite people), and she recently told me a story. Here it is, in Donna Mae's own words.

I was standing in my kitchen when I heard a noise through the screen door. At first it almost sounded like the whimper of a cat or a dog, so sad and foreign. I walked to the door and looked out to try to see what was going on. I couldn't see anything out of the ordinary, but then I heard it again, this time louder and more urgent. Now it was more like a wail, and I had a feeling I knew where it was coming from.

I turned around, headed back through the kitchen and down into my garage. The garage door was up, and as I walked alongside the car, I heard the noise again, loud and strong. This time I could make out words through the sobs and the wails: "Why me? Oh, God. Why is it always me? I just wanna be okay. Oh, God! Help me, please."

As I passed the end of my car, I saw Austin. He was splayed out on his side, struggling to put on one of his size thirteen shoes and crying hard. His braces were lying on the ground next to him. As I walked up to him, he went still.

I knelt down and reached for him.

"Austin, sweetie, are you okay? What can I help you with?"

His words came out in a rush. "I can't get my shoes on. My feet and ankles hurt so bad and with my braces it's so hard to get them on. My legs and feet always hurt. I don't understand why it's always me. It's not fair. I just want the pain to go away! This makes no sense. Why does God let me hurt like this?"

I sat down there on my driveway and held Austin, pain on his face and tears in his eyes. He cried on my shoulder as we sat there and rocked. He continued to sob, and I could feel the pain and hurt radiate from him. All I could say was, "It's going to be all right, Auz. It's going to be all right."

I am grateful Donna Mae was there to comfort Austin in that moment. She gets Austin. She has a kind and patient heart and I love her dearly.

When I think of Austin sprawled in her driveway, it stirs up so many questions. How does he take the continual broken bones, hospital trips, and pain? I suppose he never gets used to it, but how does he rebound so quickly? Even when he broke his back in the swing-set accident, the full-torso cast barely slowed him down. These ups and downs are Austin's world. He can break a bone one moment and the next he's laughing his guts out, blowing bubbles out his nose, always trying to make someone else's day better no matter what his problems are.

When phone calls come and our world turns upside down yet again, we've learned to laugh with Austin. A broken bone, a trip to the emergency room, another high or low, we always seem to get past it when we laugh together. I am sure we laugh at some things that nobody else would ever understand, like Austin saying something peculiar yet again. We may laugh at another broken bone, but in the end, maybe that's what helps us get by.

Austin loves to ride his bike. It's a little dangerous, but he enjoys it and we let him. He has a little metal bell on the handlebars that he loves to flick, and the sound makes me smile. One day I saw Auz take off down Donna Mae's driveway and zoom past our front yard, ringing the bell in time to his feet on the pedals.

Ding, ding, ding! I couldn't help but smile as I watched him ride down the street. He was headed for my brother Kent's house a few blocks away. I turned back to work on the weeds in the flowerbed, the sound of the bell starting to fade away.

Then the *ding-ding-ding* picked up speed and turned frantic. I heard screeches and screams. It sounded like a hyena, so I thought it was another of Auz's sometimes funny but maniacal-sounding laughs. I ran toward the sound and stopped when I saw what was going on—a little dog was chasing Austin on his bike. It was a ferocious-looking rat terrier with his own bell dangling from his collar and making little clinking sounds. He was relentless, growling and snapping at the tires.

Austin pedaled hard, careening across the street from curb to curb and between parked cars trying to lose the dog. He was scared to death, riding as if the hounds of hell were after him.

Austin's cackles had turned to frightened cries. He was still ringing his bell, faster and faster. I ran after him. And then he crashed, hitting a big 4x4 truck parked on the side of the street. Head-on.

Ohhhh no! I went into a full-blown sprint as I pictured the worst.

I ran up to the truck and saw Austin, now lying on the ground, still astride his bike. He had that oh-so-familiar look of pain in his blue-tinted eyes, big tears streaking down his cheeks, and panic at the ferocious little dog now sniffing around at the scene of his crime. The little bell on his collar tinkled as he investigated.

I reached down and carefully helped Auz to his feet. He had a cut on his ankle and a bruise on his forearm, but otherwise he looked no worse for the wear. I had him stand as I searched for any unseen injuries and asked him if anything else hurt.

I checked his helmet and saw a nice crack in it. If anything, he learned the value of a good helmet. He'd obviously hit part of the massive pickup with his noggin. Thank God for the lid.

Austin looked over at the little mousy dog, now barking again off to the side.

"You are a mean dog!" he said loudly. "How could you chase me? Someone should have you on a leash."

And just like that, he was off again on his bike, ringing the bell, and pedaling furiously back to the house.

I turned and looked at little Cujo. Then I shook my head and snorted a chuckle as I walked back. I found Austin in a familiar place, sitting on Donna Mae's driveway. He was talking to her, and she was listening, comforting him and carrying on like those two do. I walked on by as they looked deep in conversation.

Donna Mae told me later that after Austin told her about the dog, their talk went something like this:

"Donna Mae, do you have a boyfriend? Are you really getting married?"

"Yes, Austin. John is my boyfriend, and we are getting married."

"But aren't you too old?"

"No, Austin. I'm not too old to get married."

"Well, are you going to have any babies?"

Donna Mae just smiled.

"No way!" Austin started laughing. "I know you're too old for that stuff!"

Austin had been injured again, but he'd already moved on to more important matters. I'm beginning to understand that's how Austin's life will be as he continues to ride his bike and ring that bell. I am just as sure we will have more broken bones and pain in our future. That's part of who we are. Austin is going to keep having adventures, and some of them are going to have happy endings and some of them are going to end in a crash. But Teresa and I are learning to laugh more and panic less. And we know we are becoming a stronger family as we go through this crazy life of ours together.

24

GLOW STICKS

All greatness of character is dependent on individuality. The man who has no other existence than that which he partakes in common with all around him, will never have any other than an existence of mediocrity.
—JAMES FENIMORE COOPER

We pulled up to our friend's house for his annual Fourth of July party, and I stared across the street at the crowd of eighty thousand people streaming into Memorial Park in Omaha. The annual concert features bands like Boston, Styx, and Foreigner. Austin and I both love '80s music, but I'm always concerned about crowded settings with lots of noise and so many unknowns that can spook him. But before I could shift into park, Auz was out the door, headed to the house. We let him go.

"Let's see how it goes this time, T." She smiled and rolled her eyes just a bit.

Austin and Logan bounded ahead of us into the backyard. There would be a lot of people we didn't know, but we also had plenty of friends and family in attendance. I let myself begin to relax; Auz would be safe here.

Austin seemed to be doing well, and we all were having a great time. Before long, Austin trotted over to me with a middle-aged gentleman in a straw hat. I took notice of the hat because it reminded me of the kind that golfer Greg Norman wears. A beautiful hat with a wide, fire engine–red band, it was kinda cheesy and I loved it. Austin and the man were all smiles, and looking like long-lost school chums. Austin was gripping a typical heaping plate of food, enough to make even Guy Fieri blush.

Before I could open my mouth, the man said in a piercing voice, "I had to come over here and meet this fine young gentleman's father. He tells me you were a fighter pilot in the navy. It's really nice to meet you, Scott." He stuck out his hand.

"I have been enjoying the company of your wonderful and fascinating son for the last hour," Straw Hat continued. We talked a bit about my time in Officer Candidate School and then flight school, although I couldn't call myself a pilot. He also asked about the family. Then it was my turn to ask him some questions.

I learned his name was Kevin, and he worked for the air force. "All I do is drive a big gray steel desk all day pushing a pencil for the government."

Austin is an avid Ken Burns fan and adores WWII documentaries and movies, so the three of us were just settling in to talk military stuff when a bug landed on that straw hat. And not just any bug. A ladybug.

I saw it first, and time stood still. Austin is terrified of bugs. Not just bees and wasps and critters that sting and bite but anything that flies. Moths and butterflies are bad. And ladybugs? Those are the most terrifying. This was going to be worse than the terrier-bike attack. Way worse.

My adrenaline was rushing, and I could picture what was about to happen. Everything slowed down. Austin turned toward Kevin, and I saw it in his eyes—he'd spotted the ladybug.

I looked back over at Kevin and then back to Austin, who was winding up for a big right hook to Kevin's head. He connected square on and—*Thwack!*—knocked the straw hat and the offending bug ten feet into the air. I froze.

Kevin looked at Austin, and Austin looked back at Kevin. They paused, and then both burst out into rolling fits of laughter. It was infectious and before long I was laughing too. We carried on about it, reliving the moment, and then they walked off together, lost in something funny, while I stood alone watching them go wondering what, exactly, had just happened. The last thing I heard was Austin asking his new buddy if he could come to Red Oak for a sleepover at the house.

"Hey, Scotty! How's the general doing?" a friend standing nearby asked. "You do know who your son's new best friend is, don't you?" He chuckled and strode off, leaving me even more bewildered. I ran after my friend to find out what he was talking about.

It turned out the man in the straw hat was actually General Kevin Chilton of the United States Air Force and the most recent commander at USSTRATCOM, or United States Strategic Command, in Bellevue, Nebraska. He was a four-star general, an astronaut, and one of the most decorated officers in the world. Kevin was a real-life hero. I shook my head. It was as if my son had just smacked General Patton in the head and invited him to a slumber party. On top of that he'd convinced the general I was a navy fighter jock.

Suddenly something occurred to me—Austin will never need to find himself. Unlike most teenagers, he already knows who he is. He is comfortable in his own skin, and he fully inhabits each moment, no matter where he is or who he's talking to. It's like a state of hyper focus—Austin will immediately become consumed with any new person.

This approach doesn't always go as well as it did with the general. For example, on a typical visit to a restaurant, I'll find myself anxiously smiling as Austin turns to a man in line behind us and says, "Hi, my name is Austin, Richard Austin LeRette. What are you going to have? I'm having the number eleven." The man usually looks a little confused but wears a polite smile.

"That's the ten-piece nugget meal with fries and a drink," he continues, talking loud and fast. "I plan on getting the Hi-C for my drink and for the fries I will get salt and pepper and ketchup. I like the ketchup packets, not the stuff you get out of the machine, just like my mom likes the packets. It tastes better that way. For the nuggets I will have ranch, honey mustard, buffalo, sweet and sour, barbecue, and more ranch, of course. Please, thank you, and you're welcome. Oh, I'll get a lot of napkins too."

By now the stranger's look will turn from polite to annoyed. "Who is this guy?" is the expression I often recognize on Austin's latest target of friendship.

I don't interrupt Austin in this common ritual. To top it off, he will most likely invite the random stranger to our table to eat lunch with us. And all this in less than sixty seconds, with the guy never even getting a chance to talk.

Regardless of what a person looks like, where he or she comes from, how old the person is, how much money he or she makes, or what kind of car the person drives, Austin will offer instant and complete friendship. I have noticed over the years, however, his very closest friends do happen to be the prettiest girls around.

Whenever I see Austin and a new friend, they

are usually rapt with attention at some story or yarn that Auz is spinning. More often than not he's wearing one of his trademark hats and an enormous grin to match.

For the longest time Teresa and I were consumed with monitoring and restricting Austin in social settings like the Fourth of July party. We were so worried he would say something inappropriate or personal. I'm still haunted by the possibility of this kind of potential humiliation from time to time. But we have learned to just let him be.

And maybe Austin and General Chilton had more in common than I first thought. One thing I will never forget about my time in the navy was the discipline instilled in us. Every last second was regimented and ritualized, just like Austin operates on a daily basis.

The way Austin gets dressed every morning could not be more regimented if it had come out of the operating procedures at the Naval Academy. From top to toes, every last detail of his appearance has to be in one-hundred-percent-perfect order for him to walk out the door. Not right? Not going out. Even if that means being late for school, church, or whatever.

Austin doesn't dress to impress anyone. He does it because it makes him feel good and secure and comfortable. While I sometimes worry about my appearance, Austin couldn't care less about what others think; he just dresses his way. Austin seems to make his style be in style in spite of any prevailing trend. Because no one dresses quite like Austin.

When he was in middle school, I remember people approaching us to say they wished their kids would dress as well as Austin did. I started to enjoy watching Austin wear a stylish outfit he'd put together, without the slightest idea of the impact he was making.

I have come down the stairs to go to church and met Austin arranged in full ensemble: coat, matching pants, tie, and a fedora, while I was slouching around in my jeans and a polo shirt. I'll take one look, then head back upstairs and change my clothes. Somehow Austin leads others, and even me, without saying a word. Now before we go somewhere I check to see what Austin is sporting and gauge my attire accordingly.

There are some drawbacks to him always wanting to dress just right. Once he tries on an article of clothing, it is considered dirty. The shirt or pair of pants, even if worn for a few seconds, cannot be allowed to go back in his closet. His dirty clothes hamper can fill quickly when he tries on three or four outfits to find exactly the right one.

But as I sit and watch Austin prepare for school, a lunch date, or a trip to the movies, I see a boy becoming a young man. And unlike most young men, Austin seems immune to peer pressure and doesn't care about the status quo. *Knit beanies are in? I'll wear my jester hat.*

Auz doesn't care what car another kid drives or if he has the coolest headphones. Sure, he likes nice things like all kids do, but he doesn't judge people by what they own or wear. Austin only wants love and friendship.

That night at the Fourth of July party, I watched as Austin buzzed around the backyard. It was getting dark, and I couldn't actually see his face, but I could tell it was him running around because he had about fifty shiny neon glow sticks hanging from his neck. All afternoon he'd been collecting them as people left the concert and walked by the party. By the end of the night he had too many to count.

Soon Austin strolled up to me where I sat with my chair parked against the fence, and the glow sticks were gone from his neck. Every single one.

Where did they go?

"Dad! Come here!" he yelled, pointing. I got up and looked. My mouth dropped open. The backyard was alight. Almost every person at the party, more than a hundred, had one of Austin's glow sticks hanging from his or her neck. For the last twenty minutes, Austin had been going from person to person, draping each one with a glow stick. Almost like a blessing.

Austin doesn't care if you are a four-star general or a friend from school or the guy standing behind him at McDonald's, the guy living under a bridge, or the king of a country. He loves you no matter who you are or what you do. He's different from anyone I've ever met. His life touches everyone he meets. And he doesn't even know it.

But if he did know, would it change him?

All I know is this one simple thing—he makes people smile. He's a quick little kiss from God, a cool breeze from a different time and place. He's a touch of light.

25

THE TIGER

I'm a lion in a strange land.
—CRISS JAMI

"Aaaaaahhhh! Aaaaahhhh!" *"Chugga-chugga-chooooooooo!"*

It's five forty-five in the morning, and Austin is screeching at the top of his lungs. Now that he's a teenager, his voice is deeper and louder. I put my pillow over my head. *Make it go away.*

"Casa gouda, casa gouda. Tanaka-too-too. Doobie-da-doo! Chicka-chicka-chicka-saw, saw-saw, saw-saw."

I have no idea what those words mean or why my son is singing and screeching and pumping his arms like a locomotive. Or why he gets up so early, turbocharged and demanding my attention every single moment of every single day. If Austin is awake, everybody knows it.

Some mornings go okay, but most are hard. Really hard. It almost seems like he has to burn off some energy stored up overnight.

He cranks it up again. *"Took-took-took-took-took! Coo-coo-coo-coo-coo! Nee-nee-hee! Nee-nee-hee! Haaaahhhhh!"*

Yelling at him doesn't work. I know that. But this morning I'm not a happy camper, and I'm having a hard time feeling charitable when it's still dark outside. Austin doesn't help matters when he runs up to my bed and punctuates his bellowing call-to-arms with a fresh spray of Polo cologne right in my face. But I start yelling at him anyway.

"Austin, shut it up!"

I am exhausted. So is his mom. But the more we all bark at him, the louder and more intense he gets. Austin is going into overdrive.

Logan stumbles by on his way to the bathroom. "Freak," he mutters, rubbing his eyes.

I get up, wondering if Austin is past the point of no return.

Logan goes down to the kitchen to warm up a toaster strudel and get out of the house. Teresa's making coffee. Then Austin skips into the room, screeching gibberish to no one in particular.

"Austin, you are killing me," Teresa says. She needs a break and heads back upstairs. I hear the bedroom door click shut.

If I can just get Austin out the door, into the car, and safely tucked away at school, we might have a chance. I can't explain it but school offers him a release valve. He decompresses and does some kind of mental reset.

I bribe him to finish getting ready with the promise of a Skillet Burrito at McDonald's, then throw on my clothes, rush him to the car, and get him to school.

He launches out of the car in his jester hat and trots into school, high-fiving kids along the way.

Whew.

I drive to work in a daze, shell-shocked yet again.

Later in the morning the phone rings at the house. Teresa picks it up.

"It's Austin," says the principal. "He's here in the office on the couch, inconsolable. He thinks he's killing you."

Austin takes everything literally. Sometimes he makes us laugh, sometimes he makes us cry, but he always wears us out with his intensity. He lives large.

One weekend Auz and I were alone and planned a movie night. We started off with meat loaf at Grandma and Grandpa LeRette's house. It was delicious, and Austin had a good time investigating Grandma's kitchen cabinets for more than an hour. She knew how Austin liked to reorganize kitchens and pilfer any favorite snacks along the way. Then it was time to head back home for a movie and a snack in my room.

Austin has the exact same bed that we do, but he believes ours is ten times more awesome than his. Nights routinely begin with this not-so-small-anymore kid crawling in with us when we have just fallen asleep. For some reason, Austin thinks the more people in a bed, the more cozy and restful it can be.

While I got the movie ready, Austin decided to make popcorn. What should've taken just a few minutes stretched out into a half hour. I waited and finally Austin made his grand entrance.

Okay, now I see why this took so long! He was balancing a bowl of popcorn, a plate of chips and salsa, an entire package of Jimmy Dean microwave sausages, a jar of peanuts, cheese sticks, and for dessert? Yoo-hoos. One man's feast is another man's snack, I suppose. For Austin, mass quantities of gastronomic goodness are essential for a good time, and tonight he was ready to party hard.

I looked down at Austin's feast spread out on the bed and laughed so hard I snorted. I laughed so hard I fell down on the bed. I laughed so hard I needed to catch my breath. Our evening was just getting started, but he was already wearing me out. I decided to take a time-out in my quiet place before the movie.

I got off the bed and went to the closet in my office where I retreat when I need some solace. Five minutes is usually all I require.

I opened the closet door and jumped up on the carpeted shelf, reclining back on my neatly folded sweaters and jeans.

Ahhhhh . . .

I closed my eyes and breathed a quick prayer, thanking God for my son and asking Him to please help me be patient and make it through the coming Auz-fest. I was in the closet for the sum total of one minute when I heard Austin come into my office. The catcalls started in his excited, high-pitched, cackly voice.

"Come on, you snickerdoodle. I know you're hiding. Where are you, Dad? You can't hide forever. I will find you!" He was having a ball searching for me. I stayed in the closet, breathing deeply, practicing some quick relaxation. When I emerged, to Austin's glee, we headed back to start our movie. That night it was Rowan Atkinson's *Johnny English*, the bumbling secret agent. I couldn't help but see the parallels to my boy. The quirky, oddball agent somehow always ends up saving the day through his kindhearted but misguided efforts, rather than his skill and finesse. We watched the unlikely hero and laughed, slurping down our Yoo-hoos.

Austin is the Johnny English of his high school. Most everyone knows him because he is impossible to ignore. He's made lots of friends, and some enemies too. But his friends watch out for him. Everyone loves to watch him dance, and he doesn't hesitate to steal center stage. "At dances, we make a spot for Austin in the middle," a friend of his told me. "Everyone cheers and yells, 'Go, Austin! Go, Austin!' He has style."

Austin's dancing is impossible to describe. Think Johnny English, John Travolta, and Gomer Pyle all rolled into one.

During Austin's sophomore year, Miss Angie, the dean of students, invited Austin to serve as the mascot for Red Oak High School. He accepted and proudly wears the full furry tiger costume, complete with a giant grinning tiger head, at football, basketball, and volleyball games. He dances with the cheerleaders, stopping to fix and readjust the Velcro tabs on his costume whenever his OCD tendencies get out of control. Once, in full tiger regalia, he couldn't get the seat of his pants adjusted and kept trying, keeping the kids around him in stitches as they watched the giant tiger scratching his butt.

Miss Angie told me about walking down the school hallway with Austin past a display of Tiger quotes and school memorabilia. One Tiger quote said, "Finish strong. Signed, The Tiger."

"The Tiger wrote that note," Miss Angie said.

"No, he didn't." Austin looked at her with a big goofy grin.

"Yes, he did," she said.

"No, he didn't. No, he didn't! I'm the Tiger. He didn't write that because I didn't write that."

One memorable night Austin was in full gear for the Red Oak Tiger ladies volleyball team, hosting St. Alberts. Our team is a perennial powerhouse that competes at the highest level, and on this night, the Tigers were thumping the opposing team. Toward the end of the game, St. Alberts took their last time-out. Up hopped Austin. He approached the opposing team, thinking he'd join the team huddle and give them a little pep talk. The coach took it as a taunt. To Austin, of course, it was nothing of the sort. The coach gave Austin an earful before Miss Angie could get over there and rescue him. The crowd loved it, and he really was trying to cheer up the team.

Another night after a game, Austin was having a hard time getting out of costume and his giant tiger head was stuck. It's difficult for anyone to get in and out of. He asked for help, then reached out to Miss Angie with one big, plush paw and grabbed her hand. She pulled him along, and the dean of students and the furry tiger skipped down the hallway together.

Then Austin stopped and froze. Miss Angie stopped too. Austin turned to her and said, "This school loves me."

"What?" she asked, not sure she heard him right. She knew Austin didn't often talk about his feelings.

"Can't you feel it? This is my favorite school. Can't you feel it?"

"Feel what, Austin?"

"This school loves me."

Most of the time Austin doesn't pick up on what students or parents think about him. He just blasts through life like he's on some kind of mission.

One night Teresa and I went to the last home football game and had a great time. Nothing unusual happened—Austin did his thing, but this time I was watching the game more than the tiger. Once home, I discovered a surprising string of Facebook and Twitter comments.

This was from the parents of a little three-year-old boy who reminded me so much of Austin at that age:

> Austin LeRette makes an awesome Tiger Mascot! Taking Jeremy to a football game with lots of people could have been a disaster. He started saying, "I need go home," but Austin caught his attention and gave him several fist bumps and Jeremy started loving the evening. He had to keep going over to get attention from the Tiger, keeping him distracted from really being bothered by the noise and the crowd. We don't always have this successful of an outing with Jeremy, but they are becoming more of the norm rather than a meltdown, leading to leaving in defeat. Part of this is due to living in a small town with awesome people who

tolerate a boy walking in front of them to see a tiger, and a mom retrieving her boy so he doesn't drive the tiger wild.

I wrote back, tears in my eyes, "Glad Austin got to be Jeremy's hero tonight. No matter who you are, you are some kid's hero."

26

STRAWBERRY SHAKES AND SUNNY SNEEZES

Happiness is when what you think, what you
say, and what you do are in harmony.
—MAHATMA GANDHI

"Dad, you just don't get it. Put it down and—
Wait. Stop. Stop it! Look at me." I had no idea
what was going on, but Austin would not relent
and it made me laugh.

"Listen to me, please, thank you, and you're
welcome. Just listen, Dad!" The more I chuckled,
the more intense he became.

"Stop it! This is important." I stifled my laugh
and tried to listen.

"Look at me, Dad. You're not looking at me."

"Okay, what is so important? I'm all ears. I am
here, and I am looking at you! What's up?" I
waited. I've learned to listen to the Auzman.

What happened next was another watershed
moment in my life. But first, let me back up. I love
that Austin has a passion for food and for
cooking, and we do everything we can to
encourage him. Auz has wanted to be a chef for
as long as I can recall. I will always remember

221

watching Chef Emeril Lagasse on TV with Austin, when he was still a toddler, screaming along with Emeril, "Bam, Bam, BAM!" Of all the TV chefs, though, Guy Fieri is at the top of his favorites. Austin has every episode of *Diners, Drive-Ins and Dives* (aka "Triple D") on his iPad. He watches them over and over, drinking in every detail.

So what is it that draws him to Guy and Triple D? I'm pretty sure it started when Austin watched an episode featuring a restaurant called Big Mama's in Omaha. Auz searched for the address on his iPad, and we ate a meal there—the first of many Triple-D dives we would visit. I had the pig's ear sandwich (Guy had eaten three of them, and raved about it). I didn't like it quite as much. In fact, I almost threw up—something about eating a food that still has hair on it . . . I still get nauseated thinking of it.

Austin is a big-time foodie, and that's a true fact, as he would say. Someday he wants to be a chef, meet Guy Fieri, and open his own restaurant.

On this just-listen-to-me-Dad day, Austin had been riding with me on an errand to Omaha when one of my buddies called to talk to Austin. He'd located a vintage Nirvana concert poster. It was an original and he thought Auz would love to add it to his collection. However, he broke one of our cardinal rules, born out of necessity, and told Austin.

Austin has a skewed sense of time and finds it very hard to wait, so he talked about the poster for the next hour. Whether he was getting the poster in five minutes or five days didn't matter. We've learned never to tell him about an event or a gift in advance unless we're prepared to be pestered incessantly.

We pushed on to Omaha, my ears worn out with talk about the promised poster, and ended up on Seventy-Second Street.

"There! That's it!" screamed Auz. The vintage Nirvana poster was forgotten; Austin had spotted Burger Star. "I think I saw it on Triple D!"

I'm a burger lover, so I gave in to Austin's pleadings, and we pulled into the parking lot. The moment we walked in the door I knew we'd stumbled onto a gold mine full of everything Austin loved. Fancy vintage guitars and memorabilia covered not only the walls but the ceilings and booths too. Classic rock blasted from the speakers and music videos flickered on wall-mounted big screens. A big two-sided fireplace was in the center with big screens on each side, and a Guitar Hero video game was set up for anyone who felt the need to jam.

Music, videos, and food—it was the Austin trifecta.

We both ordered burgers, of course. Austin loved the order process—customers used a little pencil to check off ingredients on a little sheet and then handed it to the cashier, who then pushed it back to the grill via a little zip line. I had my burger slathered in coleslaw with pepper jack cheese and pickles, along with an order of fries and a drink. Austin checked off every ingredient, adding the entire salad bar to his burger. He topped off his order with onion rings and a shake.

Soon, the feast arrived, enormous, fat, beautiful burgers, along with greasy, rustic, and crusty hand-cut fries. Austin had an enormous mound of breaded Vidalias. My salivary glands kicked into overdrive and I prepared to dig in. As usual, Austin was already sucking down the strawberry milkshake before I could even take a bite.

That's when it started. "Dad, stop what you're doing," he said. He insisted on my utmost attention. I tried to sneak a first bite but gave up when I realized his gaze was firm, fixed, and determined. I had no idea what was coming, but Austin was as intense and excited as I had ever seen him. I raised my hands in surrender.

"You just don't get it, Dad. This shake. Oh my gosh. This is amazing. You have to believe me. The utter smoothness, the texture. It is so creamy and, oh man, it's just like heaven."

I started laughing again.

"No! I mean it. This is the best strawberry shake you will ever have. I know milkshakes are great, but there is just something about a strawberry shake that is the bomb. No other flavor does it for me, Dad. And this one is perfection. Do you get it? The shake makes the deal. It makes everything better, everything!"

Then he screamed it out: "This is the best day of my life!"

Believe me, I was listening now. So was the entire restaurant. I hid a small smile and raised my monster burger for a bite.

And just like that, Austin was done. Quiet. Totally engrossed in his strawberry-milkshake bliss and then onto dipping fries into the gargantuan bowl of ranch dressing he'd ordered. I ate and watched Austin as he hummed and grunted his way through his meal. He was in his own cosmos, somewhere far away.

When we were done, Austin grabbed the greasy paper order ticket they'd tucked under the fries and we were off.

As we left Burger Star, I couldn't stop thinking about the strawberry shake and the Burger Star food ticket clutched in Austin's right hand. I'm sure it meant something to him and whatever it was, I think it was probably very important.

I sat in the driver's seat, quiet. I took my hand off the key and watched Austin as he buckled in. *How can a boy be so happy over such simple things as a hamburger and a strawberry shake?*

I sat there musing for a few more moments until Austin nudged me.

How can this be the best day of his life?

Then I thought about how I'd acted with my wife and boys for many years—selfish and self-absorbed—so many words that started with the word self. A new thought nudged me. Even though I was well into my forties, maybe this boy next to me was helping me grow up. It didn't make sense, but it seemed true.

What have I been doing all these years? Have I missed other moments like this?

As we headed out onto Highway 34, Austin stirred from his food-induced coma and stared into the southern sky as the brilliant sun made its way west. He continued gazing out the window. And I just drove, with no satellite radio, AM–talk radio, or any other distractions. I had enough going on in my head. I also felt a small, peaceful smile on my lips.

"Auz, what are you doin', man?"

"Just staring at the sun," he said.

"Why?"

"I'm trying to make that sun thing happen to your nose. You know, if you stare at the sun, your nose will get all tickly, and if you look at it long enough it will let you sneeze." He spent the next twenty minutes staring at the southern sky, waiting for the elusive sneeze.

While he waited on the sun, feelings streamed through me.

I am so glad I have my family. I love everything

about them. After all the pain and heartache and frustration I have brought to my family, I know now what I have.

Every day Austin and Logan show me what I am supposed to be doing as a dad. They tell me I need to be present, and they teach me how to be grateful for the blessings that have been before me all these years. I finally own my life. So what I do with it matters.

As I drove, I thought about how Austin owns and fully inhabits every moment, no matter how small and inconsequential, moments that would slide by most people unnoticed. He celebrates every milkshake and sausage biscuit because to him, what's in front of him is the greatest thing in the world on the greatest day of his life.

Austin drifted to sleep with his head resting on the door, his face pointed up at the sun.

How blessed I am. In spite of the drama, pain, and expected trials we've had to endure, we've overcome. Teresa and I are together and strong. We have to be to navigate what we have been given. We are where we are for a reason. My family is the exact family we were made to be.

As I thanked God, I had a strange idea. Maybe all these years it wasn't Joe I was talking to, but Him. The feeling grew and I felt stronger in this new knowledge. It had been God looking out for me all along, not some imaginary friend.

The hairs stood up all over my body as I looked

back to Austin, and this is what came to mind: *I have fought a good fight, I have finished my course, I have kept the faith.* This has been my favorite scripture for so many years. And ironically, I don't think I could love a verse that is more appropriate for my family and me. Keeping faith and staying true to the course in times of adversity and question have developed perseverance in us.

As we approached the Emerson Overpass, I was still making sense of my day. As I passed underneath, I looked back. It's something I always do. Always. I never forget to do it, and I've never known why. Maybe it's an OCD tendency, but today I fixated on the image of the overpass in my rearview mirror and realized I could leave behind all the mistakes and poor decisions I'd made, the bad things I'd done, and all the pain we'd lived through. Because, as Logan puts it, "You're half dead, Dad! So live."

I may not ever forget my past—I do think it is absolutely important to remember it—but I never have to live in it again, ever.

From this day forward I will remember crossing under the overpass. But I don't ever have to look back at it again to know that life is good, as is my God.

A strawberry shake and the hope of a sunny sneeze can make it the best day of your life. Austin was just being himself, but it was everything I needed.

27

CLOSE YOUR EYES

The real problem is not why some pious,
humble, believing people suffer,
but why some do not.
—C. S. LEWIS

Some days I want to shout to people how great
life is, how we are only here for a moment, and
how, like Austin, we need to drink in every detail.
It is so hard to contain myself when I feel blessed
with an abundance of good things in my life,
and I know that my decisions and choices after
the dreaded night at the country club enable me
to walk in faith with my family today.

My walk continues, and slowly I have sensed
the four of us becoming one solid, faith-filled
body. I do like clichés, and one I have heard many
times is, "The family that plays together stays
together." I like this one even better: "The family
that prays together stays together." My family
loves church and they love me. And I'm starting
to understand the connection.

Logan and Austin have taught me and shown
me how to live and how to live right. While I'm
their father, and I hope they follow my example

today, it's pleasing to know that my children are also growing into leaders.

On a recent Sunday, another unexpected benefit of being part of a church became very clear to me. Teresa and I were sipping coffee and talking to friends while Austin darted around the sanctuary. Logan was in a Sunday school meeting elsewhere and getting ready for Praise Team. We made our way into the sanctuary and sat down to soak up the positive energy, love, and peace.

I leaned over to T and said, "You know something great about church? Two hours of freedom."

"What are you talking about?" She looked at me, eyebrows raised.

"Austin rarely sits with us. We get a little bit of respite straight from God," I said. "We're blessed with a son with autism who is social and who prefers to sit with other people during church service."

Maybe that doesn't sound like the kindest thing to say. But with Austin, sometimes it's those little breaks that help us maintain sanity.

The service was about to start and Austin was nowhere to be found. By now most folks at church have a good understanding of how to work with Austin, so we have no problem letting him be a social butterfly. At the last minute I spotted him across the sanctuary sitting by our good friends Jenni and Chris. I caught Jenni's eye and gave her a questioning head tilt, and she shot me back a thumbs-up. I relaxed and returned an okay sign.

As I settled in next to Teresa, I thought back to a conversation with Austin I'd had a few weeks earlier. I'd been in church with Austin, Logan was in Praise Team, and Teresa was out of town. About halfway through the service Austin asked me why people raise their hands.

"You don't do it, but why do they do that, Dad? Can I do that? Should I be doing that?"

"You can do that too," I said. "It's for any time you feel close to God. It stands for many things. To me it shows that He is above us and we are reaching up to the Lord in thanks and praise. It doesn't have to be at church. You can do it anywhere you like," I explained.

"Oh, okay," he mumbled. End of conversation and his hands stayed down. I'd forgotten about that discussion until the moment when I looked over at Austin during a popular praise song by Casting Crowns. We'd seen the band in concert a few times, and I knew Austin loved their songs.

I tapped Teresa on the shoulder and said, "Look at your son." I stood with my mouth open for a second, then stifled a laugh as I waved and tried to get his attention.

Austin was swaying and bending to the music, and he had his right arm extended like a bad Nazi salute. It didn't look right, and I shouldn't have been laughing, but with him bouncing and be-bopping, I couldn't resist. Then he looked at me with the biggest typical Austin smile plastered on his face. He watched while I raised my own arm, reaching up. Austin caught on and mimicked me, lifting his arm up to the skies. Teresa grabbed my other hand and squeezed it when she saw what was happening. It was vintage Austin. He ended up with a straight-arm salute that was not your typical Christian palms to the sky.

At another church service, I sat with Austin on one side and Teresa and Logan on the other. I had my eyes open, hands folded below my chin, and head bowed in prayer. Out of the corner of my eye, I could sense Austin looking at me.

"Dad," Austin whispered.

"What, Auz?"

"Dad, you can't see God if your eyes aren't closed."

"Uh, I can't?"

"You might be able to, but the best way to see Him is to have your eyes closed so you can only see Him and nothing else. No distractions," he said in a loud voice.

I looked up and turned to him. He had a point —a good one. I've always prayed with my eyes open, but maybe Austin was right. Maybe I needed to take it all to my God and shut myself off from all the distractions and dedicate that prayer time to Him and Him alone, eyes closed.

As I meditated on Austin's words, I thought of

Narnia, the magical land created by C. S. Lewis in his books. The Lewis books and movies are some of our favorites, and we've seen them over and over. So I broke a rule, one that I get so mad at Logan for, and I got out my phone right there in church and Googled C. S. Lewis. (Don't tell the pastor.)

I was looking for some of the author's words that make me think of Austin, my family, and our journey. Here's one I found:

We are what we believe we are.

The past eight years my family has shown me that if we act like we are happy and full of joy, then we are. I've also learned if I am angry and sad, then that, too, is true. By following and allowing my wife and boys to show me how to live, I have been able to grow and be the man and father and leader I was supposed to be.

I am not the man I once was, nor do I ever want to return to being that man. My faith and family now sustain me and show me what life on earth is supposed to be about. I am becoming the man I am supposed to be. Just like Austin is the boy he was supposed to be. And each day is another step in faith and sobriety and love and living. Lewis understood:

What saves a man is to take a step. Then another step.

Austin lives every moment of every day, and I strive to be like him. It is hard, but I must remember each day is a step in being a better . . . well, a better everything—teacher, husband, father, and disciple.

My sobriety and faith are inexorably linked. I know they cannot be unbound. If one fails, the other would surely follow. Together the two form a strong and secure bond on which I now rely to ensure I will and can continue my walk. I am still stumbling, but I don't fear the fall any longer. I have my Rock, my faith, and my family, who are always there to rescue me and pick me up. Always.

Here's another:

The task of the modern educator is not to cut down jungles, but to irrigate deserts.

I am to be here for my family and, just as important, I am to be an example in my life and live for others. Especially the unusual, the unlikely, the unpopular, and the unwanted.

Where I once was fumbling and stumbling, now I am able to more clearly see where I am going. I see the purpose and path I am supposed to be walking. It all started with me admitting I had a problem, casting off my denial, and accepting help and hope.

One last thought from C. S. Lewis:

I gave in, and admitted that God was God.

Lead on, Aslan!

28

BOO

The first-born in every family is always
dreaming for an imaginary older brother or sister
who will look out for them.
—BILL COSBY

Skinny and small for his age, the twelve-year-old
boy gulped as he walked through the doors of
his middle school. He was a good kid with a
sweet nature. He was used to the typical teasing
about his size, but there was one mean boy who
seemed to have it in for him. The bully wasn't
much taller, but tall enough. And for some reason
he liked making fun of the smaller boy. Soon it
became a daily ritual.

The little boy never told his mom or dad about
the bully and instead chose to go it alone, keeping
the relentless taunts, jibes, and cutting laughs
bottled up inside. Every day he faced the
onslaught alone.

One day the boy's mother peeked her head in
the door of his bedroom just before time to leave
for school. She was surprised to see her son
stuffing handfuls of candy into a bag. It was the
week after Easter, and he was carefully emptying

his stockpile of sugary delights from his Easter basket into the bag. She asked him what he was doing and he told her. Then off they went. She dropped him off at school and drove back home with a small smile, although her eyes were a little sad.

The boy fidgeted with his sack of candy while he talked to the school secretaries behind the counter. "My mom told me I had to come into the office and ask if it was all right for me to do this," the boy said. The principal came out to find out what was going on, and when she heard the story, she immediately summoned the bully to the office.

"Uhhh . . . what am I doing here?" The bully looked up at the principal, his target standing quietly nearby.

The little boy spoke up. "Listen. I know you don't like me, and every day you are mean to me."

The principal looked on, eyebrows raised. The bully turned white.

"And I heard you say you weren't doing anything for Easter," the little boy continued. "So I brought all of my candy . . . for you." He offered the bag to his persecutor.

"Why in the heck would you do that for me?" The bully looked at the bag, his face now red and his eyes brimming with tears. For a moment, all was quiet. Then he added, "I'm mean to you every day, and I know you can't stand me. Why are you doing this?"

"Because I know . . . because that is what God told me to do. It is the right thing to do, and I forgive you," said the little boy. His voice was quiet but strong.

Silence. Then the stifled sobs of two little boys and four grown women.

That little boy who gave away his Easter candy was Logan. Sometimes we call him Boo.

People ask me a three-word question all the time. "What about Logan?" The answer is pretty simple. Logan takes it all in stride. Our family life is all he's ever known, and he's lived it with supernatural patience and grace. Over the years he was handed off dozens of times to a handful of trusted and much-loved friends and family members when we needed to tend to Austin's injuries or take him to yet another medical appointment. From the earliest days of his life, Logan's mettle was tested and tested often. We may never know the true impact on our younger son of passing through the fires of an autistic, chaotic, and somewhat crazy family.

Logan was a gift, an easy baby who rarely cried. Teresa and I had agonized for years about our parenting skills with Austin. Were his problems and quirks our fault? Was it true we just needed to be firmer with him and use stricter discipline, as many suggested? Should we implement a black-and-white, tough-love policy?

When it comes to disciplining the boys, our way is a slight departure from the way I was brought up—usually a spanking or rap on the hand with the rings on Mom's dominant left hand. But in our home, any type of corporal punishment for Austin could have meant a broken bone.

Many times we felt like failures. Then along came Logan. Same parenting, same skills, yet he was a breeze, always smiling, and a complete gem. Very rarely did we ever feel it necessary to even consider smacking his behind. What worked the best with him was a serious look and he immediately straightened up.

One day Teresa had a revelation. "Maybe we've been good parents all along," she said. "We're doing the same things with Logan that we did with Austin, yet Logan is a piece of cake. Austin, not so much."

I felt it too and my heart got just a little bit lighter that day. Logan was our confirmation on two fronts—we are good parents, and our son Austin is most definitely unique and special.

After the Easter-basket encounter, Logan never had to deal with that bully again. The small gesture changed something inside the other boy, and he began to treat Logan with a bit of respect and compassion. Logan's decision to use his heart and not his fists changed everything.

I've always had intense conversations with Logan, but a few years ago he said something that startled me. "I feel like I'm the older brother and Austin is my little brother."

"What do you mean, Boo?" I asked.

"Dad, it's because I know more about the natural* life than Austin does. Some things he just can't understand. Or maybe he really does, but in a different way. I don't know. But I feel like his big brother."

Sometimes I catch myself expecting too much from Logan. I can relax a little and not worry as much when Logan is with Austin. I rely on him, and I think of Logan as a rock, but he is still a kid. And not once have I ever heard him complain about our family life. Yes, he complains about typical adolescent stuff, but never about the life we lead and how different we are.

I got curious and asked him once, "What does it all mean to you, Logan? You know, growing up in our home with Austin and everything else?"

"Well, I know his autism causes him to have a real hard time with listening and directions. And I know he gets stuck on so many things— probably his OCD stuff. And it's crazy that no one will ever know what my brother's really thinking or know what's going on in his brain.

---

* We hate that *normal* word. What's *normal* anyway? There's no such thing.

"But it's all I've ever known, Dad," he said. "He's crazy, but he's so stinkin' funny and off-the-wall and fun to be around, even while he's driving you absolutely nuts. What's not to love about him? He's my brother and will always be my best friend."

Hang on for a minute while I blow my nose. Must be my allergies.

From day one, the time and energy required to care for Austin has been almost superhuman, with very little downtime or respite. To get some time to ourselves, we've all become night owls, even Logan. When Auz is asleep, we all breathe out and relax a little bit more, and we often spend that time with just the three of us. But Teresa and I wonder—we always wonder—are we giving Logan the attention he needs?

"You guys give me much more than I probably deserve," he said. "This is how I've grown up, and this is just who our family is."

Austin and Logan have fights and argue like typical brothers, but Logan feels an extra responsibility that most little brothers don't feel. "I watch Auz all the time," he said. "When he is in a large group, he has everybody cracking up and laughing. But I remember seeing a kid do the whole limp-arm, chest-slap thing and call him a retard and a freak. I got right in that kid's face."

Then he didn't want to talk about it anymore. I

get it. It's painful. But I know Logan takes care of his brother when he needs to, and I really don't need to know all the details.

Logan is not only wise but great at academics, sports, and music. Last year he was selected for All-State Choir. Although he's not the biggest kid around, he has an awesome bass voice. Teresa, Auz, and I drove to Des Moines to watch him perform in the Hilton Coliseum in front of thousands of other students and their families. We ended up waaayyyy up in the nosebleed seats, so high and so steep that Teresa could not get up there. Thanks to a kind soul who gave up his seat, she was able to sit near the orchestra pit.

Austin sat with me, next to a school principal from another small town, and had a wonderful time chatting with him. Then the program started and we sat, waiting for Logan's choir to come onstage. At about the hour mark, while the orchestra was clearing the stage and Logan was about to perform, Austin started kicking the seat in front of him. I could feel his tension and anxiety, and as he continued the slow slide into a behavioral meltdown, I began to get just a little bit irritated.

"Come on, Auz. Please!" I whispered. "I want to see your brother." It didn't work.

Nothing about what Austin was doing was unusual, but I was getting mad just the same. Logan would be onstage within minutes, but I knew we wouldn't be able to stay in our seats.

Austin kicked harder, fidgeting and twitching as his whispers got louder and louder. "Can we go? I can't do this. I can't sit here anymore. Can we go?"

When he goes into this mode, I can feel it, right at my sternum. My chest gets tight, my face gets hot, and it's like there's a direct emotional line between me and Austin and I can feel his anxiety like I'm inside his head and his heart.

Then come the concerned looks from people nearby and the stares that turn to murmurs. "Who is this kid? Why can't his dad control him?"

"Can we go, Dad? I wanna go. Dad! Can we go?"

Each onlooker's irritated look and murmur etched its way into my heart and my face grew hot. I glanced over to the principal. "Is there something I can do to help?" he asked.

"Thanks. No. We'll be fine," I said. Then I gave up. I helped Auz to his feet and got in front of him for the trek down the steep stairs.

I shouldn't have done it, but I turned to the group where all the looks came from. "I am so sorry for my autistic son," I said, trying to keep my voice calm. "He's done really great sitting here for over an hour, but that's all he can handle. I hope you enjoy the choir."

That night it was just too much. We started down the steps as a chorus of apologies and kind words followed us. Austin's anxiety was taking over and he was almost in tears. As we neared the bottom, I noticed his steps were slowing and he was getting lethargic. I knew he'd be out within seconds.

We ended up sitting on the floor of the circular hallway outside the floor with the stage where the students were performing. I quickly rolled up my leather jacket to make a pillow and got Austin settled. He lay on a metal ventilation grate up against a cool window, his head on my jacket. He was out before his head hit the leather.

I made sure he was comfortable and then got up, walked fifteen feet to one of the doorways, and stood. I watched as Logan and the rest of the choir belted out *"Dominus Vobiscum."* The rafters rocked with the wondrous sound. Even from my odd vantage point, I could see Logan up in the front row, and it was beautiful.

When the song was over, I walked back to Austin. I wasn't angry anymore. It really was a typical night out, and with our divide-and-conquer strategy, Teresa was inside enjoying watching her son sing. I sat down again and Austin put his head in my lap. I sat by the cool window and rocked Austin while I listened to Logan sing.

Logan is now an accomplished runner, an honor student, and can play most stringed instruments. He's the drum section leader for marching band, and he recently sold his Apple iPad to buy his own violin. Last year he attended a youth leadership conference in Washington, DC, and recently he received an invitation to sing at Carnegie Hall.

But even more important, Logan is kind, gentle, and caring.

One of the ways Teresa and I have tried to cut Logan some slack is by letting him stay up late at night with us. He clearly has a later curfew than most of his peers and trust me, we've heard about it. But when Austin goes to bed, for Teresa, Logan, and me, it's time to play.

Logan does hide away in his basement bedroom on occasion. And the time he spends on school activities is sometimes an escape. I get it. That's how he copes. But when I look at Logan, I still see that little boy giving away his Easter candy to another boy in need.

The other night I was relaxing in my room when Logan came in to talk. He'd discovered Austin had been sending chat messages to people on Facebook he didn't know very well and he'd been inviting them over to our house to eat, play, and hang out. One was a young man who has used drugs and had trouble with the law. Alarmed, I called Austin in to tell him that wasn't such a good idea.

"Dad, he is a good person. He's just had some bad times growing up." He began to cry, frustrated. "I don't understand, Dad. Why can't I be friends with him? He needs friends!"

He got louder. "I just want people to like me. I want to be like other people and I want to have friends." He cried louder, waving his hands. I was overwhelmed with his sudden intensity and not sure how to answer.

Then Logan stepped in. His voice was gentle. "Auz, I only have two or three true friends."

Austin's sobs quieted a bit. He was listening.

"Asking strangers to our house is not such a good idea. We have to know them and trust them. How do you think Mom and Dad would feel about these people walking into our house out of the blue?"

Still talking, Logan turned and walked out of the room. Austin followed. They ended up in Austin's bedroom, and I could hear their voices rising and falling. Logan's voice was quiet, slow, soothing. Austin's voice mirrored his younger brother's and quieted too.

I sat on my bed and bawled. It had been a long time since I'd seen Auz this upset, but Logan knew what needed to be done. I realized our youngest is growing up, and when things begin to unravel, we can call in the little brother SWAT team.

Ten years ago Austin almost killed his little brother. But now there's something invisible, mighty, and wonderful binding these two brothers together. And no power on earth can break it.

29

CLOUDS

It always rains on tents. Rainstorms will travel
thousands of miles, against prevailing winds,
for the opportunity to rain on a tent.
—DAVE BARRY

*Boy Scout campout? Forget it. There is no way
I'm going.*

It was autumn and already looked like it was
going to rain. The temps were dropping and we'd
be out in the middle of freezing nowhere. Also,
full disclosure, my Oklahoma Sooners would be
playing their opening-day football game that
same weekend. *No stinkin' way I'm going to miss
that.*

Even if I did go, I wouldn't be able to follow
the game on my cell phone or iPad without a cell
signal. I was pretty sure the Scouts wouldn't be
bringing along a television either. Nor was I
excited at the thought of sleeping in the mud,
snarfing on eggs-in-a-bag, building lean-tos, or
slogging through the woods for three long days
with Austin and hundreds of other boys from
around the Heartland.

But Austin loved being a Scout, and there was

no way I was getting out of this trip. I still dreaded it, though, and mumbled cranky thoughts to myself as I packed. Austin gleefully packed everything he would ever possibly need, and then some. He was ready to go by the Monday before the trip. Austin barely slept the whole week and asked, "Is it time to go?" almost every hour on the hour. By Friday morning, he was revved and ready to go—a wound-up and tightly coiled ball of energy.

Austin and I headed out under sunny blue skies, contradicting the weatherman's call for thunderstorms. Sure enough, upon arriving at Little Sioux Scout Ranch, Mr. Sun went away and the black clouds rolled in as if on cue. The gloomy skies matched my mood to a tee. The weatherman confirmed my fears—the weekend would be wet, boring, muddy, and more wet.

The park was beautiful, however, and gleamed after recent renovations. Just a few years prior, on June 11, 2008, the North Valley section of Sioux Scout Ranch had been devastated by a massive tornado. Four young Scouts were killed and forty-eight wounded. The tragedy made world-wide news and touched hearts around the globe. This opening weekend was a recommissioning of sorts, with Scouts filling the ranch once again and bringing life and laughter with them.

When we rolled in, news crews and cameras were setting up to record the grand reopening of the devastated area. Although the weather was turning, I couldn't help but sense the energy and anticipation of the weekend to come. I wished I felt it too.

Before I could put the car into park, Austin flung open the door and burst out as usual. A moment later I followed, just as the rain commenced. I knew we faced a gentle, half-mile hike to our campsite. *This won't be so bad,* I told myself. I knew I'd be carrying the lion's share of the load since the uphill hike in and of itself would be a challenge for Auz. His leg problems, along with the micro-fractures, chronic pain, and meds, cause him to tire easily. On top of that, some of the meds cause reactions when he gets too much UV exposure, while others make him tired, with overexertion often leading to seizures or drowsiness.

I decided to watch him closely as we got ready to set out. If I detected a flushed red face, silence, or lethargy, I knew we'd need to resort to plan B. I just didn't know what plan B was yet.

A moment later I looked up, and Austin was already one hundred feet up the trail, fully loaded down with his pack, a large bag, and his pillows and blanket. *Hmm, I better scramble.* I hurried to grab my gear, locked the car, and trotted after him. And I kept trotting because he was scooting right on up the trail. It went up and up and up. And Austin kept trucking up and up and up.

As Austin marched up the trail, I could see how eager and focused he was on this trip. I also noticed he was one of only a handful of Scouts dressed in full Scout uniform with khaki shorts, button-down shirt, sash, hat, scarf, and even socks. He looked sharp! Later he told me, "You gotta walk the walk, Dad."

When we arrived at the campsite Austin barely looked winded, but his face was a little red so I kept watch. The next step was to choose where to pitch our tent. One of the Scout leaders popped out of a nearby tent and told us Austin would be sleeping in a tent with another Scout who was alone. Apparently Scouts can't camp alone. Austin thought this was a great idea, then surprised me by taking the lead and pitching my tent for me.

Immediately I started to worry. Austin's sleep-overs and nights away from home have never ended well. Most attempts result in a phone call at about nine or ten at night to come and pick him up, either because he is homesick or scared or the other kid doesn't know how to play Austin's way.

But so far everything was going well; the evening campfire and simple meal were relatively quiet and uneventful. Other troops straggled in to find their campsites and set up before bed. Then, about eleven, the first thunderclaps shook the camp. *It won't be long now.* I knew Austin would be scared, and as I waited for him to scramble into my tent with his pillows and blanket, I gazed through the clear plastic tent canopy at the light show outside, enjoying the incredible brilliance of dozens of lightning strikes.

But the tent flap stayed closed, with no sign of Austin. I finally gave in and got in my bag. Soon I felt a drip on my forehead. Then another. *Drip . . . drip . . . drip . . .*

No way! This tent is waterproof. What's going on? I rolled over, bringing my sleeping bag with me, away from the leak to the far side. *At least I brought the air mattress.*

I still couldn't figure out where the water was coming in so I rolled back over, reached up, and touched the clear plastic canopy at the top. A stream of ice-cold rainwater sluiced down my arm, over my body, and continued to parts farther south. It was cold!

I moved again, worming farther back into the corner.

And still no Austin.

As I peered up through the plastic canopy, I saw tiny cracks in the plastic when the lightning flashed. *That's how the water is getting through.* I was not going to be dry anytime soon. I thought of Austin again, but quickly turned my thoughts to how nice and dry and warm Logan and T were in their beds at home. The rain was dampening my spirits with every drop.

A couple hours later I was still awake, and still no Austin.

The storm finally relented as the dark became light and the hushed chatter of eager Scouts started to filter into my tent.

Riiiiip! My tent flap flew open. "Dad! What's up? What an awesome night. How'd you sleep? Are you ready to rock? What'd you do all night? Do you love these tents? We had a blast. This is going to be great. Are you hungry? I am. Are you ready to go? Let's do it, man!" He went on and on and on. I guess *his* tent didn't leak.

"By the way, Dad, was that storm cool or what? That was so awesome."

Humph.

The sun was flirting with the clouds but hadn't yet shown up. I prayed a tiny prayer that it would emerge soon to help me dry out. I felt soggy and wet all the way to my bones. And I was cold. No one else looked cold. I continued to complain to myself. I wasn't answering, but I was talking plenty.

Saturday's schedule consisted of events and workshops scattered over the entire North Valley. The first one Austin had signed up for was a Civil War reenactment. Auz and about fifty other Scouts were placed in different spots as active battle participants.

Austin was chosen for artillery. The center-piece of the artillery division was an authentic,

813-pound Civil War–era cannon. Austin was prepped in how to prime the fuse, insert the black powder, and, when so ordered, let 'er rip by pulling the cord to fire.

The first time he pulled the cord, the cannon boomed and I swear the earth shook. Of course there was no cannonball, only powder, but I had visions of soldiers from both South and North caught in a grueling struggle, with hand-to-hand combat and raging *ka-booms,* clanging bayonets, and soldiers' cries ringing out through a haze of sweat and smoke and fodder.

The cannon belched out another round. This time I admired the enormous plume of smoke mixed with sulfur as a massive fireball shot forth. It was an amazing sight.

After the battle concluded, the Scouts got to hang around the reenactors, decked out in vintage Union and Confederate mufti. When it was time for questions, of course Austin's hand shot into the air.

"What was it like being in the Civil War?"

The soldiers smiled, then laughed so hard a few of them came to tears. It was a friendly laughter and it didn't bother Austin one bit. One soldier put his arm around Austin and told him it was an awesome and brutal thing, but an important part of our country's history.

No other hands were raised. So Austin asked another question, and another, and another. Even though all the other Scouts were quiet, they listened as the soldiers had a blast answering Austin's endless string of questions. I laughed right along with the soldiers.

Austin was genuinely interested in what the soldiers had to say. He wanted to hear their stories, and I was so proud and impressed with his focus and sincerity. Soon, it was clear the other Scouts were ready to go, but the soldiers seemed in no hurry to leave any of Austin's questions unanswered. I loved it. Cool with a capital C.

Next, we strolled around the different reenactors' tents and stands to check out the wartime daggers, bayonets, and tools. I was pretty sure we'd be heading back up to camp next for a nap since Austin is easily winded. But it wasn't to be.

The soldiers thanked and hugged Austin, and as we walked away I couldn't help but think of what I'd just witnessed—Austin being inquisitive, caring, unafraid, engaged, and leading the way in front of a group of boys either too shy, too bored, or too apathetic to care. I'm not sure exactly why, but I felt really happy.

As we walked Auz grabbed my hand.

What is happening? Just a few short hours ago I was dreading everything about this weekend, but now the weekend seemed different. I felt shaken. I think my son's joy and sense of purpose had exposed something still quite ugly in me. I felt a flash of revelation—I had come to this place with a self-serving and unloving attitude. I didn't realize and couldn't have known that I would be seeing a little glimpse into Austin's future.

My son is growing up. He is soon to be a man. Every minute I have left with Austin and Logan matters. Every breath counts, no matter what.

Then I felt a surge of joy, my own joy.

What teenage son holds his father's hand?

I was walking with Auz and it felt good. We slogged onward in our muddy boots. I had no idea where or to what event Austin was leading me, but he seemed to know exactly where he was going. And I hurried to catch up.

30
STARS

The clearest way into the Universe is
through a forest wilderness.
—JOHN MUIR

I caught up to Austin in time to see a big sign
labeled Archery. *This should be interesting.*
Inside, I saw Auz hopping back and forth, a wide
grin on his face. And then I saw why—Xavier!
Austin gave him a big high five and a bear hug.

"We're going to battle, Dad. Mano-a-mano,
head-to-head, straight up, one-on-one for all the
marbles, baby!" I looked over at Xavier.

"You got it," said Xavier. "I have to finish
working my station but I can take a break in a
little while, and then the heat is on."

Austin first met Xavier a year earlier at another
Scouting event in southwest Iowa. He was in a
different troop but they quickly became fast
friends. He knew just how to get along with
Austin and I appreciated him so much. Xavier
was one of the brave and courageous Scouts who
survived the deadly tornado. He'd been through
some horrific trauma, and my understanding is
that he helped triage and possibly save the lives

of several of his peers. He was a real hero, an Eagle Scout, and a freshman at the United States Military Academy at West Point.

The archery range was set up in stations. First, you picked up your equipment, then proceeded to the first target, then the next, and so on. Each target had a line of boys, each waiting his turn. Austin paced himself and waited patiently in line, always keeping an eye on Xavier. Austin and I worked our way through three complete loops of the range. Each time around Austin looked hopefully at Xavier, but each time Xavier shook his head because he couldn't take a break yet. "Dad, I know it's going to be the next time. I can just feel it," Auz said several times.

Finally, on our fourth circuit, Xavier flashed a quick grin and nodded to Austin. "Yes!" Austin screamed. Game on.

As Austin inched closer in line to Xavier's station, I noticed he was smiling big and tapping the seams of his pants over and over. He was excited beyond measure and I started to worry again about overstimulation.

We made it to the front and Austin now stood beside Xavier. I grinned so big it hurt.

I knew Austin was excited to be with his buddy side by side on the range. But when I turned to see him, he was in a different zone. The Auz Zone. Totally dialed in and focused on the bow in his hand and the targets downrange.

So far on his three previous tries he'd hit a target or two, coming up all but empty. But it didn't matter. I sensed a new energy and focus I hadn't ever seen before. Others sensed it too, and the Scouts gathered around, watching silently as Austin and Xavier lined up to battle.

Austin calmly nocked his first arrow. *He sure looks like he knows what he's doing,* I thought with surprise and a tiny bit of pride. He slowly drew the bowstring back and, *swish!*

The arrow flew free and . . . *Oh, wow, you are kidding me!*

Dead in the center. Bull's-eye. Ten points for Austin, along with a few gasps of surprise from the onlookers.

Next, Xavier was up. He shot, hitting just outside the bull's-eye for nine points.

A few of the Scouts started urging Austin on. "Come on, Austin, you can do it . . . Get another one, man . . . Go, Auz."

Quiet and focused, Austin nocked his second arrow. *Swish!* His arrow flew right at the target, striking just outside the bull's-eye, this time for nine points. In return, Xavier ripped another one downrange for a perfect bull's-eye.

Xavier shot again, his third arrow landing one more time just outside the bull's-eye for nine, with a grand total of twenty-eight points. Pressure was on—Austin needed a nine to tie and a bull's-eye to win outright.

The gaggle of Scouts had grown quite large and the range was at a standstill as the battle raged. Austin prepared his last arrow. Then the chant started. "Austin, Austin, Austin . . ." It grew louder.

Austin released his third and final arrow, and we all watched as it screamed through the air . . . and landed in the dirt embankment to the right of the target. He missed by at least a foot.

Oh man. I am big-time bummed. I stared at the arrow embedded in the dirt and prepared for a sorely disappointed young Scout. But I turned toward my son and saw something totally unexpected—Austin was bear-hugging Xavier and thanking him for being his friend and telling him how he had a blast. And I realized, regardless of the score, Austin won. He got exactly what he wanted and much, much more. I was fixated on the two of them laughing and didn't even realize that Auz was talking to me.

"Dad! Let's go, dude. Time to move on."

The day wasn't over by a long shot. *Hmm. What a day this has been so far. Austin knows more than I realize about how to live life. I can't believe I'm walking around this campground learning things from my silly son.*

It was surreal. I knew God was working on me through my son.

We ambled up the road and found a fire-building workshop to try, but just as we started to listen to the directions, Austin turned around and bolted off up the road, for where, I did not know. As he ran, he looked back over his shoulder with that familiar cosmic grin of his and the twinkle in his blue eyes.

"Now this is what I am talking about, Dad. This is how we are going to complete our day."

I followed, spotting a wooden sign that said Cross-Cut Saw.

Holy guacamole. I saw an enormous saw, at least four feet long with one-inch, razor-sharp teeth running along the edge. It was made for two people and had handles on either end.

Austin was already in line, and when we stepped up for our turn, the saw looked more like eight feet long with ten-inch teeth and wicked scary. The log seemed massive, although it was really only about a foot thick. This was a timed event and so far the fastest time of the day was thirty-nine seconds.

I stood there with my right hand on the rough-hewn handle and waited, admiring Austin. He was glowing and glassy-eyed; he was so tuckered out. But he was also determined. He had a steely look in his eyes.

While we waited, the moment stretched out and I started to think deeply about the weekend and what it all meant. I really had not wanted to come and had been dragged along. But I was starting to realize that there was something else going on, working below the surface, pulling me along. I got the sense that there was a plan behind this weekend, something I needed to see and to understand. It's the same feeling I get when I look back on that night at the country club, which I now knew was probably the single most important moment of my life—a crossroads after which everything changed.

Another cog seemed to tumble into place. *I am supposed to be here this weekend.* Yes, it was a Scouting event and everything was for the Scouts, but I had a moment of clarity inside as I was getting ready to rip into this log. Then the words came, deep inside, flowing into my heart.

I love my life, crazy and flawed and messed up as it is. I closed my eyes for a brief moment and took a deep breath.

"Are you ready for this, Auzman?" I snapped out of my moment and focused on my son. I had a feeling he was about to show me a thing or two. He had that look, like he knew something I was not privy to.

"Dad, we're going to do this. Can't you see? We are going to beat that time . . . so hold on and *Casa Gouda!*" I laughed at one of his favorite nonsensical words. He'd screeched it and that told the starter we were ready.

"Pull when I say pull," Austin reminded me. "Don't forget, Dad. It's absolutely important or this won't work."

The whistle blew. "Pull!" Austin shouted. I tried, but right away we snagged the saw. I'd pushed when I should have pulled. Austin's demeanor didn't change an iota. Complete and utter focus.

"Now pull, Dad!"

I will never forget what I witnessed. Austin was a boy transformed. He had always been a little guy with skinny legs and arms, but in that moment, every inch of his frail body turned into a shaking, swaying, synchronized piston of motion. He was driven by some force that drew me in and engaged me in the rhythm. We were rocking the huge saw now at a crazy speed. I had no idea how we kept it in the groove, but before I knew it, a thick chunk of log slammed to the earth.

Thirty-six and a half seconds. The fastest time of the day.

Hand on saw, I stood and stared at my son. I was shaking, overcome by wonder.

I was meant to be here, to experience this amazing day. Can it get any better? And then I realized I'd almost missed it. *What if I'd stayed at home?*

Again Austin grabbed my hand. I squeezed it, maybe a little too hard. We started walking and I almost began to weep. I wasn't worried about rain or the football game anymore. I had so many thoughts flying around my brain as I struggled, trying to put it all together.

We trudged back to the campsite, arriving just as the entire troop was heading out for the big bonfire. I soon realized we weren't going anywhere. It was just about dusk, and Austin climbed into his sleeping bag and lay down by our little fire. Within seconds he was sound asleep. I sat in my camp chair and thought over everything that happened that day. And it made me think of how upside down so many things in my life had been. How I had wasted years on empty pursuits. How I had distanced myself from the ones who loved me most.

I looked up at the stars and talked to the One who made them. *God, where have I been? Where have we been? You are good and gracious and most awesome. Thank You for the life I have. I am so sorry for so much of what I've been and who I was.*

I leaned back into my camp chair. Austin was growing up, but so was I.

I slipped to my knees right beside Austin. I lightly touched his face. "Thank you, Auz. I love you."

Then I sat in my chair and drank my coffee. The best cup ever.

EPILOGUE
UNBROKEN

Do I want to be a hero to my son?
No. I would like to be a very real human being.
That's hard enough.
—ROBERT DOWNEY JR.

And thou shalt love the Lord thy God with all
thy heart, and with all thy soul, and with all thy
mind, and with all thy strength.
—MARK 12:30 (KJV)

I was driving a gleaming, candy apple red 1965 Chevrolet Impala convertible. At forty-five degrees it was a chilly evening for prom, but Austin and Jessi wanted the top to stay down.

We inched toward the hotel entrance where an announcer greeted each car and introduced the couples to the throng of family and friends. The Prom Drive-In Ceremony had been a Red Oak tradition for many years, but this was my first time to attend, although I was just a driver.

I rolled up and stopped beside the red carpet. Austin scrambled out of the Chevy to open the door for the multicolored, bedazzled, and beautiful Jessi. He looked debonair in his James Bond tuxedo of black pants with silk seams and an immaculate white dinner jacket with apple green vest and bow tie. Right before we had left the house, T had pinned a turquoise blue flower on his lapel.

"Ladies and gentlemen! Welcome Austin and Jessi," said the announcer. I braked and looked over my shoulder, watching Austin revel in the moment. He was smiling, arms outstretched and waving the Hawaiian "hang loose" thumb and pinky sign.

As I slowly rolled away, the last nineteen years of my life became a blurring cascade of vibrant Polaroids. I knew we were approaching a milestone. Soon Austin would be out of high school, with Logan not far behind. Our boys were becoming men.

What does the future hold for Austin? Did Teresa and I do enough for him? Were we great parents to our boys? Will Logan become a leader? Will Austin be able to live and flourish on his own one day?

I took a drive to clear my head and feel the cool breeze. I pulled in to our driveway thirty minutes later and headed to my favorite chair on the side porch. I don't need to run to the closet anymore. I don't need to hide myself and try to wish things were better.

As I relaxed in the cool evening air, I found

myself filled with longing. I pulled a little spiral notebook from my pocket and this is what I wrote:

Dear Teresa,

I started writing a few words to describe everything you mean to me, but I couldn't do it. It's just not possible. A few pages won't do justice to the incalculable love you have opened my heart up to.

It's just like how I started writing a book about living with Austin, but I couldn't do that either. Instead, I wrote a love story—a story of pain, renewal, redemption, and ultimate grace. The story of you and Austin and Logan was simply the canvas where I was able to open up my heart and soul to be touched by all three of you. All of this you bestowed upon me with the helping hand of our Lord and Savior, Jesus Christ.

When I started writing and reliving our lives, the story began to take on a life of its own, and sometimes I wept. There were tears of pain but more often tears of joy for the love we have forged through it all. Yes, there were times we acted more like college roommates, or Oscar and Felix from *The Odd Couple*, but a couple we were.

I started off wanting to write about a boy's diseases and quirks and challenges, but instead my eyes were opened and I never felt so alive. Each chapter I wrote built upon the last and ripped open raw emotions—exposing me to the sin and pain I felt, the same things I inflicted upon you and those I loved. And something unexpected happened: I saw that through it all, you were there, always there, the constant variable for us all.

Through you and Austin and Logan, I was able to systematically dismantle my life and build it back up with you as the foundation and God as our guide. I can't put into words how much I love and appreciate you for holding it all together for all these years. I will never understand how anyone could be the pillar of faith you have been to me.

At first, I focused on all of Austin's defects. Oh, how wrong I was in that. I also realized how much of myself I see in Austin, and how much of Austin I have in me. Maybe I was as broken in mind and heart and spirit as the broken bones you and Austin have to deal with.

Our family is quite crazy. If we weren't crazy, we'd be insane. We're more like the Addams Family than the Cleavers. But it's all we've ever known. Our meeting was no accident; neither was Austin's birth. He was born the boy he was made to be, just as we are the family we were made to be.

You know how I'm never without a book? I read one awhile back called *Writing Down the Bones* by Natalie Goldberg. The cover image was a bottle of the blackest ink spilled onto a stark white background. Instantly I knew it was an apt metaphor for our family—we live in the darkest and brightest of margins. There is no gray and no middle ground for us. Where the dark and light collide is what binds us together and makes our lives a series of those soaring highs and crushing lows, just like our Austin.

Let me show you what I mean in a different way. An old friend shared a poem called "On Joy and Sorrow" by Khalil Gibran. Here is the line that rocked me back: "Your joy is your sorrow unmasked." I thought of how you led me through the process of waking up and getting my life back. How you walked with me as all the pain and hurt peeled and scraped away, along with the poor decisions and bad luck.

Did I have to endure, struggle, and fail to become the husband and father and disciple I am today? Maybe. Probably. Yes.

Another line I want to show you: "The deeper that sorrow carves into your being, the more joy you can contain." I see in that poem the transformation that allowed me to come back to you. In order to have joy and grace and love, I had to stumble, fall, and almost die. The fire and flames, mostly self-inflicted, set me up to see and feel and live this joy like I never would have been able to otherwise. And you were always there. You could have walked away, but you believed.

I have such a hard time even thinking, let alone talking, about that night at the country club. And you *had* to be there for it. Your steady hand let me experience the second best thing to happen to me in my life—sobriety, second only to my faith.

While I've come to grips with my brokenness, it has only shown me the contrast between me and Auz. He is not broken, and he doesn't need fixing. There is so much right about our unbreakable boy. He has the struggles and angst of any teen, but how he receives, processes, and transmits is so unique. I know it is not all sunshine and rainbows for our son Richard Austin, but his ability to overcome and accept his lot is something I think we can both learn from.

Honey, I had it all wrong. I had love defined for me as the physical and lustful thing you see in the movies or read about in magazines. I couldn't have been more wrong. I did not love you when I met you. How could I? We didn't know each other. And my priorities were so upside down, they blotted out any real chance of my knowing true love, even when it was right in front of me.

Today I look in your blue eyes and see a glow and a spark and a fire, a font full to the brim. What I see in your eyes is love.

You are what is me. And I am slowly becoming you. We are a team and lovers and best friends. You led me to the doorstep of Christ. You endured and kept pointing to it. You allowed me to crash on the rocks that night to have that door crack open, even if just for a moment, so I could get a glimpse of what could be.

Each day I see Him more and more. And just as our love soars to lofty levels I never thought possible, I know it's God who's binding us together.

Teresa, I only want us to live and be more like our boys. We need to live more like Austin. I want us to be able to have his compassion and love for all people. If we base our relationship on this love and faith, there can be no room for drama, greed, or selfishness. We can both let go and become the person Jesus Christ intends for us to be.

It all starts with love . . . the love you showered upon me, even when I wasn't there.

We love and we survive. Unbroken.

Scott

THE UNBREAKABLE BOY
RESOURCES

AUTISM SPEAKS
www.autismspeaks.org

Autism Speaks is the world's leading autism science and advocacy organization. Visit their website for a wealth of resources, including information about the latest autism research, autism awareness events, and autism advocacy programs.

OSTEOGENESIS IMPERFECTA FOUNDATION
www.oif.org

Learn more about osteogenesis imperfecta, read the stories of people with OI, and discover resources for managing OI and connecting with others in the OI community.

WALK TO EMMAUS
emmaus.upperroom.org

Walk to Emmaus is a program established by The Upper Room for those seeking Christian spiritual renewal. The program begins with a three-day weekend experience where participants learn about the spiritual disciplines, their spiritual gifts, and more. Singing and fellowship are other key aspects of the weekend. After the weekend, participants join a small group, where they can continue to grow in their faith. Walk to Emmaus events take place throughout the world; visit the Walk to Emmaus website to find a chapter in your area.

GUIDEPOSTS
www.guideposts.org
Visit the Guideposts website for inspirational stories that will encourage you in your faith.

CHRISTIANITY TODAY
www.christianitytoday.com
Read articles about theology, church, culture, and many more topics relevant to Christians today.

FAITHGATEWAY
www.faithgateway.com
Learn how to grow and share your faith through articles from top Christian authors. The site also includes daily devotionals, webinars, giveaways, and book excerpts.

BOSTON RED SOX
www.redsox.mlb.com
Scott's favorite baseball team.

THE UNBREAKABLE BOY WEBSITE
www.unbreakableboy.com
Check out the companion website for this book.

THE UNBREAKABLE BOY
FACEBOOK FAN PAGE
www.facebook.com/theunbreakableboy

Become a fan of *The Unbreakable Boy* on Facebook.

AUSTINTISTIC, SCOTT'S BLOG ABOUT LIFE WITH AUSTIN
www.austintistic.blogspot.com

Visit *Austintistic* to see the blog that inspired this book.

AUSTINTISTIC TWITTER PAGE
https://twitter.com/ScottLeRette

Connect with Scott on Twitter.

ADDITIONAL INFORMATION

- Centers for Disease Control and Prevention, "Facts about dextro-Transposition of the Great Arteries (d-TGA)." Updated June 5, 2013. http://www.cdc.gov/ncbddd/heartdefects /d-tga.html.
- Osteogenesis Imperfecta Foundation | OIF.org. "Fast Facts—Osteogenesis Imperfecta Foundation | OIF.org." Accessed February 9, 2014. http://www.oif.org/site/PageServer?pagename =fastfacts.
- Autism Speaks. "What Is Autism?" Accessed February 9, 2014. http://www.autismspeaks .org/what-autism.

- Neil Kaneshiro, MD, MHA, Clinical Assistant Professor of Pediatrics, University of Washington School of Medicine, "Osteogenesis imperfecta: MedlinePlus Medical Encyclopedia," *National Library of Medicine—National Institutes of Health.* U.S. National Library of Medicine, August 2, 2011. http://www.nlm.nih.gov/medlineplus /ency/article/001573.htm.

AUSTIN'S FAVORITE MOVIES

Austin's room is his safe place. There he is secure, comforted, and in control. He has an extensive movie and music collection, and his DVDs and CDs are his prized possessions. Many of them are mine, but since they've migrated to his room, they now belong to him. He knows the cover art, titles, and credits for the moviemakers and the musicians by heart. He's also a treasury of movie one-liners and musical snippets.

You can often hear Austin talking in an odd manner, using different voices and taglines—he's actually reciting movie dialogue, extensive word-for-word recreations and character embellishments. Much of his conversation in real life weaves in one-liners and insights from his media collection. Little do the original writers and lyricists know they are supporting characters in one autistic boy's life!

Here are Austin's all-time favorite movies (including the names of his favorite actors):

1. *Star Trek*, with Zachary Quinto
2. *Ghost Rider: Spirit of Vengeance*, with Nicholas Cage

3. *The Avengers*, with Chris Evans and Robert Downey Jr.
4. *Iron Man 3*, with Robert Downey Jr.
5. *Goonies*
6. *The Lord of the Rings*
7. *The Hobbit*
8. *The Crow: Salvation*, with Eric Mabius
9. *Toy Story*, with Tom Hanks
10. *The Vampire Diaries*, with Paul Wesley
11. *Twister*, with Bill Paxton
12. *Without a Paddle*, with Seth Green and Matthew Lillard
13. *Big*, with Tom Hanks
14. *The Dark Knight Rises*, with Christian Bale
15. *Arrow* (TV series), with Stephen Amell
16. *X-Men*, with Hugh Jackman
17. *Ghostbusters*, with Bill Murray
18. *The Emperor's New Groove*

OUTTAKES: LIFE WITH AUSTIN

If the LeRette family goes to a movie, we never miss the credits, and we always hope for an extra scene. Here are some of our very favorite outtakes from life with Austin, our own, real-life superhero.

A SINGLE, SOLITARY QUESTION

Have I told you that Austin likes to talk? Unlike many people with autism, Austin is extremely verbal and even more social. Is this a blessing or a curse? Some days I think the answer is a definitive Yes! to both. He is social and verbal to a fault. Boundaries are something with which Austin has extreme trouble comprehending. Personal space is a concept that does not register for my son. And he loves to hug and tell you he loves you, regardless of the setting.

Just as Austin reaches for the sky in everything he does, he also knows no limits or boundaries when it comes to going over the top on anything and everything he does. A prime example is when Austin asks a question. It can quickly become a trying conversation.

AUSTIN: What's that?

Is that meat?

Is that pot roast or poop with white
  sprinkles?

ME: Uhh . . .

AUSTIN: When is dinner?

Is that what's for dinner?

Hey, are werewolves real?

What if we had one in Red Oak?

I just know they are real.

Dad, I think I have a migraine.

Do you have a migraine?

Why do we get migraines?

What is a migraine?

Should I take something for it?

It's probably because I talk too much and
  my cortex can't keep up.

I am such a dork.

I'm a dork, aren't I?

Do you love me, Dad?

Please tell me you love me.

ME: Auz, I . . .

AUSTIN: We're really having that for
  dinner?

Werewolves must be so cool.

I bet they have one at the zoo.

If they don't I'd be so mad.

Dad, if they don't you have to get them one.

I would love to meet a werewolf and
  invite him to lunch.

That would be so cool.

Am I frustrating you?

ME: Umm . . .

AUSTIN: I don't like the soap we use. Is
that Irish Spring?

I don't really care for it.

Is Bruce Lee Chinese?

Oh, I know he is.

If he were alive would he still be
Chinese?

Or is he Japanese?

Either way . . . he could come to lunch.

Whatcha' doin'?

ME: Well . . .

AUSTIN: Bruce Lee's son, Brandon,
died from an accident on a movie set.

I know which one it is.

Do you want to watch that Brandon Lee
movie?

I'm really busy sorting my ties.

I better go.

So that's what we're having for dinner,
huh?

We're really going to eat that?

Dad, it looks really good.

Even if it looks like poop with sprinkles.

I told Sabrina she's the sprinkles on my
cupcake.

She thought that was sweet.

She is a really good person, Dad.

Tell me when dinner's ready.
See ya' later alligator.
ME: After a while crocooooooodiiiiile . . .
   I love you Austin.

Whew—true story. It happens multiple times, every single stinkin' day. Some days I wish I were a werewolf!

FISH ON!

My brother Kevin and I took four-year-old Austin with us for a day of fishing on the Chesapeake Bay. It was an awesome-looking weekend with clear blue skies. The conditions were perfect for catching Striper.

"I'm going to catch a monster fish," said Austin.

We drifted at about seven miles out as Kevin prepared the outriggers and planes for four to six lines. He and I also had enormous gold Shimano reels we'd be casting by hand.

Austin was in the Captain's chair, decked out in his madras Polo shirt, khaki shorts, and a pair of boat shoes, completed by a little life jacket. Kevin topped him off with a Bill Fish hat, and I wrapped my windbreaker around him and behind the chair, securing him in position.

Kevin threw all the lines out but one, baiting a brand-new Incredible Hulk fishing rod for

Austin to use. It was about three feet long and had about fifty feet of line that looked like cheap dental floss. Austin was so excited just to hold it.

Uncle Kevin told him what to do when a fish was on the line. What we weren't prepared for was Austin screaming, just five minutes later, "Fish on! I got one, and it's a huge shark. Hurry up, Uncle Kevin, and help me haul it in."

Kevin and I stayed in place, grinning at each other. We knew he was just having fun imagining. But then he screamed at us again, "Guys! Fish on. Help me!!"

Kevin did a double take and then lunged for Austin. The little green rod was bent at a severe angle. Just as he got there, the pole snapped and the reel rocketed through the air. Thankfully, Kevin had on his fishing gloves and snagged the broken reel in both hands.

Austin definitely had a *fish on*.

Inch by inch Kevin pulled in the line, and whatever was on it, to the boat. I followed Kevin's commands with the throttle, reversing course to help him take up the slack and not break the fragile line.

"Oh my gosh" was all Kevin said. Then he pulled in a three-foot sand shark as Austin squealed with joy.

We ended the day with Austin tied into the Captain's chair as we made our way back to shore. Austin was propped upright, sound asleep as the wind whipped his hair, and I think I saw a little smile on his lips. Fish on!

CRANK IT UP

On any given day it's fun to watch Austin immersed in organizing his music and movie collections—first by alphabet, then by genre. I have even seen him do it by color of the jacket or sleeve. Usually, the TV is blasting at high volume, accompanied by a song on the stereo playing even louder. Austin seems comforted when he is enveloped by the sound and noise and closeness of it all. On the other hand, he can get anxious and even have a seizure in social settings that are too close and loud and stuffy.

But when his OCD and ADHD tendencies get the best of him, it can be hard to watch. A few years ago at Christmas he spent almost three hours arranging his DVDs. When I stuck my head in his room, I saw him sprawled on the floor in full meltdown. He was making very little noise, but it was easy to see the marks of epic levels of frustration and angst on his face and body.

"I can't get them sorted the right way, Dad. It's just not working like I want it to," he said.

There was little to do but comfort and love on him. He'd spent his day trying to arrange several hundred CDs and DVDs, only to end up on the floor with an impending seizure, all because he couldn't do it the perfect way—his way—even if he knew what that was.

HE FLOATS

I asked Austin what God looks like.

"Straight up, Dad, He's got a white beard, white hair, white robe with a tannish type of skin. And He floats. I saw that on *The Simpsons*, Dad!"

BUSTED AT TARGET

One time, before we got started shopping at Target, the two of us ran into the men's bathroom, just inside the front doors.

All that was available was a stall so we both jammed ourselves into it and proceeded to take care of business. Then Austin looked up at me.

"Dad?" he whispered. I could barely hear him. "Dad, are those men's shoes?" he asked, pointing.

I looked down. In the stall next to ours was a bright red stiletto heel. I looked at Auz, my mouth in a huge *O*. I put my finger to my lips.

"Are we in the ladies' restroom?" he asked, much louder.

There came a rustling from the other stall.

"Let's get outta here, now!" I whispered back. We stopped everything we were doing and sprinted for the door. Before we got out, Austin had already broken out in one of his trademark raucous laughs.

"Dad, we forgot to wash our hands . . ."

Busted.

"Wanna go back?" I asked.

"No way, Jose!"

BEDTIME FOLLY

Just as mornings are routine and predictable, so are evenings. When Austin prepares for slumber there are certain steps, procedures, and rituals that must be completed. If not, sleep cannot and will not commence.

First, Austin gathers up as many as twenty water bottles and lines them up on the nightstand. Each must be full to the brim. The sheer quantity must help him feel secure.

Next, the pillows. The last time I checked he had fourteen pillows on his bed. Austin uses the pillows to create a protective cocoon so he can burrow down between them. Each part of his body must stay in contact with at least a part of any given pillow.

And then there are his blankets. Easily a good dozen grace the top of his bed, punctuated with an electric blanket, winter or summer. The blankets puzzled me for the longest time. I got the pillow thing, but the blankets were something that kinda freaked me out.

After some research on the Internet, I discovered weighted blankets. Folks with autism and others with sensory and stimuli issues use them for the secure and safe feeling they induce.

So, the weight and size and comfort of everything on the bed aids Auz in preparing for bed. If we were to strip the bed to a top sheet, a single pillow, and a cup of water, I think we might see WWIII.

The pillows and blankets will stay.

THE LAWN-MOWER INCIDENT

I was in the garage when I saw Logan by the front steps, frozen in place. I wondered what in the world he was so taken with. I walked over to get a look and I, too, stared at the spectacle before me—Austin mowing the lawn. He was sixteen but this was his first time ever mowing. I'd always been quite nervous about letting Austin loose on a machine with razor-sharp blades of death spinning just in front of his big clunky feet.

I had my hand in the air ready to give Logan a pat on the back, but it hung in the air, mid-pat, as we both watched what was unfolding.

Austin marched, arms stiff and straight, elbows locked and head down. His legs were just as rigid and moving at a fast pace. His right leg swung a little out to the right, as it is wont to do.

He was dominating this machine, driven by some unseen force, and I decided I would not get in his way.

Logan and I watched as Austin sliced and diced and made quick work of the turf. He went from corner to corner and through the middle, and then back around for another go, featuring U-turns and starts and stops. There was not a single straight line to be seen, and renegade sprigs of grass popped up here and there.

I have always enjoyed mowing, and I usually try to vary the cut from either long or short to diagonal, always leaving a nice pattern. Well, Austin was definitely following my lead and making his own mark on our yard.

We couldn't stop watching, and he had no idea we were there. I ducked my head in the front door and yelled for Teresa. This was too good to keep to myself. By this time Logan and I were almost on the ground crying with tears of laughter. My sides hurt from the show our dear son was offering us.

Teresa joined us, and before she'd even made it down to the last step, she was entranced by Austin's lawn-mowing skills. Her mouth dropped open and in minutes, she was laughing with us. It was one of the funniest things I have ever witnessed.

Austin finished the front. He was covered in grass from head to toe, drenched in sweat, and flushed red as a beet. He walked past us all and into the house as if we weren't even there. Austin was done.

He left patches of rough grass and ragged patches as far as the eye could see. I didn't touch it; he'd done the job and put his heart and soul into it. So who was I to touch it? Instead, I rolled the mower to the back and finished, for Austin.

And he's never done it again.

JOGGING

One day I decided to go for a run. The spring air was cool and made my skin tingle as I ran through the neighborhood. But the sky was blue, the sun was on my back, and a light, sweet breeze tickled the trees.

Austin was with me. He's never run more than a mile before, but today he joined me to run my usual three-mile course. I could see he was on a mission.

"I want to be like you, Dad."

I laughed at this. "No, you need to be you, Auz. I would rather be more like *you*."

Austin loped ahead of me with his long, lean legs. I noticed how he strained to swing his left leg forward—it takes a little extra effort because of the length differential. I know it hurts him when he runs too far or too hard, so I let him set the pace. How far we got or how fast we got there didn't matter. I was just proud and happy Austin wanted to be with me, doing something together.

We jogged about a block, toward Division Street, when he came to a stop. He was about ten feet ahead, frozen in place.

What now? Then he turned, took two steps, closed in, and enveloped me in a bone-crushing bear hug. Only then did I realize he was crying. Tears flowed down his flushed cheeks, but he couldn't talk yet—he was still breathing too hard. I held him, right there in the middle of the road.

"I'm going to get fat and out of shape," he sobbed, after he caught his breath. "I could die if I don't get in tip-top, peak performance. I heard you and Mom talking about me gaining weight, and I don't want to die."

Teresa and I did talk about how he had grown a bit of a pooch this last year, but we weren't concerned because he had been so skinny and frail for so long. But Austin lives in a very literal world. If you tell him something, he takes every word at face value. Innuendo, sarcasm, and subtle humor mean nothing.

BEST FRIENDS?

Meanness goes right over Austin's head—an unintended blessing. One day at bowling league, the three boys on his team were absent, leaving Austin with four eighth-grade girls. They were doing their thing, bowling and cutting up, having fun, but then the girls went into a huddle, whispering together. They broke up, and the leader of the girls went over and talked to Austin in a hushed voice. I watched as Austin looked back at me with a huge grin and a thumbs-up.

Then he rushed over. I could tell he was excited about what the girl had said to him. "Did you see my friends, Dad? They are my new best friends. All I have to do is shut up and they will like me. Isn't that cool?"

My heart hurt for him, but at the same time, I realized he was immune to the meanness. Not a bad way to live. Austin interprets everything as goodwill. When a boy screams insults at him, like idiot or 'tard, Austin immediately tries to explain it away. "He is really a good guy, Dad. He really didn't mean it. Don't get mad at him, Dad. He's my friend." I scratch my head and wonder, *Is his perception reality? Because Austin thinks it, is that loudmouth boy actually his friend?*

RUN, FORREST, RUN

One day on a trip to the beach, Austin talked his Uncle Jay into tossing the football around. I'm not sure why—Logan likes football way more than Austin—but this day Auz had his heart set on playing football. Jay told Austin to go out for a pass.

"How far?" Austin asked.

"It's going to be a long bomb, Auz," said Jay. "So go wayyyyy long. I can throw it a mile."

Austin takes everything you say literally. If you say you can throw a mile, then he believes you can throw the football a mile. So he took off running. He ran and ran and ran. He'd still be running if we didn't go and retrieve him. He's the Forrest Gump of our family. Remember that Tom Hanks movie where he played the quirky character who decided one day to get up and run around the United States for a couple of years? "Run, Forrest, run!" was the mantra of everyone who met him. But no one ever knew why he started, and one day his trek was over as abruptly as it had begun. He stopped when he was done.

Don't stop Austin from running. Let him run. I know I'll be following.

ACKNOWLEDGMENTS

SCOTT LeRETTE: I thank my mother and father. I love you both more than the world. I also want to thank my in-laws, Doug and Sandy Houser, who've been a blessing in my life. Thank you to my family for allowing me to be me the last nineteen years. Austin and Logan, in your own special way I know you supported me but couldn't care less if Dad had a popular blog that he went on and on about. Austin, you slay me the way you tell anyone and everyone about this book and blog although you've never read a word of either one. Logan, you are just the steady Freddy, always there and supporting me even though you had a million other things more important than whatever it was Dad was working on.

Even during the roughest years of my life, Teresa, you were always there and are still standing steadfast beside me. And today you remain the rock supporting me even when we may have disagreed. You are my greatest critic and most ardent champion. We are standing together with a love I never thought imaginable, only surpassed in knowing that we grow each day loving more and building a stronger walk together with God. I love you more than yesterday but not as much as tomorrow.

I thank my brother Kevin for inspiring me to take this silly little blog and make a book. You seeded the thought that grew into what you are now holding in your hands. Even though you are many miles away, your concern, compassion, and interest in my family, and especially Austin, will always hold a special place in my heart. I love you, brother. To my brother Kent, who is always there to sweep Austin away and calm his fears. In your own special way, you have a calming and nurturing way in loving Austin. Lastly, brother Brian—thank you for always being there. You were a constant we could always count on.

Mayra Fernandez is a special lady I was introduced to by an old long-lost friend, Chad Smith. Mayra, you helped me when I had some rough and tumble stories about my family. You read them all and guided me in wading through the gold and the superfluous. You made my stories better, and I hope you see some of those things in what I ended up writing.

I met this really cool dude while looking for resources I thought I might need if I ever wanted to write a book. Mark Malatesta and I ended up on the phone for an hour one day, and I think he may have been more exuberant about the possibilities of my story than I was. Mark, your infectious passion is only rivaled by your industry knowledge and literary acumen. You made me a better writer and made the path to publishing a journey that I slowed down to enjoy, realizing this was a life-changing event. It never was about business for either one of us. Thank you, friend.

Closer to home, an old schoolmate of mine, Jayne Schram, helped me think through many things while giving advice and grammar and etiquette lessons as a bonus. You are an awesome cheerleader and incredible sounding board.

Special super-duper thanks go out to Stephany Evans at Fine Print Literary for taking a risk with me. I know that's what you did, so don't deny it. And when you placed me with your rock-star agent, Becky Vinter, the process went into hyper-speed. She led me every step of the way and threw in her own editing expertise whether I asked for it or not. Becky, you are a class act, and I will miss you greatly on the next book.

I pause here to collect myself as I think of the words to describe and acknowledge a person who helped me take my book from okay to good to better, to levels I couldn't have envisioned. Susy Flory is the best-selling writer who has been with me since the first days at Fine Print. We looked at many writers and for some reason I just knew you were the one who would enable me to be me on the page. I had this gut feeling that working with you would allow me to write my book in a way that people would someday say they could hear me saying the words. And the readers group proved that. I would not have this book if not for you. Somehow I knew during the process that your voice was the one that would make mine shine. You have become a dear friend to my family, and we are richly blessed that you are part of it.

Andrea Sharaf, you were the incredible unknown that came up with those diamonds in the rough. Your input to me and Susy was invaluable. You were the third set of eyes that helped in the eleventh hour. I can't tell you how important the "ah-ha" moments were—gold.

The Unbreakable Boy readers group was a piece of this puzzle that filled in so many of the gaps to make everything better. I appreciate all your hard work, and the critique was so eye-opening and sometimes humbling. Thank you, Barb Wright, Carolyn Rech, Cindy Cox, Debbie Graber, Jayne Schram, Joan Lamb, and Jodi Vegors.

Thank you to Matt Thayer, the first person ever to read my blog. You're like a brother to me.

To Bix Skahill, thanks for the industry wisdom. Especially for the words, "Hey, man. The hometown wants you to win!" It all meant more than you know.

Rick Auten and Trinity United Methodist Church in Charlotte, North Carolina, will forever be a part of this story and our lives. The memories are a part of who we are today, and the seeding of my faith lies within the walls of Trinity.

Our North Carolina support system of the Currents, Putkians, Serdinskys, and Glanklers— we cherish all of you.

Jim—you are a friend always in need indeed. You have impacted and made an indelible mark on Austin LeRette. You are a true cool breeze.

Angie Spangenberg—when Austin transitioned to the high school you were there for him from day one. You showed me that regardless of the training and degree, the person with the biggest heart gets my vote every time. And you have the heart of a lion. Your compassion and care and love for our son were evident and beautiful. You showed us how people should be with any person who may be "different."

Alison Aufdenberg, Makelti White, and Jessi Redd are three of Austin's gems. You ladies are a part of Austin's and my family circle that we are very thankful for. Thank you for being the awesome friends you've been to the Auzman.

Much love and thanks to Jedd Sherman, an outstanding school principal and one of the good guys . . . that gets it.

Nathan Guffey, William Griffey, Donnie Torbett, and Gavin French will always be as goofy-crazy and full of unabashed friendship and unconditional love to Austin. We are grateful for your kind hearts and infectious and hilarious attitudes.

It's a privilege to work with Brian Hampton, our editor Kristen Parrish, Katherine Rowley, Chad Cannon, Stephanie Tresner, Tiffany Sawyer, and the rest of the exceptional team at Thomas Nelson, HarperCollins Christian Publishing. I'm grateful to Chip MacGregor of MacGregor Literary for introducing us.

And to all those who made a difference in our family and Austin's life—all the doctors and nurses and staff in the ERs and ORs, Autism Speaks, Kerry Magro, David McGrew, Kim Photography-Omaha, Pete Walker and Craig White, Babble.com, Facebook, Twitter, Wallace Chapman, Myrna and Carol, My Care Credit Team, Cherry 7 Up and RC Cola and Pepperidge Farms Goldfish, Coach Switzer, Rudy Reutigger, General Kevin Chilton, Chris Deter, Curt Adams, Jenny Stauffer, Donna Cody, Miss Jenny, all the readers of Austintistic, and some more I probably missed.

And to all the fine ladies running the show at ROHS—Jeannie, Crystal, and Beth.

I'd be crazy if I didn't mention my Emmaus Group. You all are part of something that changed my life, and I will always know that.

Kudos to my REBOS group. You know who you are. You helped get my life back.

And last . . . I thank God.

Susy Flory: My thanks to Becky Vinter, formerly of Fine Print Literary, for introducing me to Scott LeRette and his amazing family. I know they have a special place in your heart too. And thank you to Chip MacGregor, my agent and friend, for joining this project with gusto. I appreciate your straight-up, wise advice and guidance. We'll get the Mel Gibson story—just wait.

To the Thomas Nelson/HarperCollins team, I'm so thrilled to work with you again. Thanks to Brian Hampton, Kristen Parrish, and Katherine Rowley for giving this story wings.

To Austin's friends and family, thank you for embracing me and making me feel so welcome on my trip to your beautiful city. Teresa and Logan, thank you for telling me stories and making me laugh. I wish I lived closer so we could go bowling in crazy hats more often!

Scott, thank you for trusting me with your story. You're an incredible father, husband, and human being. Your story is going to help a lot of people, and that's what this is all about. Go Sox!

Austin, when I first met you, you told me I was the most beautiful woman in the world (after your mother). Thank you for that. Then you said, "I love you. Do you love me?" Yes, I do. And I want to be more like you too.

Andrea Sharaf, my assistant and right hand on this project—thank you for settling in and taking on some of the load with me. You have a bright future in publishing, and I'm cheering you on. Also, a very big thank-you to the *Unbreakable Boy* readers group—your input was invaluable: Cathi Bobbitt, Ed Glasscock, Ellen Cardwell, Jeanette Hanscome, Julie Elder, Kelly Conley, Kristy Rose, Melanie Crawford, and Peggy Loofbourrow (my high school English teacher!).

And to my friends and mentors: Gini Monroe, Lorena Bathey, Kathi Lipp, Cheri Gregory, Jon and Bev Drury, Andrea Meyer, Mark and Tracy Teyler, Debbie Blake, Shannon Boyer, Taeko Lemke, Tammy Gomes, Annette Chin, Rita Hassna, Jeanette Hanscome, and Joe and Anita Santos—I'm so grateful for your prayers, support, and encouragement.

And last, I wouldn't be able to do this without my family: Robert (my coach, mentor, and number-one fan), my son Ethan and his wife Angela, my daughter Teddy, Mom, Jerry and Alice, Aunt Stella, Dave and Bea, Jeff and Sheila, Lou and Teresa, and my dear nieces and nephews. Thanks for supporting me and putting up with my stories. I love you a million bazillion.

ABOUT THE AUTHORS

SCOTT LERETTE is an ordinary man with an extraordinary son. As a sales executive for GE Capital, he's been a consistent top producer for the company as long as he's been there. Prior to working at GE Capital, Scott was a top performer with Allergan, a pharmaceutical company selling surgical and pharmaceutical products. Sitting in a cubicle under fluorescent lights would drive him nuts. He is a people person and loves to share life with anyone and everyone.

Before that, Scott was selected as a member of the United States Navy's Aviation Officer Candidate School (AOCS—think *An Officer and a Gentleman*) where, upon graduation, he received his commission as an officer. He was selected for advanced jet training as a radar intercept officer (RIO); his job was to sit in the backseat and tell the pilot where to go and when and where to target bombs. Scott holds a business degree from the University of Oklahoma and is a rabid Oklahoma Sooner fan, especially when his team is playing any team from Texas. His favorite team of all time is the Boston Red Sox.

Scott and his wife, Teresa, have been married for seventeen years. They live in Red Oak, Iowa, where Scott was born and raised, along with Austin (eighteen), Logan (sixteen), and a number of pets, including Boomer, Austin's tiger rescue cat, and Stella, the French bulldog. Scott is an accomplished chess player and plays acoustic guitar in a band. He's an avid gamer and loves shooter and adventure games, as well as electronic board games. He's actively involved with his church where he helps organize youth and high school missions and community service projects.

He wrote *The Unbreakable Boy* to raise awareness of special needs, but his story goes much deeper than that. Scott sees us all as broken, flawed, and imperfect, and he wants to use his speaking and writing to encourage people that embracing "different" is right and sound and good. He challenges us to shed fear and ignorance and know that even if faced with enormous obstacles, decisions, and setbacks, you can come out stronger.

Scott's wife, Teresa, and his son Austin both suffer from a genetic bone disorder called osteogenesis imperfecta, or brittle bone disease. Austin has also been diagnosed with autism and has multiple heart defects. Scott started a blog called *Austintistic* to share some of his stories of life with Austin. "I love life, even with all the chaos," said Scott. "I didn't choose it, but it's mine. So, like Austin, I embrace it and make it mine."

Susy Flory is a *New York Times* best-selling author who grew up on the back of a quarter horse in Northern California. She took degrees from UCLA in English and psychology, and has a background in journalism, education, and communications. She first started writing at the Newhall *Signal* with the legendary Scotty Newhall, an ex-editor of the *San Francisco Chronicle* and a one-legged, cigar-smoking curmudgeon who ruled the newsroom from behind a dented metal desk where he pounded out stories on an Underwood typewriter. She taught high school English and journalism at Redwood Christian Schools, then quit in 2004 to write full-time. A journalist at heart, Susy seeks out epic stories and loves happy endings (especially involving dogs or horses).

Susy is the author or coauthor of eight books, including the runaway bestseller *Thunder Dog: The True Story of a Blind Man, His Guide Dog, and the Triumph of Trust at Ground Zero* (Thomas Nelson, 2011), cowritten with Michael Hingson. Thunder Dog captured the number one New York Times ranking for nonfiction e-books the week of September 11, 2011, and has been translated into fifteen languages. She lives in the San Francisco Bay Area with her husband, Robert. They have two grown children, Ethan and Theodora, and a new daughter-in-law, Angela. In addition to writing books and articles, Susy consults for Lightside Games, teaches at her local church, and is a popular speaker and founder of the So Long Status Quo leadership group for emerging women leaders.

Center Point Large Print
600 Brooks Road / PO Box 1
Thorndike, ME 04986-0001 USA

(207) 568-3717

US & Canada:
1 800 929-9108
www.centerpointlargeprint.com

Science Experiments You Can Eat

VICKI COBB

Science Experiments You Can Eat

REVISED AND UPDATED

illustrated by David Cain

HarperCollins*Publishers*

Acknowledgments

The author extends heartfelt thanks to the following people but accepts full responsibility for the accuracy of the text: Louise Slade, Ph.D., G. Curtis Busk, Ph.D., and Caroline Fee of Nabisco Biscuit Company; Dr. Jeffrey Stamp of Frito-Lay; Duane MacDonald of General Mills; and Dr. Ann Hollingsworth of Bil Mar Foods.

Library of Congress Cataloging-in-Publication Data
Cobb, Vicki.
    Science experiments you can eat / Vicki Cobb ; illustrated by David Cain. — Revised and updated.
        p.   cm.
    Includes index.
    Summary: Experiments with food demonstrate various scientific principles and produce an eatable result. Includes rock candy, grape jelly, cupcakes, and popcorn.
    ISBN 0-06-023534-9. — ISBN 0-06-023551-9 (lib. bdg.)
    1. Science—Experiments—Juvenile literature.   2. Cookery—Juvenile literature.
[1. Science—Experiments.   2. Experiments.   3. Cookery.]   I. Cain, David, date, ill.   II. Title.
Q164.C52   1994   93-13679
507.8—dc20   CIP
                                                                                AC

Typography by Elynn Cohen
1   2   3   4   5   6   7   8   9   10
❖
Revised Edition

To the memory of Paula Wolf, my mother,
for whom cooking was an act of love

Contents

Science Experiments You Can Eat

Food for Thought

Think about food often? Who doesn't? Imagine a hot fudge sundae, how it smells and looks and tastes. Are the juices flowing in your mouth yet? Thoughts of food can do that. You probably think about food at least ten times a day—whenever your stomach growls, or you read a menu, or pass a bakery, or smell a deli, or follow a recipe, or plan a party, or go to the supermarket.

When my two sons were growing up, planning meals and shopping for food were part of my job. I experimented with recipes to make the job interesting for myself. One day a friend called and suggested that we collaborate on writing a cookbook for kids. I said, "Let me think about it." I hung up the phone and walked to the window. As I looked out over the Hudson River, I thought, "I don't want to write a cookbook for kids. I want to write science books for kids." The words "science experiments you can eat" popped into my head. Suddenly I had a whole new way to think about food. One that opened up countless possibilities for experimenting in the kitchen. The book was published in 1972 and has new readers every year.

But a lot has happened since then. Microwave ovens are now popular. New fruits and vegetables have come onto the market. A few items have disappeared from supermarket shelves. I've kept on learning. It was time for me to take another look at experimenting with food.

So here is an updated version of *Science Experiments You Can Eat*. It has all of the old experiments plus lots of new ones. The purpose of this book remains the same: to use food and cooking to learn about science.

If you're not hungry to learn about science, this book will whet your appetite. It is designed to nourish your curiosity and feed your mind. The ideas in this book are as easy to digest as the food. In a way, it's like a cookbook. You can use it to prepare many different dishes, although you might change your mind about eating them when you get your results. (I've done every experiment, but I must confess that I haven't eaten every experiment.) This book combines learning about science with eating—two of life's greatest pleasures. And it gives you a legitimate reason to play with your food.

EXPERIMENTING WITH FOOD

Next time you sit down to eat, try to figure out how all the things on your plate began. All foods were once alive or produced by a living thing. Sometimes the food on your table has no resemblance to the animals and plants from which it came.

Many changes in food take place before it reaches your home. Some foods are prepared from only a part of a living thing, such as wheat germ, lard, or sugar. Many foods are processed so they will keep longer without spoiling. Chemicals are often added to breads and cakes to keep them moist and to crackers and potato chips to keep them dry and crisp. Fruits, vegetables, and meats are canned, dried, or frozen to keep harmful bacteria from making them unfit to eat. But in some cases, the growth of bacteria or other microorganisms is necessary, such as in the preparation of bread, cheese, yogurt, and vinegar.

Cooking changes food still further. Heat makes some food softer and some food firmer. It changes the color of many foods. Different flavors blend when heated together. Heat destroys harmful bacteria and makes certain foods easier to digest.

It's easy to produce changes in food, and producing change is part of what science is about. If you can produce a change in a certain food, you can learn something about the properties of that food by studying the way it changes.

All of the experiments in this book are designed to show changes. Sometimes the changes are not obvious, and you have to look closely to see if one has even occurred. But when you know what you are looking for, even a small change can be very exciting. Every experiment has been tested, but the materials you use and the conditions in your kitchen may be slightly different from those described in this book. If you don't get the expected results, try to think of what factors might have caused the different results, and how you can redesign the procedure to produce the expected results.

HOW TO USE THIS BOOK

Be sure you know *what* you are doing in an experiment and *why* you are doing it. Every chapter has a short introduction that discusses the subject you will be investigating. Every experiment also has a short introduction that asks a question you can answer by doing the experiment.

The materials and equipment needed are listed at the beginning of each experiment. Collect everything before you begin. This way you will not be caught without some important item at a critical time during the experiment.

The procedure section tells you how to do the experiment. Often, reasons for doing a certain step are discussed as you go along. Since timing is important, you should read and understand the whole procedure section before you start the experiment.

There are certain standard practices for safety and use of equipment in every laboratory, and your kitchen is no exception. Consult the cook in your house before you start experimenting and ask for help with any procedures you are not sure about.

After the procedure section there is a brief discussion of what your results mean. Often, you are directed in your observations by questions. I don't always tell you what your results should be. This gives you the opportunity to get answers for yourself from your experiments, just as real scientists do.

As you do these experiments, questions of your own will occur to you. You may get ideas for experiments of your own design. So do them! Don't worry that you are getting sidetracked. Believe it or not, finding something interesting and getting sidetracked is the goal of every working scientist. Your own discoveries are what make science an adventure! This book is your road map. Bon voyage and bon appétit!

Solutions

The "stuff" that makes up food, you, and everything else in the universe is called *matter*. Chemists are scientists who study matter and how it changes. They define matter as anything that has weight and takes up space.

When scientists first tackled the study of matter, they had to deal with the problem that matter in its natural state is complicated. Very little matter in nature exists in a pure state. Most matter exists mixed up with other matter. A *solution*, such as seawater, is an especially interesting kind of mixture. One amazing thing about a solution is that it is evenly mixed or *homogeneous*. In a pail of seawater, a cup taken from the top has exactly the same amount of salt in it as a cup taken from the bottom. Another amazing thing about solutions is that they become homogeneous *all by themselves*. No stirring is necessary.

Chemists have a way of thinking—a model—about solutions that accounts for their interesting properties. They say that solutions, like all matter, are made up of tiny particles too small to see. These particles are arranged in two phases. One phase is called the *solvent*. Water is the most common solvent around. The solvent phase is *continuous*. This means that the water particles are in contact with one another. The other phase is called the *solute*. Salt is a solute in seawater. The solute phase is *discontinuous*. Solute particles may occasionally bump into each other but for the most part they are surrounded by solvent particles. Salt water is a simple solution with one solvent and one solute. But seawater has a number of solutes. A solution may be made of one or more solvents and one or more solutes.

When a solute dissolves, the solute particles move through the solvent in a process called *diffusion*. You don't even have to stir. See for yourself. Drop a lump of sugar (a solute) into a glass of water (a solvent) and let it stand for a while. What happens to the lump of sugar? When you can no longer see any sugar crystals, taste the top of the solution with a straw. How can you tell that the sugar is present? Use the straw to taste the solution near the bottom of the glass. To do this, cover the top end of the straw with your finger before you lower the other end into the solution. When the bottom of the straw is where you want to take your sample, carefully move your finger to let a small amount of the solution rise in the straw. Keep your finger on the top of the straw as you raise the bottom end of the straw to your mouth. Lift your finger to let the solution run into your mouth. With this technique you can taste samples from all parts of the solution. But be careful to keep the disturbance to the solution as little as possible when you insert the straw. Is the solution homogeneous? If it isn't, wait a while and taste again.

Solutions are important in the study of matter. You can often discover what a substance is by the solvent it dissolves in and by how much of it dissolves. Many chemical reactions take place in solution that will not take place in air. The experiments in this chapter will introduce you to some different solutions and some of the ways solutions are used to learn about matter.

ROCK CANDY: RECOVERING SOLUTE CRYSTALS

It's easy to recover a solute if you don't care about keeping the solvent. Leave a water solution open to the air and the solvent will evaporate, leaving the solute behind. To recover the solute from all kinds of beverages, put small amounts in shallow dishes. The water evaporates from the large surface area.

Some solutes form *crystals* as the solvent evaporates. Crystals are solids that have a regular geometric shape, with many sides or faces. Take a close look at sugar and salt crystals with a magnifying lens. They have very different shapes.

Rock candy is simply very large sugar crystals. Grow some in the next experiment.

Materials & Equipment

+ $\frac{1}{2}$ cup water
+ I cup sugar
+ a measuring cup
+ a small saucepan
+ a wooden spoon

+ 3 or 4 small shallow dishes (aluminum foil dishes work well)
+ a magnifying glass

Procedure

1 Pour the water into the saucepan. Measure out a cup of sugar. Put just a spoonful of this sugar in the water and stir. Use a wooden spoon to stir; it won't get hot the way a metal spoon would when you heat this solution later. Continue to add sugar by spoonfuls, stirring after each addition until the sugar dissolves. How many spoonfuls before the sugar stops dissolving no matter how much you stir? When this happens the solution is called a *saturated solution*.

2 Set the saucepan on low heat for a few minutes. What happens to the undissolved crystals as the solution gets warmer?

3 Turn off the heat and remove the saucepan from the stove. Add sugar again, spoonful by spoonful. How many spoonfuls do you need to make a saturated solution in hot water?

4 Pour all the remaining sugar from the measuring cup into the pan. Put the saucepan on the stove again and continue heating gently until all the sugar is dissolved. Then bring it to the boiling point and boil for about a minute. The solution should be thick and clear and contain no sugar crystals. Pour the solution into the small dishes while it is hot. It's not important to distribute the solution evenly.

Observations

Watch the solution as it cools. Be careful not to jolt it or disturb it in any way. Does the solution remain clear? If it becomes cloudy, take a close look at it with a magnifying glass. A clear solution that contains more solute than would normally dissolve at that temperature is said to be *supersaturated*. Supersaturated solutions are very unstable and the slightest disturbance will cause crystals to form, removing them from the solution.

Some candy, like fudge, depends on the formation of millions of tiny crystals. When you beat fudge, tiny crystals form quickly from a super-saturated solution.

If you don't beat fudge hard enough, the crystals will be larger and the fudge will feel grainy in your mouth.

To make rock candy, you want large crystals to grow, and this takes time, sometimes weeks. Let the solution stand undisturbed at room tempera-ture for a week or more. Every day, carefully break off the crust of crystals that forms at the surface so that the water can continue to evaporate.

Rock candy crystals will form around any small object you put in the solution. Make rock candy lollipops by putting a swizzle stick in a glass of supersaturated sugar solution. They will also quickly form around a crystal of sugar dropped into the solution. Such a crystal is called a *seed crystal*. You might want to try using a colored crystal sprinkle as a seed crystal in a supersaturated solution.

The formation of crystals is one way chemists know when they've got pure matter, either an element or a compound. Crystals are also a clue to the structure of a substance. Scientists figure that the perfect shape of crystals is not an accident but is the result of a regular arrangement of the smallest particles of a substance. These particles, *atoms* and *molecules*, have a size (although it's way too small to see even with the strongest microscope) and a shape. The arrangement of the atoms or molecules of a crystal produces the shape of the crystal much as closely stacked bricks can produce only a rectangular stack.

Compare the shape of the rock candy crystals to the crystals of granulated sugar with a magnifying glass. Are they the same shape? Do sugar crystals have the same shape as salt crystals? Would you expect sugar molecules to have the same shape as salt molecules?

ICE POPS AND THE FREEZING POINT OF SOLUTIONS

One question that comes up over and over again in the laboratory is: How do you know when you have a pure substance? One way to answer this question is to see how a substance you know to be pure (usually because a manufacturer says so on the label) behaves differently from a substance you know to be a mixture (because you made it yourself). It is well established that pure water freezes at 32° Fahrenheit or 0° Celsius. Does a solution freeze at the same temperature as pure water? Do the next experiment and find out.

Materials & Equipment

- 1 cup of a clear, not cloudy, canned or bottled fruit juice (cherry or grape or apple works well)
- water
- 6 5-ounce paper cups
- a pen

- 6 circles of cardboard big enough to cover the cups
- 6 swizzle sticks or wooden sticks
- 2 measuring cups (each cup should hold at least 1 liquid cup)

Procedure

When you set up this experiment you will put different amounts of fruit juice in each cup in a systematic way and then freeze all the cups. The first ice pop will be undiluted fruit juice as it comes from the can, the second will be ½ fruit juice and ½ water, the third will be ¼ fruit juice and ¾ water, and so on. This systematic changing of the amount of water in a solution is called *serial dilution*. Laboratories in many industries use serial dilutions to test the strength of a substance to find out, for example, how much detergent to put in a washing machine or how much aspirin to take when you are sick.

Since the freezing point of the ice pops is to be compared to the freezing point of pure water, you will also make an ice pop that is pure water, without juice. This ice pop is called the *control*. A control is treated just like every other part of an experiment but does not contain the thing being tested so it can be used as a basis for comparison.

1 Start by marking the cups: Juice, $\frac{1}{2}$, $\frac{1}{4}$, $\frac{1}{8}$, $\frac{1}{16}$, and control.

The purpose of the cardboard circle covers is to hold each stick upright until the ice pop has frozen. The covers should be large enough to cover the tops of the cups without falling in. Punch a hole just large enough to insert a stick in the center of each cardboard circle. Place a stick in each hole.

2 Measure $\frac{1}{2}$ cup of water and pour it into the cup marked "control."

Measure out 1 cup of juice. Pour $\frac{1}{2}$ cup of this juice into a second measuring cup. Then pour remaining $\frac{1}{2}$ cup of juice into the paper cup labeled "Juice."

Add $\frac{1}{2}$ cup of water to the second measuring cup to bring the volume up to 1 cup. Mix well. Use the first measuring cup to get $\frac{1}{2}$ cup of this dilution. Pour this into the paper cup marked "$\frac{1}{2}$."

Add $\frac{1}{2}$ cup of water to the first dilution to again bring the volume up to 1 cup. Mix well and use $\frac{1}{2}$ cup of this dilution to make the next ice pop in the cup labeled "$\frac{1}{4}$."

Follow the same procedure to make ice pops that are $\frac{1}{8}$ juice and $\frac{1}{16}$ juice.

3 Put the covers and sticks on each cup. Adjust the sticks so that they just touch the bottoms of the cups.

4 Put all six cups in your freezer. It is important to place them at the same depth so they will all be at the same temperature. After about 40 minutes, check to see how freezing is progressing by jiggling each stick back and forth. As freezing occurs, you can feel the ice forming. Keep checking about every 20 minutes. Which pop freezes first?

Which ice pop takes longest to freeze? Does it require more or less time to freeze a solution?

Observations

On the basis of your experiment, why is salt put on sidewalks in winter? Why is alcohol put in car radiators before the cold weather sets in? How can the temperature at which a solution freezes be used to tell how pure a substance is? Handbooks for chemists always list the freezing points of pure solvents. If they test the freezing point of a liquid in their lab and they don't get the freezing point they expect, they know that other substances must be present.

When the ice pops are frozen solid, which may take several hours, your experiment is completed and you may eat them. Although some of the ice pops will taste better than others, even the control can be refreshing on a hot day. Just tear off the paper cup and enjoy!

FRUIT DRINKS AND DISSOLVING RATES

Ever notice how some solutes dissolve faster than others? Can you think of some of the variables that cause some solutions to form faster than others? In the next experiment see how temperature affects the rate at which a solute goes into a solvent.

Materials & Equipment

+ ½ cup ice water
+ ½ cup room-temperature water
+ ½ cup boiling water
+ 1 package of unsweetened Kool-Aid
+ sugar
+ 6½ cups cold water
+ a measuring cup
+ 3 clear glass tumblers
+ a 2-quart pitcher

Procedure

1 Put ½ cup of ice water in the first glass, ½ cup of water at room temperature in the second glass, and ½ cup of boiling water in the third glass.

2 Drop a small pinch of Kool-Aid into each glass. Watch how the Kool-Aid diffuses into solution.

Observations

In which glass does it dissolve most quickly? How long does it take for the Kool-Aid to diffuse evenly through the water?

Try this with other colored solutes like instant coffee or food coloring.

After you have finished the experiment, you can prepare the Kool-Aid to drink. Pour all the solutions into a 2-quart pitcher. Add the remaining Kool-Aid and the amount of sugar suggested on the package. Add 6½ cups of cold water to bring the volume up to 2 quarts.

SOUR-BALL ADE

How does the amount of surface area of a solute affect the rate at which it dissolves in a solvent? The next experiment explores this idea.

Materials & Equipment

- ✦ ¾ cup water, room temperature
- ✦ 3 pieces of dark-colored hard candy (grape or cherry)
- ✦ 3 small glasses
- ✦ a measuring cup
- ✦ waxed paper
- ✦ a hammer or rolling pin

Procedure

1 Put ¼ cup of water into each glass.

2 Wrap one candy in waxed paper and tap it lightly with the hammer or rolling pin so it

breaks into several large pieces. Wrap another candy in waxed paper and smash it so it is like granulated sugar.

3 Drop the whole candy into the first glass, the broken candy into the second glass, and the smashed candy into the third glass.

Observations

Which candy has the most surface area? Which candy dissolves first? How do you think the amount of surface area affects the rate at which a solute dissolves? How do your findings explain why superfine sugar is used to sweeten iced drinks?

You can make a refreshing drink from this experiment. Pour all 3 solutions into one glass and add a few ice cubes. An orange slice adds a festive touch.

RED-CABBAGE INDICATOR

A sour taste is one indication of a type of solution called an *acid*. The word *acid* comes from a Latin word meaning sharp or biting to the taste. Acids also conduct electricity. A light bulb connected by wires to two electrodes will light up when the electrodes are submerged in an acid. Acids are not the only solutions that conduct electricity. Bases, also called *alkalies*, do the job as well.

Acids are present in many of the foods we eat. Lemon juice and vinegar are good examples. We also eat certain bases, although they are not as common as acids. Baking soda, for example, is a base when it is dissolved in water.

There are, of course, many stronger acids and bases that we don't eat because they are poisonous or extremely damaging to living tissues. Tasting is not a test used by chemists to determine whether or not a substance is an acid or a base. Instead, they use a dye called an *indicator* that changes color depending on what the solution is. Litmus paper turns blue when it is dipped in a base and pink when it is dipped in acid.

The pigment in red cabbage can be used as your own personal "litmus." Here's how to make some red-cabbage indicator.

Materials & Equipment

- ✦ 1 whole red cabbage
- ✦ water
- ✦ a knife
- ✦ a grater
- ✦ 2 large bowls
- ✦ measuring cups and spoons

- ✦ a slotted spoon
- ✦ a strainer
- ✦ a very clean glass jar and cover
- ✦ a small white dish

Procedure

1 Cut the cabbage into quarters. Grate it section by section into a large bowl. Add between 1 and 2 cups of water, enough to cover the cabbage. Let the cabbage stand in the water, stirring occasionally so that all the cabbage is moistened.

2 When the water is a strong red, remove as much of the grated cabbage as you can with the slotted spoon and save it in your second bowl. Pour the water solution through the strainer into the

glass jar. Add the strained cabbage to the rest of the cabbage you have saved.

3 Put about a tablespoon of your cabbage-juice indicator into a small white dish. Test for an acid by adding a substance you know to be an acid to the cabbage juice. Notice the color it becomes in acid. Now use a fresh sample of cabbage juice and add a substance you know to be a base (baking soda). Again notice the color change. Pretty gorgeous! Now add acid to the base-and-indicator mixture to reverse the color change. What happens when you add base to the indicator showing the acid color? An acid and a base will react with each other to neutralize each other. The original color of the red cabbage is pretty close to neutral. Now you can test some foods to see which category they fall into. Here is a list to get you started:

✦ Cooking water from boiled vegetables, including beans, peas, onions, carrots, turnips, celery, asparagus, etc.
✦ Liquids from canned vegetables and fruits
✦ Cream of tartar
✦ Soda pop
✦ Egg whites
✦ Fruit juices
✦ Tomatoes
✦ Cottage cheese

You can use the grated red cabbage raw in a salad or cole slaw, or you can experiment with it further.

Materials & Equipment

- ✦ shredded cabbage from above experiment
- ✦ 1 tart apple
- ✦ water
- ✦ a knife
- ✦ a wooden spoon

- ✦ 2 aluminum pots (The pot metal may be written on its underside. If you're not sure, ask the cook in your house.)

Procedure

1 Divide the cabbage evenly between the two aluminum pots. Cut the apple into quarters and remove the core. Cut the apple into chunks and add it to one of the pots. Add just enough water to cover the bottom of each pot ($1/4$–$1/2$ cup).

2 Then cook the cabbage over low heat for about 20 minutes, stirring occasionally.

Observations

Which cooked cabbage is redder? Which one contained acid? How do your findings support the idea that small amounts of aluminum combine with water to form aluminum hydroxide, a base? What did the apple do to this base?

You can also prepare your indicator from cooked cabbage but, of course, you can't cook it in an aluminum pot. Put raw grated cabbage in a stainless steel, porcelain, or glass pot and cover with water. Cook over low heat until it boils for 3 or 4 minutes. Then drain off your liquid. It will be a darker red than the uncooked indicator. Compare indicators to see which one you prefer using.

Mixed with salt, pepper, and butter, the cooked cabbage goes well with pot roast.

OPTICALLY ACTIVE SYRUPS

One characteristic of a true solution is that it is perfectly clear when you shine a light through it.

If you shine a special kind of light, called *polarized light,* through a syrup, you can see a pretty interesting property of some solutions. One way to create polarized light is to shine it through a lens of polarized sunglasses. It's hard to understand just what polarized light is because it involves three dimensions. Here's a way to think of it. Ordinary light is made up of waves, or beams. Imagine a single beam coming right at you. The beam would be a dot viewed from the end. Now imagine rays of light coming out of the beam at every possible angle. This should give you a mental image of how light travels in every direction. But when light strikes a polarized lens, only the rays traveling in one certain direction can pass through. The light that emerges from one polarized sunglass lens might be traveling in a vertical direction. If another lens is put on top of the first and it is rotated so that it only allows light traveling in a horizontal direction to pass through, then the incoming light will be completely blocked. If you rotate one lens on top of the other, varying amounts of light will pass through.

Certain sugar solutions are *optically active*. This means that they have the ability to rotate polarized light. The next experiment is not a recipe but it shows pancake syrup in a new light.

Materials & Equipment

✦ various syrups in clear containers (maple, pancake, and corn syrups; diluted molasses; the sugar solution you made for rock candy)

✦ 2 lenses from a pair of polarized sun-glasses (make sure you get permission before you sacrifice a pair of sunglasses to science)

✦ a flashlight

Procedure

1 Line up the flashlight, one lens, a clear container with syrup, and the other lens as shown in the picture. If the syrup doesn't come in a clear bottle, pour it into a clear drinking glass.

2 Rotate the lens near your eye. An optically active syrup will produce a rainbow of colors, one at a time as you turn the lens.

Observations

Polarized light (emerging from the first lens) that passes through the syrup is rotated from its entering position as it emerges from the syrup. Light contains waves of all different colors, but taken together they appear white. Even a beam of polarized light is made up of different waves. When light passes through the syrup, each colored wave is rotated by a slightly different amount. When you turn the second polarized lens in front of the syrup bottle, it filters out the separate waves so you see a sequence of colors through the second lens. The concepts of polarized light and optical activity are quite complicated, and you may want to read more about them in an optics book.

Biochemists use a device called a polarimeter to measure how optically active a sugar solution is. *Glucose*, one of the most important sugars we eat, is also called *dextrose* because it rotates polarized light to the right ("dextro" means "right"). *Fructose*, another kind of simple sugar, often found in fruit, is sometimes called *levulose*, because it rotates polarized light to the left. The optical activity of sugars is an important method in biochemistry for identifying sugars and understanding the structure of sugar molecules. The way a sugar solution acts in polarized light is directly related to the structure of its molecules.

Unlike the syrup you made for rock candy, the syrups you buy for pancakes are designed to remain crystal free. Syrups that contain different kinds of sugars will not form crystals easily because the different sugar molecules don't fit together.

Suspensions, Colloids, and Emulsions

Matter is found in all kinds of mixtures, including mixtures with water. Figuring out all the different parts of mixtures is a challenge for scientists.

Water is called the universal solvent because more things dissolve in water than in any other liquid. But not everything dissolves in it. Some water mixtures, such as mud, contain particles that are heavy enough to settle on the bottom after being stirred up. This kind of mixture is called a *suspension* because the material is suspended only temporarily in the liquid. You can separate the liquid from the large solid particles in a suspension by letting the particles settle and then by pouring off the liquid as shown in the illustration. This method of separation is called *decanting*. If a suspension contains very small particles, it may take days or weeks to settle. Decanting either isn't practical or won't work with these mixtures. Instead, you can separate the particles by pouring the mixture through a strainer or filter. Filtration can also be used to determine the size of the suspended particles.

Do the next experiment to discover more about suspensions and the way they are handled by scientists.

BORSCHT COCKTAIL: SEPARATING SUSPENDED PARTICLES

A *puree* is a suspension of food particles in a liquid. Purees are made with food processors or blenders or by pushing soft food through a strainer. Usually the pureed food particles are so small that they take a long time to settle. Pea soup, tomato sauce, and applesauce are examples of purees. Jarred beet soup, or borscht, is good for beginning a study of suspensions involving a beet puree.

Materials & Equipment

- ✦ a jar of borscht
- ✦ 1 tablespoon sour cream
- ✦ a watch with a second hand
- ✦ a strainer

- ✦ 2 glass jars
- ✦ some coffee filters
- ✦ a large spoon
- ✦ a wire whisk or an eggbeater

Procedure

1 Shake the jar of borscht. Use the watch to time how long it takes for the beet particles to settle on the bottom. Do some beet particles stay suspended longer than others? Which ones stay suspended longer?

2 Pour about a cup of the settled liquid through a strainer into a glass jar.

Observations

Are any beet particles caught by the strainer? What is the size of particles that pass through the strainer? Are they smaller or larger than the holes in the strainer?

Procedure

1 Rinse out the strainer. Put a coffee filter in the bottom of the strainer and place it over the second glass jar. **2** Pour the liquid you have just strained from the first glass jar through the filter paper and let the mixture drip through.

Observations

What evidence do you have that the filter paper has holes even though you can't see them? Are there any beet particles on the filter paper? Are these particles smaller or larger than the holes in the filter paper?

Taste the liquid that you have just filtered. Is there sugar in borscht? How can you tell? (Confirm your observations by reading the list of ingredients on the label.) What can you say about the size of sugar particles compared to the size of the (too small to see) holes in the filter paper?

Procedure

1 Remove the filter paper from the strainer. Take 2 large spoonfuls of beets from the bottom of the jar of borscht. Push them through the strainer with a spoon into the liquid in the glass jar. Be sure to scrape the beets off the outside of the strainer. You can use some of the liquid from the jar you are straining into to wash the pureed beets through the strainer.

2 Stir or shake the pureed beets into the liquid.

Observations

How long does it take these particles to settle? Do they all settle eventually? How does the settling time compare with the time for the pieces of beet before they were pureed? (If you find it difficult to see the beets, work in front of a strong light.)

From the results of your experiment, can you explain how settling rates and filtering can be used to find the size of particles? Can you think of how these procedures can be used to identify different substances as well as to separate them? Can you design an experiment to test the speeds on a blender or the blades on a food processor by creating purees with coarser and finer particles?

You can make a delicious cold soup with your experiment. Chill the pureed mixture. Beat in about a tablespoon of sour cream with a whisk or an eggbeater.

LIQUID FOOD AND THE TYNDALL EFFECT

Solutions and suspensions are both mixtures with two phases. One phase, the solvent, can be thought of as *continuous*. That is, all the particles are in contact with each other. The second phase, the solute, can be thought of as *discontinuous*. The solute particles are separated from each other by the solvent. The main difference between true solutions and suspensions is the size of the particles of the solute phase. In a solution, solute particles are approximately the size of single molecules. In a suspension, the particles are made up of countless numbers of molecules and are large enough to be filterable.

SOLUTION

A *colloid* is a third kind of mixture with two phases. The suspended particles in a colloid are larger than single molecules but small enough to remain in suspension permanently and be homogeneous. It is hard to tell the difference between a colloid and a solution just by looking at them. There is, however, a

SUSPENSION

COLLOID

simple test that does tell the difference. All you need is a clear glass and a flashlight.

If you pass a beam of light through a colloid, and you look at the beam from the side, you can see the beam. This is because the particles in a colloid are large enough to act as tiny mirrors and reflect light. This light-scattering ability is called the *Tyndall effect*. You can see the Tyndall effect in a beam of sunlight in a dusty room or from car headlights on a foggy night. Fog and dust particles are large enough to reflect light while air molecules are too small.

You can see the Tyndall effect in liquids we drink. Pour a small sample of a liquid into a clear glass. Hold the glass against a dark background and shine a flashlight beam through it. (A pen flashlight works especially well.) Look at the beam from the side. If you can see the beam as it passes through, the liquid is a colloid. If you can't see the beam from the side, the liquid is a solution.

Which of the following liquids are colloids and which are solutions? Tea, cranberry juice, syrup (colorless), orange drink (not juice), coffee, salt water, Jell-O, Kool-Aid, consommé, vinegar (distilled), egg white, cider.

Protoplasm, the living material of all cells, is a complicated colloid. What would you expect if you shone a beam of light through a cell?

SALAD DRESSING:
A LIQUID SUSPENDED IN A LIQUID

If you shake oil and water together and then let them stand, they will separate into two layers. Liquids that do not form solutions are said to be *immiscible*.

Classic French salad dressing (or vinaigrette) is a mixture of oil and vinegar and seasoning. Vinegar is a water-based substance (an acid) and is immiscible with oil. In order for all the flavors of the dressing to be evenly spread through a salad, it must be thoroughly mixed. A vinaigrette is usually given a number of hard shakes and immediately poured on a salad before the two liquids have a chance to separate.

This experiment is designed to answer the question: Does the size of the droplets of two immiscible liquids affect the rate of separation into layers?

Materials & Equipment

+ ⅓ cup vinegar
+ ½ teaspoon salt
+ ¼ teaspoon pepper
+ ¼ teaspoon garlic powder
+ ¼ teaspoon paprika
+ I cup salad oil
+ measuring cups and spoons

- ✦ a jar with a tight cover
- ✦ watch or clock with a second hand
- ✦ a small bowl
- ✦ an eggbeater or electric mixer
- ✦ a magnifying glass

Procedure

1 Put the vinegar in the jar and add the salt, pepper, garlic powder, and paprika. Screw the lid on tight and shake.

2 Pour in the salad oil and let the mixture stand for a few minutes.

Observations

Where does the oil go? Which do you think would be heavier, a cup of water or a cup of oil? Can you think of a way to check your guess?

Procedure

1 Cover the jar and shake about 10 times. Use the watch to see how long it takes for the mixture to separate. Can you see which is the continuous phase and which is the discontinuous?

2 Shake the jar hard about 20 times. Does the dressing take more or less time to separate? Look for droplets of vinegar suspended in the oil.

3 Shake the jar different numbers of times and examine the size of the droplets immediately after shaking. When does the dressing have the smallest droplets?

4 Put the mixture in a small bowl and beat hard for about 4 minutes with an eggbeater or an electric mixer. Quickly pour the dressing back into the jar. Examine the droplets with a magnifying glass. How long does the dressing take to separate into two layers? What did shaking and beating do to the size of the droplets?

You can use the French dressing over a tossed green salad. Mix well and use just enough to coat the leaves lightly.

EMULSIONS

If milk, fresh from a cow, is allowed to stand, the fat rises to the top as cream. When milk is homogenized, it is forced through tiny holes in a screen.

This breaks up the butterfat into very tiny droplets. Why doesn't the butterfat separate from milk when it is homogenized?

A suspension of two immiscible liquids that doesn't separate on standing is called an *emulsion*. The word *emulsion* comes from a Latin word that means "to milk out." Emulsions have a milky or cloudy appearance. Cream is an emulsion in which droplets of butterfat are suspended in a water-based continuous phase. The watery part of milk or cream contains some milk proteins and sugar. If you put heavy cream into a jar with a tight cover and shake hard for a few minutes, you will produce the opposite result from the French dressing. When you make French dressing, shaking causes the discontinuous phase (the vinegar) to break up into tiny droplets and disperse throughout the continuous phase (the oil). If you shake heavy cream, you cause the tiny droplets of butterfat (the discontinuous phase) to come in contact with each other. This will be explored in the next chapter when you make butter.

MAYONNAISE: A STABILIZED EMULSION

When oil and vinegar in French dressing separate,

the vinegar droplets grow larger and larger, and the oil droplets grow larger and larger. The large oil droplets float to the surface of the vinegar. If, however, you add a certain third substance to a mixture of oil and vinegar, you can stabilize the mixture and prevent the separation. The result is a stable emulsion of two immiscible liquids and the substance that keeps the two liquids from separating is called an *emulsifying agent.*

One example of an emulsifying agent is soap. When you wash greasy dishes, hot water turns the grease into an oil. One end of a soap molecule attaches to the grease and the other end is soluble in water. Each grease droplet is held in suspension in the water by countless soap molecules. The emulsified grease is easily washed down the drain. Try washing greasy dishes in cold water and in hot water without soap to see how emulsifying by soap works. Can you get the dishes clean?

Mayonnaise is an emulsion of oil in vinegar. Vinegar is an acid in water. In the process of making mayonnaise, you disperse five parts oil into only one part water. The vinegar forms a thin coating around the oil droplets. The emulsifying agent is egg yolks. Making mayonnaise is a real challenge to many who pride themselves on being good cooks, but it is not difficult to make if you understand what is happening as the emulsion forms.

Materials & Equipment

+ 2 egg yolks (see pages 197–98 for how to separate eggs)
+ ½ teaspoon prepared mustard
+ ½ teaspoon salt
+ 3 tablespoons vinegar

+ I cup salad oil
+ measuring cups and spoons
+ a small bowl
+ an electric mixer or a friend and an eggbeater

Procedure

Have all the ingredients at room temperature. Cold oil does not flow as quickly as warmer oil, and cold egg yolks will not emulsify as much oil as warmer egg yolks. (Can you think of experiments to check these ideas out?)

Put the egg yolks, mustard, salt, and 1 teaspoon of the vinegar in the bowl and beat at a medium speed until the egg yolks are lemon-colored. The egg yolks are now thoroughly mixed with the water in the vinegar and are ready to receive the oil.

2 Add the oil drop by drop while beating constantly. If you do not have an electric mixer, you can make the emulsion by hand with a friend. One of you does the beating with an eggbeater while the other adds oil.

The idea in making mayonnaise is to spread tiny droplets of oil evenly through the egg yolks. Egg yolk coats these droplets as they form and prevents them from coming together and forming a separate layer. If you add the oil too fast, or too much oil at one time, the droplets will come together before they can be forced into the egg yolks and the mayonnaise will "curdle" or separate. If this happens, you can correct the situation with a fresh egg yolk, but add the curdled mayonnaise to the yolk rather than the other way around.

You can tell when the emulsion has formed because the mixture gets thick. This usually happens after about one third of a cup of oil has been added.

3 Once the emulsion has formed, you can add the oil slightly faster until the full cup has been beaten into the yolks. If the mixture gets too thick, add a teaspoon of vinegar. Beat in the remaining vinegar at the end.

Homemade mayonnaise is thick, yellow, and

glistening. It spoils easily and should be stored in the refrigerator. Cover it so a skin doesn't form on top.

Several cookbooks make the claim that mayonnaise is difficult to make on a rainy day or when a thunderstorm is threatening. But mayonnaise is made commercially on every working day regardless of the weather. You might want to do some experiments to check this out.

STRAWBERRY BOMBE: A FROZEN EMULSION

Ice cream, bombes, and other frozen desserts contain water and cream. Separation of the fat in cream is not a problem because the fat droplets are very small. In frozen desserts the problem is to keep the water droplets small. Large water droplets form large ice crystals and give the dessert a grainy texture. As long as the ice crystals are tiny, the dessert will be smooth.

Suppose an emulsifying agent that attracts water is an ingredient in a frozen dessert. Do you think it can keep large ice crystals from forming as egg yolks keep large oil droplets from forming in mayonnaise? Discover the answer by making the strawberry bombe in the next experiment.

Materials & Equipment

- 1 teaspoon unflavored gelatin
- 4½ tablespoons cold water
- 1 9- or 10-ounce package frozen strawberries, defrosted
- 1 cup sugar
- 2 teaspoons lemon juice
- 1½ tablespoons boiling water
- 2 cups heavy or whipping cream
- measuring cups and spoons
- a small dish or cup
- 3 small bowls
- a spoon
- pen and labels
- an electric mixer or eggbeater
- a rubber spatula
- 2 1-pint containers (plastic ice-cream containers are good)

Procedure

1 Put the gelatin in the small dish or cup and add 1½ tablespoons cold water.

Does the gelatin attract water? How can you tell? You may have to wait a few minutes before you can answer these questions.

2 Put the strawberries in one of the bowls and add the sugar and lemon juice. Mix well and then pour half of the strawberry mixture into a second bowl.

3 When the gelatin has softened and absorbed all the cold water, add 1½ tablespoons of boiling water and stir until all the gelatin dissolves. Add the gelatin mixture to one of the strawberry mixtures and stir well. Stir 3 tablespoons of cold water into the other strawberry mixture as a control. Label the bowls so you know which one contains the gelatin.

4 Refrigerate the strawberry mixtures until the gelatin starts to thicken. It should not be firm but only slightly gelled. Start checking after 15 minutes. When the gelatin mixture is ready, remove it from the refrigerator.

5 In the third bowl whip the cream until it stands in soft peaks when you raise the beaters. Put half the whipped cream into each strawberry mixture.

6 Gently combine the strawberries and cream by using a rubber spatula to bring the mixture from the bottom of the bowl to the top. Repeat this motion again and again, until the whipped cream and strawberries are well mixed. (This is what is known as folding two ingredients together.)

7 Pour one strawberry-and-cream mixture into each pint container. Be sure to label the one containing the gelatin. Put the containers into the freezer for about 12 hours. When the desserts are frozen, taste them.

Observations

Is there a difference in texture between the dessert containing gelatin and the one without?

Let a few tablespoons of each dessert thaw and then refreeze them. Which dessert has a grainier texture? What do you think the gelatin does in a strawberry bombe?

CONSOMMÉ: CLARIFICATION BY FLOCCULATION

Canned broths and bouillon cubes are staple foods in almost every kitchen. But true chefs pride themselves on their "stock pots," the broths they create with leftovers from daily food preparation. It takes time to create a broth—hours of simmering on the stove. Broths are cloudy with all kinds of suspended particles. They are complicated suspensions and colloids with many kinds of particles in the discontinuous phase. A true bouillon or consommé is clear and sparkling. The word *bouillon* comes from the French word for *boil*. The word *consommé* comes from a word that means the *highest*. In the next experiment, you create your own broth and clarify it—that is, remove the particles—to make consommé. The project takes two days to complete. It will give you a real appreciation for homemade stock, and also for inexpensive, easy-to-use canned consommés and bouillon cubes. It will also show you a method for removing particles that is often used in many chemical industries.

Materials & Equipment

To make the broth:

+ 1 pound of lean sliced beef
+ about a pound of beef bones
+ water
+ 2 peeled carrots
+ 2 peeled onions
+ 2 stalks celery with leaves
+ 2 teaspoons salt
+ 6 sprigs fresh parsley
+ $\frac{1}{4}$ teaspoon thyme
+ 2 washed leeks
+ a 4-quart soup pot
+ a slotted spoon
+ a 2-quart bowl or container
+ a knife

Procedure

1 Put the meat and bones in the soup pot and add enough cold water to fill the pot about ³/₄ full. Set the pot over low to medium heat. As the liquid starts to simmer, a scum will rise to the surface. Skim it off with a slotted spoon until it stops forming. This will take about 5 minutes. It is important not to let the soup boil violently, as the scum will be returned to the broth and make it even more cloudy.

2 Add the rest of the ingredients and let the mixture simmer uncovered for at least 4 hours. The liquid will be reduced by about half.

3 Remove all the solid ingredients from the broth. They are good to eat. Pour the broth into a bowl or container. Notice that the liquid fat rises to the surface. Refrigerate uncovered overnight.

4 The next day the fat will be a hard, whitish layer on top of the broth. Remove it by cutting around the edge with a knife to separate it from the wall of the container. The whole layer of fat can be lifted out in one piece. Fish out any remaining pieces of fat with a slotted spoon. Notice how cloudy the broth is. You're going to get rid of the cloudiness with a very amazing procedure using egg whites. This is the clarification procedure.

Materials & Equipment

- 2 egg whites
- $\frac{1}{2}$ of the cold stock, about 1 quart
- 2 crushed eggshells
- a small bowl
- a wire whisk
- a 2-quart saucepan
- colander
- cheesecloth
- a large bowl
- a spoon
- a ladle

The large bowl must be one that the colander can rest in with its bottom well above the bottom of the bowl.

Procedure

Beat the egg whites slightly with a wire whisk in a small bowl. Put 1 quart of your stock in a saucepan and beat in the egg whites with the whisk. Add the crushed eggshells. Place the saucepan over low heat, and slowly, without stirring, let the soup come to a simmer so that it is barely moving. **Do not let the soup boil, or the egg white will break up and fail to clarify the soup.** The egg white and shells float to the surface of the soup, forming a "raft" that is strengthened by the eggshell pieces. The egg white is *coagulating* (more on this in Chapter 5, "Proteins") and becoming firm due to the heat. Amazingly it acts like a magnet for some

rvations

mpare the clarified broth with the original
th. If you made a mistake and boiled the egg
ite mixture, you can chill it and try the process
in with fresh egg whites. You can clarify the
er half of the broth or not, as you wish. It is per-
tly good to eat unclarified.

aste your consommé. If it is not as strong as
might like, add a bouillon cube or two. You can
cooked noodles or vegetables or meat to cre-
any number of soups from your consommé. Eat
enjoy.

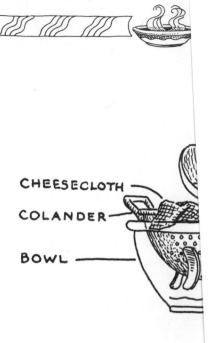

CHEESECLOTH
COLANDER
BOWL

of the larger particles floati
process of drawing out im
them in bunches is called *flo*
folks at the dinner table wit
Carefully simmer your broth
Remove from the heat and al
turbed, for about an hour.

2 Line the colander with
wrung-out cheesecloth. S
bowl. Gently push the raft to o
and carefully ladle the broth i
which will filter out any egg wh
ticles.

Carbohdyrates and Fats

Solutions, suspensions, and emulsions are all mixtures that can be separated and purified into simpler substances. One question that challenged scientists was: What are the simplest substances of all? It turns out that there are only two kinds of pure substances on earth: *compounds* and *elements*.

Elements are the simplest kinds of pure matter. Ninety-two elements have been identified in the earth's crust and a number of others have been made in laboratories. The most common elements found in food (and that also make up your body) are carbon, hydrogen, oxygen, and nitrogen. Living things also contain sulfur, phosphorus, iron, magnesium, sodium, potassium, and chlorine, to name a few.

It took a long time to discover all of the elements. This is because elements combine to form compounds, and it was hard to tell whether a pure substance was an element or if it was a compound. Water is a good example. Water is an extremely stable compound, and it takes enormous amounts of energy to break it up into its elements. So for hundreds of years, people thought that water was an element. It was a great scientific breakthrough when water was found to be a compound made of hydrogen and oxygen, two substances known to be elements.

Elements combine to form compounds very differently from the way substances combine to form mixtures. The properties of the components of mixtures don't change as a result of being part of a mixture. But most compounds have very different properties from the elements that are its components. (Think how water is different from oxygen and hydrogen. Hydrogen is an explosive gas. Oxygen is also a gas, and it supports burning and life. Water is a liquid at ordinary temperatures and neither burns nor supports burning.) Compounds are also made of fixed amounts of combined elements. Any amount of hydrogen and oxygen can be mixed together, but water forms from two parts of hydrogen and one part of oxygen. Any extra hydrogen or oxygen present from the original mixture will be left over after water has formed.

Sugars and *starches* are compounds that are important kinds of food. They are made of only three elements— carbon, hydrogen, and oxygen. When sugars and starches are broken down into these elements, there are two atoms of hydrogen and one of oxygen for every atom of carbon. Two atoms of hydrogen and one atom of oxygen are the same as a molecule of water. For this reason, sugars and starches were called *carbohydrates*, which means "watered carbon." This chapter investigates some of the properties of this interesting group of compounds.

SYRUPS:
SOLUTIONS THAT DON'T CRYSTALLIZE

One property of sugar is that it dissolves in water. If it didn't, you couldn't make rock candy. Actually, making rock candy involves recovering solute crystals from solution, not dissolving them. Corn syrup, molasses, maple syrup, and honey are all examples of sugar solutions. Do the next experiment to see if you can recover sugar crystals from these solutions.

Pour a small amount of each syrup into small shallow dishes and let them stand for several days. In some cases no crystals will form and you will be left with a thick, sticky material in the bottom of the dish. Scientists are always looking for testable questions, ones that can be answered by experimenting. Answering the question "Why don't sugar crystals form from some syrups?" could lead to other testable questions.

Perhaps the syrups are not reaching the supersaturated condition necessary for crystallization to occur. Does syrup absorb water from the air even while water is evaporating from its surface so that most of the sugar remains in solution?

To test this idea make a supersaturated sugar solution as for rock candy (see Chapter 2, pages 13–14). Divide the solution into two dishes. Leave one dish exposed to the air and cover the other with a cake cover or large glass bowl. Before you cover the second dish, sprinkle some calcium chloride on the table around it. Calcium chloride absorbs moisture from the air and will keep the air above the dish dry. You can get calcium chloride in hobby shops.

Perhaps crystals form more slowly from solutions containing several solutes than from a solution containing only one solute?

Materials & Equipment

- ✦ 1½ cups water
- ✦ 2 cups sugar
- ✦ 7½ tablespoons white corn syrup
- ✦ ½ teaspoon cream of tartar

- ✦ a saucepan with a cover
- ✦ a wooden spoon
- ✦ a candy thermometer
- ✦ 3 foil dishes

Procedure

1 Put ½ cup water, ⅔ cup sugar, 2½ tablespoons corn syrup, and ¼ teaspoon cream of tartar into the saucepan and stir over medium heat until dissolved. When the mixture starts to boil, cover it briefly so that the steam washes all the sugar crystallized on the side of the saucepan back into the solution.

2 Uncover and put in the candy thermometer.

Continue to boil without stirring until the temperature reaches 290°F (143°C). Carefully pour the syrup into a foil dish.

3 & 4 Make two more batches of syrup with new ingredients and these small variations: In the second batch, leave out the cream of tartar. In the third batch, use the cream of tartar but heat the mixture only until all the sugar is dissolved. As the solutions cool, you can tell when crystals have formed because the solution becomes cloudy. Close examination with a magnifying glass will reveal thousands of tiny, needlelike crystals.

Observations

Where do crystals form? They should form in two of the syrup batches, while one should remain clear.

There are a number of different kinds of sugars. All are sweet and they all dissolve in water. Some sugars contain only five or six carbon atoms per molecule. These are called simple sugars, and they include *glucose* (sometimes called dextrose) from beets, *fructose* from fruit, and *lactose* from milk. Table sugar is called *sucrose*. It is not a simple sugar because each sucrose molecule is a two-molecule chain of one fructose molecule and one glucose molecule linked together.

When a sucrose solution is heated to a high temperature, it begins to break down into glucose and fructose. This breakdown is speeded up with the addition of an acid such as cream of tartar. The result is a syrup containing a mixture of three sugar solutes—glucose, fructose, and sucrose. Crystals will not form in such a mixture because a crystal is the result of a regular arrangement of identical molecules. When there are several different kinds of molecules in a solution, similar molecules have a harder time getting together.

The syrups you have made can be poured over ice cream or popcorn.

HYGROSCOPIC COOKIES

Ever notice how cookies lose their crispness when they've been exposed to air for a while? Cookie manufacturers have. That's why they seal their products in packages that keep them from being exposed to water vapor in the air. The ingredient in cookies that is chiefly responsible for absorbing moisture is sugar. Such a substance is described as *hygroscopic*, which means "wet looking."

Is one kind of sugar more hygroscopic than another? The next experiment compares cookies made with granulated sucrose and those made with honey. Taste honey and sugar. Which is sweeter?

Materials & Equipment

- ✦ 2 cups flour
- ✦ 1 teaspoon baking powder
- ✦ $\frac{1}{2}$ teaspoon salt
- ✦ 1 stick ($\frac{1}{2}$ cup) unsalted butter
- ✦ $\frac{1}{2}$ cup sugar
- ✦ 1 egg
- ✦ 2 tablespoons water
- ✦ $\frac{1}{2}$ teaspoon lemon juice
- ✦ $\frac{1}{4}$ cup honey

- ✦ measuring cups and spoons
- ✦ a flour sifter
- ✦ a fork
- ✦ 4 bowls
- ✦ electric mixer or eggbeater
- ✦ waxed paper
- ✦ greased cookie sheets
- ✦ a metal spatula
- ✦ wire cooling racks

Procedure

1 Preheat the oven to 400°F. Sift 2 cups of flour onto waxed paper. Measure out 1 cup of this sifted flour and resift it together with $\frac{1}{2}$ teaspoon baking powder and $\frac{1}{4}$ teaspoon salt into a bowl.

Resift a second cup of flour with $\frac{1}{2}$ teaspoon baking powder and $\frac{1}{4}$ teaspoon salt into a second bowl. Set dry ingredients aside.

2 Put $\frac{1}{2}$ stick of softened butter into a third bowl. Beat until creamy with an electric mixer or eggbeater. Add $\frac{1}{2}$ cup of sugar to the butter and continue beating until thoroughly mixed.

3 Beat the egg with a fork in a measuring cup. Put half the egg into the butter-sugar mixture. Also add 1 of the bowls of dry ingredients, water, and lemon juice. Blend until smooth.

4 Now prepare the batter with honey. Put the remaining ½ stick of softened butter in a fourth bowl and beat until creamy. Beat in the honey. Add the other half of the egg and the second bowl of dry ingredients to the butter-honey mixture. You do not need to put in lemon juice, as honey already contains an acid. Mix until well blended.

5 Drop small spoonfuls of the batter onto greased cookie sheets, leaving about 2 inches between cookies. Bake until brown around the edges, about 7 minutes. Be sure to keep track of which cookies contain sugar and which contain honey.

Let the cookies cool for a few minutes on the sheets before moving them to a wire rack with a metal spatula. When they are completely cool, store the cookies in airtight containers.

Observations

When they are cool, eat a sugar cookie and a honey cookie. Are they about the same crispness? Are they the same color? Which is browner? Leave one of each kind of cookie exposed to the air. Take a bite of each every few hours. Which cookie loses its crispness more quickly? If you wanted to make a cake that would stay moist for a long time, what might you use to keep it moist?

STARCHES

Sucrose is a two-molecule chain of simple sugars. A starch molecule is made of long chains of simple sugar molecules. Plants make starch molecules as a way of storing sugar because it can be easily converted back to sugar when needed. If you have any doubt that starch is made of sugar, an experiment using a chemical made by your own body can give you the answer. Do the following experiment and see for yourself.

Materials & Equipment

✦ a soda cracker, saltine, or other plain flour cracker

✦ your tastebuds

Procedure

I A soda cracker is made of flour (a starch), water, and baking powder. It contains no sugar. Check the ingredients listed on the box to make sure. Chew a soda cracker well and hold it in your mouth, without swallowing, for 5 minutes.

Observations

Does the taste of the soda cracker change? There is a special chemical in your saliva that breaks the links in the starch chains so that sugar molecules are released. You should be able to taste this change.

Compare some of the properties of starches and sugars. How is the taste different? Try putting different starches in water. In addition to flour, common starches include arrowroot starch, cornstarch, and potato starch. Which dissolves most easily? In general, smaller molecules dissolve more easily than larger molecules. Sugar dissolves more easily than starch.

Like sugar, starches also absorb water. When starches are heated with water, they swell. This property, called *gelatinization*, makes them very useful as thickeners for sauces and gravies.

Many different foods contain starch. There is a

simple chemical test for starch. Put a few drops of iodine solution (called tincture of iodine, available in most drugstores) on the food. If starch is present, the iodine changes from reddish-brown to a blue-black. **Don't eat any food on which you put iodine! Iodine is poisonous.**

TAPIOCA

Tapioca is a starch that comes from the root of a Brazilian cassava plant. Cassava flour is rolled into little balls, which are sold as dried "pearls." Tapioca pearls are used to make thick puddings.

Put a drop of iodine on a tapioca pearl. Does it give a positive starch test? Discard the pearl you tested. Take $\frac{1}{4}$ cup of tapioca pearls and put them in $\frac{3}{4}$ cup of water. Let them soak for 12 hours. How does the size of the soaked tapioca compare with dried pearls? How is this evidence that starches swell with water?

Make tapioca pudding with the soaked pearls.

Materials & Equipment

+ $\frac{1}{4}$ cup tapioca pearls soaked in $\frac{3}{4}$ cup water
+ $2\frac{1}{4}$ cups milk
+ $\frac{1}{4}$ teaspoon salt
+ water
+ 2 eggs
+ $\frac{1}{2}$ cup sugar

- ✦ 1 teaspoon vanilla
- ✦ a double boiler
- ✦ a wooden spoon
- ✦ 4 dessert cups
- ✦ measuring cups and spoons
- ✦ a small bowl
- ✦ an eggbeater
- ✦ plastic wrap

Procedure

1 Test a small sample of milk, salt, eggs, sugar, and vanilla for starch. **Don't use any of the ingredients you have tested when you are preparing the pudding.** Is starch present in any of these ingredients?

2 Put the soaked pearls in the top of a double boiler with the milk and the salt. Fill the bottom of the double boiler about three quarters full with water and set over medium heat. Cook the tapioca mixture, uncovered, over boiling water for about an hour, stirring occasionally with a wooden spoon.

3 In a small bowl, beat the eggs with the sugar. Mix a few spoonfuls of the hot tapioca mixture into the egg-sugar mixture. This will warm up the eggs slowly. If you were

to put the eggs directly into the hot tapioca mixture, they would cook and you'd have scrambled eggs in your tapioca.

Add the warmed egg-sugar mixture to the tapioca in the pot. Cook about 3 minutes more.

4 Remove the double boiler from the stove, and set the top aside to cool for 15 minutes. Then mix in the vanilla. Divide the pudding into four dessert dishes, cover with plastic wrap, and chill.

5 Test part of the pudding (not a pearl) for starch. Then pick out a pearl from the pudding, wash it off and test it for starch. What has happened to some of the starch that was in the tapioca pearls? What has this starch done to the liquid milk? Again, **don't eat** anything that has iodine on it.

GRAPE JELLY: HOW PECTIN ACTS

Pectin is a starch found in especially high amounts in green apples and the white underskin of citrus fruits. When pectin is cooked with sugar and acid, it swells to form a clear, thick jelly.

Pectin is prepared commercially and is sold in a package with an acid. Is the added sugar necessary for the formation of a firm jelly? Or can a pectin-acid combo do it alone? That's what the next experiment is designed to find out.

Materials & Equipment

- ✦ 3 cups sugar
- ✦ 1 6-ounce can of grape juice concentrate (thawed)
- ✦ 2 cups water
- ✦ 1 package of Sure-Jell (commercially prepared pectin and acid)
- ✦ measuring cups and spoons
- ✦ a large saucepan
- ✦ a wooden spoon
- ✦ 4 6-ounce glasses or jelly jars
- ✦ a metal spoon
- ✦ melted paraffin for sealing off the jelly jars (not necessary if you will eat all the jelly within two weeks)

Procedure

1 Put 3 ounces of juice concentrate, 1 cup of water, and ½ package of Sure-Jell (2½ tablespoons) in a saucepan. Cook over high heat, stirring constantly, until bubbles form all around the edge.

2 Add 1 cup sugar all at once and stir. Bring the mixture to a rolling boil and allow it to boil without stirring for 1 minute.

3 Remove from the heat. Use a metal spoon to skim the scum that rises off the surface. Pour into two glasses. If you plan to store the jelly, pour melted paraffin on top to seal it closed. Sealed jelly doesn't need to be refrigerated. Unsealed does.

4 Make a second batch of jelly with the remaining Sure-Jell, juice concentrate, and water, and this time use 2 cups of sugar.

Observations

Which jelly is firmer? The softer jelly makes a good sauce for vanilla ice cream.

FATS AND OILS

Most of the compounds found in living organisms are made up of only a few of the 92 naturally occurring elements. Carbon, hydrogen, and oxygen are found in a countless number of compounds. The differences in these compounds are due to the amounts of each element that are present and the way the atoms are arranged in the molecules.

Fats and oils, like carbohydrates, are a group of compounds made of only carbon, hydrogen, and oxygen. Fats and oils are produced by animals and plants as a method of storing food. Molecules of sugars and starches become fat or oil molecules as the atoms are rearranged. Stored fats and oils protect an organism against a time when food is scarce.

You can find out if a food contains fat or oil by rubbing it on a piece of brown paper bag. If the food contains a greasy substance, a translucent spot (an area that lets light through) will appear where you have rubbed. Water in food will also produce a translucent spot, but a water spot disappears when the water dries. A fat or oil spot will not disappear.

Animal fats, such as butter or lard, are usually solids at room temperature, while vegetable fats are liquids. Vegetable oils can be made into solid fats in a laboratory by adding hydrogen gas under pressure. The terms *saturated* and *unsaturated* fats refer to the amount of hydrogen in a fat. Saturated fats contain more hydrogen than unsaturated or polyunsaturated fats. Saturated fats are usually solid, while unsaturated fats are oils. Margarine, which is advertised as being made from oil, contains some saturated fat. Hydrogen was added to make the fat solid.

There is a discussion among scientists about whether eating certain kinds of fat may affect your health. When some people age, yellowish, fatty deposits of a substance called *cholesterol* form inside the arteries, leaving a narrower passage for blood to get through. This condition, called arteriosclerosis, can cause blood clots, which may block an artery and cause it to burst. It may also completely close an artery, cutting off the blood supply to a part of the body. If this happens in one of the arteries that nourishes the heart or brain, death can result. Some scientists claim that saturated fats in the diet may increase the amount of cholesterol in the body, and unsaturated fats may lower blood-cholesterol levels. For this reason, doctors suggest that older people cut down on the amounts of butter, cheese, and fatty meats in their diets.

NUT BUTTER: PRESSING OUT OILS

Nuts contain oil, and oil burns easily with a steady flame. See for yourself by setting a Brazil nut or an almond on fire. Set the nut in the center of a pan. Hold a wooden match to the end of the nut until it burns steadily. You can toast a marshmallow in the nut's flame.

Many vegetable oils are prepared by crushing olives, seeds, or nuts in presses. The oil is then separated from the nuts or seeds. In the next experiment, you will release the oil in nuts. Since it is difficult to separate the oil without the proper equipment, you will create a mixture of oil and nuts—a nut butter—that is good to eat.

Materials & Equipment

+ ¹⁄₂ to 1 cup shelled almonds, pecans, or walnuts
+ a nut grinder or food processor
+ 2 plastic bags
+ a rolling pin
+ a spatula
+ a jar with a lid

Procedure

You can use pecans or walnuts as they come out of the shell, but almonds should be white with their outer skins removed. This is done by putting shelled almonds into boiling water for a few minutes. Drain them and let them cool. They almost pop out of their skins if your hold them at the broad end and squeeze gently.

1 Put the nuts through a nut grinder or grind in a food processor. If you haven't got either of these tools, put the nuts in a double plastic bag and pound them with a rolling pin. You are trying to break up the nuts into the smallest possible pieces.

2 After the nuts are ground, put them into a plastic bag and roll the rolling pin on them with as much pressure as possible. (Hydraulic presses are used commercially to extract oil from

olives and peanuts.) The nut particles will begin to cling together as the oil is pressed from the nut meat. The finer the nut meat, the better the butter will be.

3 When the butter is as finely pressed as you can get it, scrape it into a jar. Store the nut butter, covered, in the refrigerator, as it spoils easily.

Nut butters can be used as spreads on bread and crackers. Try a nut butter and jelly sandwich for a variation on an old favorite.

BUTTER: COALESCING FAT DROPLETS FROM A SUSPENSION

Milk has often been called the most complete food. It contains water, carbohydrates, vitamins, minerals, proteins, and fat. Butter is made by extracting the fat from the other parts of milk. Cream contains more butterfat than whole milk. Use it to make butter in the next experiment.

Materials & Equipment

+ ½ pint heavy cream
+ a pint jar with a tight cover
+ a marble

Procedure

1 Put the cream in the jar with the marble. Screw on the cover and make sure that there are no leaks.

2 Shake the jar in a figure-eight motion. At first you will hear the marble moving. Then there will be a time when the cream will be so thick that you won't be able to feel the marble moving. Then, suddenly, the butter will form.

3 Drain the buttermilk—which is also good to drink—from the butter. Wash the butter by running cold tap water into the jar to remove any trapped buttermilk. Fish out the marble and pack the butter down. Store in the refrigerator.

Observations

The process of making butter takes advantage of certain properties of fat. When milk first comes from a cow, the butterfat is in the form of droplets that are suspended in the liquid. If fresh, whole milk is allowed to stand, fat droplets rise to the top, carrying along some liquid. This is cream, and it is less dense than the more watery part of the milk.

Cream is a fat-in-water emulsion. The fat droplets are held in suspension by milk proteins. The butter-making process is the formation of a water-in-fat emulsion where water droplets are suspended in the fat.

When you make butter from cream, you force the fat droplets to come together. They form larger and larger globules until they separate from the water part of the mixture. This process is called *coalescing*. Butterfat coalesces because the fat globules are more attracted to each other than they are to the water in which they are suspended. When you shake the cream, you force the fat droplets to come into contact with each other. The marble stirs up the mixture as you shake it, increasing the opportunity of fat droplets from different parts of the mixture to come in contact with each other.

The amount of butterfat varies in cream. Light cream has much less butterfat than heavy cream. The amount of fat in cream is the most important factor in making good whipped cream. Try making whipped cream from heavy cream and light cream. Which whips more easily? Which keeps its stiffness longer?

AN ICE CREAM TASTE TEST

You may consider yourself an expert on ice cream, but do you really know a good ice cream when you taste it? Is there a real measurable difference between expensive premium brands and less expensive ice creams? How can you measure something that depends on personal opinion? The next experiment is designed to eliminate the variables that shape opinions. You will need a group of people to sample different ice creams and evaluate them. The larger the group the better, but even a group of five or six friends can give you some idea of which ice cream is the favorite.

Materials & Equipment

- ✦ 4 different kinds of vanilla ice cream:
  1 premium brand (The word "premium" must appear on the package. Usually it is expensive and sold in pint containers.)
  1 moderately priced brand that is also labeled "premium"
  1 very inexpensive brand
  1 ice milk or vanilla frozen yogurt
- ✦ 4 bowls
- ✦ labels and a pen

For each person taking the test:

- ✦ a spoon
- ✦ a glass of water
- ✦ a napkin
- ✦ a pencil or pen
- ✦ an Ice Cream Taste Test Data Sheet copied from this book

Procedure

If you are conducting this experiment, you cannot participate in the test. Here's the setup.

1 Put a different ice cream in each bowl and label the bowl with a number so only you can identify which ice cream it holds. Don't throw out the containers the ice cream came in, and also make a note of the prices paid for each brand.

2 Don't let the participants see the original containers. They should see only the ice cream in the bowls at the time of the experiment. Packaging and brand names can have a large effect on how people "taste" ice creams.

Some of the other things that could influence how people perceive the different ice cream tastes are: conversation between participants, the order in which they taste the ice cream, and leftover flavor from the last ice cream tasted. So you must instruct your participants not to speak to or look at each other. They should take a sip of water between tastes, and sample each ice cream at least three or four times, in different orders, before drawing any conclusions.

Here are some of the things professional ice cream taste testers look for:

Color—The color should be what you expect for the flavor. Vanilla is not too yellow or too white.

Melting—The best ice cream melts quickly at room temperature, and the melted ice cream is a smooth liquid without foamy bubbles.

Body and texture—The best ice cream is firm but drips easily. The "mouth-feel" is creamy smooth and chewy. Better ice creams have more butterfat and stay firm at lower temperatures. They don't feel as cold as less expensive ice creams that have such a cold feel they can give you a headache.

Flavor—Vanilla ice cream should be pleasantly sweet and you should be able to taste the vanilla.

ICE CREAM TASTE TEST DATA SHEET

FILL IN BLANKS WITH A "YES" OR A "NO."

BOWL	#1	#2	#3	#4
FLAVOR				
Too much vanilla	___	___	___	___
Too little vanilla	___	___	___	___
Too sweet	___	___	___	___
Not sweet enough	___	___	___	___
Too sour	___	___	___	___
Too salty	___	___	___	___
Cooked	___	___	___	___
Aftertaste	___	___	___	___
BODY AND TEXTURE				
Coarse/icy	___	___	___	___
Crumbly	___	___	___	___
Fluffy	___	___	___	___
Gummy	___	___	___	___
Grainy	___	___	___	___

TOTAL NUMBER OF "NO" VOTES

___   ___   ___   ___

The ice cream should not taste "cooked" like milk that has been boiled.

3 After all the tasters have finished collecting their own data, add up the total number of "no" votes for each ice cream for the group. The ice cream with the most no votes wins.

Observations

Which ice cream wins? Do people generally prefer the most expensive ice cream?

Look at the list of ingredients on the cartons. All ice cream contains butterfat (in cream), milk, sugar, flavoring, and air that has been beaten in. Premium ice creams have more fat and less air than cheaper ice creams. High fat content lets the ice cream remain firm at warmer temperatures. Premium ice creams melt without leaving behind a foam. Cheap ice creams have less fat and more air. Ice crystals tend to be larger, and the ice cream feels colder. Emulsifiers and stabilizers are added to keep the size of the ice crystals small, but they can give the product a sticky, gummy texture and a strange aftertaste. The temperature, texture, and mouth feel can tell you a lot about the ingredients. In general, premium ice creams have fewer ingredients than cheaper ice creams.

With practice, you can become a champion ice cream taster.

Proteins

In the eighteenth century scientists became interested in a substance, found in all living things, that acted differently from all other substances. When a fluid like blood or egg white was heated, it did not become a boiling liquid like water or oil. Instead, it became a solid. And, if this was not strange enough, once changed to a solid, it could never again be a liquid. Nothing could be done to return blood or egg white to its original liquid state. It did not take scientists long to realize that this strange material that changed permanently when heated was the very basis of all life. For this reason, they named it *protein* meaning "of first importance."

Proteins have turned out to be the most complicated and numerous of all the compounds found in living things. Some proteins, like egg white, dissolve in water; some, like hair, are fibers. Some, like muscle protein, are responsible for movement in animals. But all proteins have certain things in common. In addition to the elements carbon, hydrogen, and oxygen, all proteins contain nitrogen. The atoms of these elements, along with an occasional atom of sulfur, form small molecules called *amino acids*. Proteins are chains of amino acids.

Only 20 different amino acids make up most proteins. The different amino acids are like an alphabet for proteins. When you think of all you can say with 26 letters, you can see how 20 amino acids can be used to form so many different kinds of proteins. A protein molecule can be thought of as a chemical sentence or even a paragraph. And the proteins of each kind of organism can be thought of as being its own unique language.

When human beings and other animals digest food, what they are doing is breaking down the protein they have eaten into amino acids. The amino acids from food are reassembled to build new proteins that are the particular type for that organism.

Scientists have found protein to be one of the most challenging kinds of material to study. You can use some of their methods of investigation to learn how different kinds of protein behave and how some of the properties of certain proteins are important in food preparation.

MERINGUES:
THE PROPERTIES OF EGG WHITE

An egg white is a good place to start learning about proteins. It is made up of about 87 percent water, a trace of minerals, and about 9 percent protein. The protein in an egg white makes it very useful for preparing food with different textures and consistencies.

Materials & Equipment

- ✦ 3 eggs
- ✦ water
- ✦ a knife
- ✦ a deep bowl
- ✦ a plastic ice cube tray
- ✦ plastic wrap
- ✦ 2 small transparent glasses
- ✦ a flashlight
- ✦ a spoon
- ✦ an electric mixer or eggbeater
- ✦ a magnifying glass

Procedure

1 Let the eggs come to room temperature. Protein in egg white is most useful to cooks at about 79°F (26°C). (You can check this out by try-

ing to make meringues from egg whites at different temperatures.)

Separate the whites from the yolks using the instructions on pages 197–98, putting the whites into a deep bowl. Save the yolks; you'll need them for the next experiment. Put each egg yolk in its own compartment of a plastic ice cube tray, leaving empty compartments between the yolks. Cover the tray with plastic wrap and refrigerate.

2 Pour enough egg white into a glass to make a depth of two inches. Shine a beam of light through the egg white. Can you see the beam as it passes through? The beam is an example of the Tyndall effect. What does it tell you about the size of the particles in egg white? (See Chapter 3, page 40 if you don't remember the Tyndall effect.) It has been proven that protein particles are single molecules. They are among the largest molecules in existence.

3 Pour the egg white back into the bowl. Put some water in the glass. Take about a teaspoon of egg white and stir it into the water. Does the egg white dissolve?

4 Beat the egg whites in the bowl with an electric mixer or eggbeater until they are foamy but will still flow if poured. Take about ½ teaspoon of foam and put it in a fresh glass of water. Does it dissolve? What shape are the tiny particles that are suspended in the water? Use a magnifying glass.

Observations

You have just demonstrated a very important property of proteins. That is, that the shape of a protein molecule plays an important part in determining how it behaves. Protein molecules in egg whites are like tiny balls of yarn. Their round, compact shape enables them to dissolve in water. When you beat egg whites, you are, in effect, unraveling these balls of yarn. The long chains that form are too large to dissolve. The process of changing protein from its natural form is called *denaturing*. It is impossible to restore denatured egg white to its original form.

The egg whites can be used to make meringues, which show some other properties of proteins.

Materials & Equipment

- ✦ oil
- ✦ 3 egg whites, beaten foamy in previous experiment
- ✦ ½ teaspoon cream of tartar
- ✦ ½ teaspoon salt

- ✦ ½ teaspoon vanilla extract
- ✦ 1 cup superfine sugar
- ✦ a cookie sheet
- ✦ brown paper
- ✦ a rubber spatula
- ✦ measuring cups and spoons
- ✦ an electric mixer or eggbeater
- ✦ airtight container

Procedure

1 Preheat the oven to 175°F. Prepare a cookie sheet by covering it with brown paper rubbed with a little oil to coat.

2 Add the cream of tartar, salt, and vanilla extract to your foamy egg whites. Cream of tartar is an acid that makes the foam last longer. (You can test this idea with a simple side experiment. Beat two egg whites in separate bowls. Add ⅛ teaspoon cream of tartar to one egg white before you beat it. Find out which foam lasts longer.)

Beat the egg whites with an electric mixer or eggbeater until you can make peaks that stand upright. As the egg whites are beaten, the protein becomes more and more unraveled, and the foam becomes stiffer and stiffer.

3 Slowly add the sugar by sprinkling a tablespoon at a time over the egg whites. Continue beating while adding the sugar. Occasionally scrape down the sides of the bowl with a rubber spatula.

The water in the egg whites is carried along the

strands of protein. When sugar is beaten into stiff egg whites, it dissolves into this water. This is why you use superfine sugar (which dissolves more easily), and you add it very slowly to give it a chance to go into solution. If all the sugar doesn't dissolve, tiny droplets of sugar syrup will form on the surface of the finished product. Professional chefs consider such a "weeping" meringue a failure.

4 After you have added all the sugar, taste the meringue. It should not feel gritty, but if it does, beat in a tablespoon of water to dissolve all the sugar.

5 Make four separate piles of meringue on the oiled paper. Push down the middle of each pile to make a bowl shape.

6 The last step in making a meringue is to remove the water. This is accomplished by drying it in a warm oven for a long time.

Put the meringues in the oven for one hour at 175°F. At the end of that time, turn off the oven and let the meringues stay in the oven overnight.

A successful meringue is a stiff, snow-white confection that will keep for weeks in an airtight container. (Since sugar absorbs moisture from the air, meringues must be stored away from the air. Otherwise, they become soft and fall apart.)

Fill the meringues with fruit or ice cream and top with whipped cream or chocolate sauce.

HOW TO SAVE EGG YOLKS

Egg yolks contain the nutrients needed to nourish a growing chick. Since they can also provide nourishment for countless bacteria, they are among the most perishable of leftovers. One way to preserve food is to freeze it. Water in frozen food is solid ice and is not available to microorganisms. But freezing can also make the yolk unusable unless you are an inventive chef. Do the next experiment to see if there is a way around this problem.

Materials & Equipment

- 3 egg yolks
- $\frac{1}{8}$ teaspoon salt
- $\frac{1}{8}$ teaspoon sugar
- a plastic ice cube tray
- measuring spoons
- a spoon
- paper
- a pencil
- plastic wrap
- a knife

Procedure

1 Take the egg yolks you saved from the last experiment out of the refrigerator. Put about ⅛ teaspoon salt in one egg yolk and stir it well with a spoon. Rinse off the spoon. Put about ⅛ teaspoon sugar in another egg yolk and stir. Rinse the spoon again and stir the third egg yolk, but don't put anything in it.

2 Draw a diagram of the ice cube tray showing where each egg yolk is located. Cover the tray with plastic wrap and put in the freezer overnight.

3 The next day, let the yolks defrost at room temperature. Stick a knife into each one (rinsing it off between dips). See whether the egg yolk is a firm semisolid or still runny. You can use the runny egg yolks to make cupcakes. The semisolid yolk is perfectly edible, but not too tasty.

Observations

The egg yolk is about half water. The solids are mostly fats and some proteins. Some proteins are dissolved in the watery phase of the egg yolk. But most of the yolk proteins and all of the fat are in tiny round particles that are suspended in the liquid creating a thick emulsion. When you hard-boil an egg, the soft, crumbly, grainy texture of the yolk is due to the denaturing of the granular proteins.

When an egg yolk is frozen, the protein in the water solution is denatured, trapping the water and producing a solid mass when it is defrosted. If you add salt or sugar to an egg yolk, however, some of the water is removed from its close connection with protein. It is not trapped in the denatured protein after defrosting, so the eggs yolks remain runny.

A Quick Cupcake Recipe
Materials & Equipment

+ ½ stick butter, softened
+ ½ cup sugar
+ 2 egg yolks
+ 1 cup cake flour (not self-rising)
+ 1⅓ teaspoons baking powder
+ ¼ teaspoon salt
+ ⅓ cup milk
+ ¾ teaspoon vanilla
+ measuring cups and spoons
+ 2 medium bowls
+ a sifter
+ an electric mixer
+ a cupcake pan
+ cupcake liners

Procedure

1 Preheat the oven to 350°F. Beat the softened butter in a bowl with the sugar. Then beat in the egg yolks.

2 In another bowl sift together the cake flour, baking powder, and salt.

3 Pour the milk and the vanilla into a measuring cup. Add about one third of the dry ingredients to the butter-sugar mixture. Then beat in half of the milk mixture, then another third of the dry ingredients, then the rest of the milk, and then the rest of the dry ingredients. You should beat the batter well after each addition.

4 Line 4 baking cups with cupcake liners, pour the batter into them, and bake for 25–30 minutes.

CUSTARD: COAGULATING PROTEIN

The process of changing liquid protein into a solid by heating it is called *coagulation*. Coagulation is a kind of denaturing. You used coagulated egg white to clarify stock in Chapter 3 (see pages 54–55). Egg white coagulates at about 156°F (69°C). It changes from an almost colorless, transparent, fairly thick liquid to a white solid. The protein in an egg yolk also coagulates when heated.

Protein coagulation is one of the main reasons the texture of food changes when it is cooked.

Meat and fish become firm, and batters change from liquids to solids. In fact, most baked goods have a "skeleton" of coagulated milk or egg protein that supports them.

Custard is a homogeneous mixture of eggs, milk, and sugar that has been heated to coagulate the protein in the eggs and the milk. The next experiment shows how different amounts of heat affect the coagulation of these proteins.

Materials & Equipment

- ✦ $\frac{1}{2}$ cup sugar
- ✦ $\frac{1}{8}$ teaspoon salt
- ✦ 1 teaspoon vanilla
- ✦ 2 cups milk
- ✦ 3 eggs
- ✦ measuring cups and spoons
- ✦ a bowl
- ✦ an electric mixer or eggbeater
- ✦ 4 custard cups or other oven-proof cups
- ✦ a pan the cups will fit into

Procedure

1 Preheat the oven to 325°F. Beat the sugar, salt, and vanilla into the milk. Add the eggs and beat well.

2 Divide the mixture equally among four custard cups. Set the cups in the pan and cover the bottom of the pan with about an inch of water.

(This is to make sure that the bottoms of the cups are not heated more than any other part.) Put the pan with the custards in the oven.

3 After 30 minutes, remove one cup of custard. Take the second cup out after 40 minutes, the third cup after 50 minutes, and the fourth cup after one hour.

Observations

Which custard has been properly cooked? Which custard has separated and has the most liquid?

When eggs first coagulate, the protein is able to trap and hold other liquids, such as the water in the milk and egg whites. If eggs are cooked too long or at too high a temperature, they become tougher and tougher and can no longer hold water. For example, scrambled eggs from which water has separated have been either overcooked or cooked too quickly.

Properly made custard is a smooth, shiny, yellow

pudding that slices cleanly when you put a spoon into it. There is no trace of water from either the egg or the milk.

All of these custards are good to eat. Refrigerate until you are ready to serve them. The overcooked custards should be drained before eating. They can be topped with fruit.

SOUR MILK BISCUITS: PROTEIN DENATURED BY ACID

Some protein is easily denatured by acid. You can tell when this happens if solid particles form in a liquid that contains dissolved protein, like milk. The protein in sour milk makes the milk thicker and ultimately separates from the watery portion of the milk. Certain bacteria make milk sour. Their acid waste products denature milk protein. But you can make a quick version of sour milk by adding your own acid.

Bring $\frac{1}{2}$ cup of milk to room temperature. Put 2 teaspoons of vinegar, a weak acid, in another cup. Pour the milk into the vinegar and stir. Let the mixture stand for about 10 minutes. How can you tell if the protein is denatured? Stir the milk. Can you get the denatured protein to dissolve?

You can use the sour milk to make biscuits. Just

substitute it for whole milk in a package of biscuit mix and follow the directions on the box, or make your own biscuits from scratch using this recipe.

Materials & Equipment

- ✦ 1 cup flour
- ✦ 1 teaspoon baking powder
- ✦ $\frac{1}{8}$ teaspoon baking soda
- ✦ $\frac{1}{2}$ teaspoon salt
- ✦ 2 tablespoons cold butter

- ✦ $\frac{1}{2}$ cup sour milk
- ✦ a medium-sized bowl
- ✦ a pastry blender or 2 knives
- ✦ a fork
- ✦ 2 spoons
- ✦ a cookie sheet

Procedure

1 Preheat the oven to 450°F. In a medium bowl, mix together the flour, baking powder, baking soda, and salt.

2 Using a pastry blender, or two knives, cut in the butter until the mixture looks like crumbs the size of small peas.

3 Add the sour milk and stir with a fork until all ingredients are thoroughly combined.

4 Drop the dough by spoonfuls onto the un-greased cookie sheet. Bake for 12–15 minutes until golden brown.

GELATIN:
SOL-GEL TRANSFORMATION

If all protein were as easily denatured as the soluble proteins in egg and milk, life could not survive. About 40 percent of the protein in our bodies and those of other animals is considerably tougher than egg and milk protein. It already exists as a solid that will not dissolve in water. This protein, called *collagen*, is found in cartilage, the white, flexible material at the ends of bones. It is also found in tendons, which attach muscles to bones, and ligaments, which tie bones together; and it is the main protein in bones themselves. Collagen is the protein that keeps us from falling apart.

As you might expect, collagen is also found in meat we eat. Tougher cuts of meat contain more collagen than more tender cuts. The problem facing cooks is how to make the collagen softer and meat more tender.

Fortunately, this is not a difficult task. When collagen is heated with water for a while, it breaks down into a smaller, softer, soluble protein called *gelatin*. The process of changing collagen to gelatin is speeded up with the addition of an acid like lemon juice, vinegar, or tomatoes to the cooking water. (Some cooks soak or marinate tough meats in vinegar before stewing.) A tomato stew should become tender sooner than one made in meat broth alone. Can you design an experiment to confirm this?

If you would like to prepare almost pure gelatin, get two or three veal bones from your butcher. Veal bones, which come from young calves, have a great deal of cartilage. (As animals grow older, cartilage is replaced with bone.) Cover the veal bones with water and boil for an hour. Strain the broth and let it cool. You can improve the taste of the gelatin in the broth by adding tomato juice.

Gelatin is different from collagen. Gelatin dissolves in hot water, while collagen doesn't dissolve at all. You can learn about some other properties of gelatin in the next experiment.

Materials & Equipment

✦ ½ cup cold water

✦ a package of unflavored gelatin

+ 1 ½ cups boiling water
+ a package of presweetened Kool-Aid
+ a measuring cup
+ a small bowl
+ a wooden spoon
+ a clear glass
+ a flashlight
+ a small pot
+ a 2-cup mold or 2-cup container
+ a plate

Procedure

1 Pour the cold water into a bowl and sprinkle the package of gelatin over it. Does the gelatin attract the water? How can you tell?

2 When the gelatin has been softened, add the boiling water and stir. Does the gelatin dissolve? This mixture is called a *sol*.

Taste the sol. Commercial gelatin is so tasteless that it can be used to make desserts as well as meat dishes.

3 Pour some of the sol into a clear glass. Shine a light through it. Does it show the Tyndall effect (see page 40)? What does this tell you about the size of gelatin molecules?

Let the sol cool in the glass, then chill it, uncovered. The most dramatic property of gelatin is revealed when a sol cools. It changes from a liquid to a semisolid quivering mass called a gel. Shine a light through the gel. Does it show the same Tyndall effect as the sol? Is there any sign of water in the gel?

4 Put the gel in a pot and warm it over medium heat. Can you change the gel back into a sol by adding heat? Add ½ package of presweetened Kool-Aid to the sol and stir with a wooden spoon until it is dissolved. Pour the flavored gelatin mixture into a mold, cool, and then chill until set.

5 Unmold the set gelatin by changing the gel next to the mold back into a sol. Fill the sink with hot water and have ready a plate that covers the top of the mold. Put the mold into the water for about 10 seconds. Be careful not to let

any water get on the gelatin. After removing the mold from the sink, put the plate over it, turn the whole thing over, and give it a hard shake. You should hear the gelatin plop onto the plate. If the gelatin doesn't slip out, heat it again for a few seconds and repeat the procedure. Be careful that you don't heat it too much, as you can lose the sharp shape of the mold on your dessert.

A gelatin dessert can be unmolded long before it is to be served. Just return it to the refrigerator until you are ready to eat it.

Observations

The sol-gel transformation fascinated scientists. They wondered what happened to the water. Their research discovered that the water is trapped by a network of gelatin molecules that form when gelatin cools. They also discovered that as gelatin ages, it is able to hold less and less water.

See for yourself how gelatin loses moisture as it ages. Cut some of your gelatin dessert into 1-inch cubes. Leave the cubes, uncovered, on a plate in the refrigerator for several days. Every morning and evening, eat a cube to see how they begin to get tougher and tougher as they get dryer.

MUFFINS: A STUDY OF GLUTEN— THE WHEAT PROTEIN

Denatured protein is the "skeleton" that supports baked products. In cakes and muffins and other delicate baked goods, this support comes from coagulated milk and eggs. In bread, the support comes from a protein called *gluten* found in wheat flour.

Flour does not actually contain gluten. It contains two substances that can become gluten under the right conditions. The next experiment will show you some of the conditions needed to develop gluten and the effect of different amounts of gluten on the texture of muffins.

Materials & Equipment

+ 1 cup all-purpose flour
+ 2 tablespoons sugar
+ 1 teaspoon salt
+ 2 teaspoons baking powder
+ 1 cup cake flour (not self-rising)
+ 2 tablespoons butter
+ ⅔ cup milk

+ 2 eggs
+ paper muffin-cup liners
+ a 12-cup muffin tin
+ measuring cups and spoons
+ waxed paper
+ a sifter
+ 3 bowls
+ a small frying pan

◆ an electric mixer
or eggbeater

◆ 2 spoons

Procedure

1 Preheat the oven to 350°F. Put eight muffin-cup liners in the muffin tin, four on each side so you make two groups separated by four empty cups in the center. Use different-colored liners on each side or double line one side to help keep track of which cups hold which batter.

2 Sift about a cup of all-purpose flour onto a sheet of waxed paper. All-purpose flour contains more protein that can become gluten than cake flour. Measure out 1 cup of this flour and resift it along with 1 tablespoon of sugar, $\frac{1}{2}$ teaspoon salt, and 1 teaspoon baking powder into a bowl.

3 Using a clean piece of waxed paper, repeat this process with cake flour instead of all-purpose flour. Cake flour has a lower potential gluten content. This mixture will be prepared in a way that keeps the gluten from developing.

4 Melt 1 tablespoon of butter in a frying pan and let it cool. In a clean bowl, beat $\frac{1}{3}$ cup milk with 1 egg. Add the cooled butter and pour the mixture into the dry ingredients containing the all-purpose flour. Mix carefully until all the flour is moist, then beat the batter with an electric mixer or eggbeater until it becomes smooth and glossy.

5 Repeat the steps for melting butter and mixing it with milk and egg. Add this second ·mixture all at once to the bowl with the cake flour. Stir quickly and lightly until all the flour is moist. You should not have to stir more than 15 seconds. Do not beat too hard and don't worry about lumps in the batter. How does this batter look compared with the other batter?

6 Spoon the batter containing cake flour into 4 muffin cups. Then spoon the all-purpose flour batter into the other 4 cups. Bake for 15 minutes until the tops are brown. Let the muffins cool.

Observations

Cut one of each kind of muffin in half. Which muffin has the finer grain? Which makes crumbs more easily? Taste the muffins. Which is more tender? Which has large tunnels caused by larger bubbles of gas?

Gluten develops when dough is warm and there is a lot of mixing. Gluten is prevented from developing when dough is kept cold and handled as little as possible. Some bread does not contain any protein other than gluten. Why do you think bread dough is kneaded? Why should pie dough be handled lightly and as little as possible?

There are many variations of this experiment.

Try making muffins with cake flour and with bread flour. Handle the batters the same way. See if temperature affects the way gluten develops. Use all-purpose flour but use ice-cold ingredients in one batter and room-temperature ingredients in the other. Which of the following baked products do you think depend on gluten for structure and which must be fairly gluten-free to remain flaky and tender—bread, cream puffs, pie crust, cake, biscuits? Can you think up experiments to test your ideas?

Kitchen Chemistry

The first chemists, called *alchemists*, were not searching for truth about nature or looking for a system to describe all matter. They worked long, hard hours over smelly cauldrons, which often contained dangerous materials, with a single idea to keep them going—finding a way to create gold. Nothing noble here. Just another get-rich-quick scheme.

You can't blame an alchemist for trying. Suppose you had plunged an iron pot into a perfectly ordinary-looking spring and found upon removing the pot some time later that it was covered with a red coating. You might reason, as they did, that if you could turn iron into something else, why not look for a way to make gold from other metals? To this end, alchemists separated mixtures and mixed substances together. They developed many procedures used in laboratories today, and they discovered many substances no one knew existed.

But the alchemists failed in their intended purpose. No matter how hard they tried, they could not make gold. Nothing personal here. The alchemists didn't know that no one can make gold, for gold is an element—a substance that cannot be broken down. But alchemists did make many other important discoveries. Perhaps the most important were the events they observed in which one kind of matter did change into another. These events are *chemical reactions.*

There are hundreds of thousands of different chemical reactions. The flame from a gas burner, the rust on an old piece of iron, and the browning of a cut apple are three examples. Despite the obvious differences, all chemical reactions have certain things in common.

In every chemical reaction, you start with one kind of matter and end up with another. Often the products of a reaction have very different properties from the reactants you began with. For example, when propane gas in a stove reacts with oxygen in the air, the products are carbon dioxide and water vapor. This reaction can be written as a chemical equation:

propane gas + oxygen + starter heat $\rightarrow$
carbon dioxide + water + flame

All chemical reactions involve energy, which may be in the form of heat, light, or electricity. Chemists usually find heat is the easiest way to measure energy involved in reactions. All chemical reactions can be divided into one of two kinds: those that give off heat and those that take up heat. Some reactions, like burning, need a small amount of heat to get started but give off energy once they get going.

Many times a chemical reaction is not as obvious as the flame of a gas burner. There are other ways of knowing when a chemical reaction has taken place. In this chapter, you will learn some of these ways and how chemical reactions play a significant part in the preparation of food.

LEMON FIZZ:
A REACTION FORMS A GAS

Sometimes a gas is the product of a chemical reaction. If the reaction takes place in a solution, bubbles rise to the surface and are easy to see.

Materials & Equipment

- ✦ water
- ✦ 1 teaspoon baking soda
- ✦ lemonade
- ✦ measuring spoons
- ✦ 2 glass tumblers
- ✦ 2 spoons

Procedure

1 Fill one glass half full of water. Add ½ teaspoon of baking soda and stir with one of your spoons. Does the baking soda dissolve easily? Is there any reaction? Use red-cabbage indicator (see Chapter 2, pages 25–26) to test this solution to see if it is an acid or a base. Pour a little of the solution into a small amount of the indicator.

2 Fill the second glass half full of lemonade. (Test the lemonade with the indicator in another container.) Using a clean spoon stir ½ teaspoon of baking soda into the lemonade. How can you tell that there was a reaction? Drink the lemon fizz quickly before all the bubbles escape into the air.

Observations

Invent other experiments to see if baking soda reacts with other acid drinks. Try making orange fizz or apple fizz.

Baking soda is a compound of sodium, carbon, hydrogen, and oxygen. It reacts with acids to give off carbon dioxide.

CUPCAKES: HOW CAKES RISE

The changes that occur as a cake bakes are very dramatic. As the batter gets warmer, tiny bubbles of gas form in the mixture and grow larger. The batter surrounding these bubbles becomes permanently set as the protein from milk and eggs coagulates with heat. Flour strengthens the walls of these bubbles so the cake doesn't collapse when removed from the oven. Sugar and flour hold moisture to make a tender crumb. The ingredients play an important part in the structure of a cake. Perhaps the most remarkable thing about this amazing structure is that it is delicious to eat.

Since the source of the lightness and delicacy of a cake is gas bubbles, it's fun to investigate the bubble-producing reactions. Then we'll investigate how bubbles help make a cake rise.

Materials & Equipment

+ ½ teaspoon cream of tartar
+ water
+ ½ teaspoon baking soda
+ 1½ teaspoons double-acting

+ baking powder
+ measuring spoons
+ 4 glass tumblers
+ 4 spoons
+ a small saucepan
+ a candy thermometer

Procedure 1

1 Put about ½ teaspoon of cream of tartar in half a glass of cold water. Stir to dissolve. Is there any reaction? Test a small amount of the solution with red cabbage indicator. Is it acid or base?

2 Add about ½ teaspoon of baking soda to the cream of tartar solution. Be sure to wipe off your measuring spoon before you dip it into the baking soda box and use a clean spoon to stir the mixture.

Observations

Is there any reaction? What gas is released? How would your findings from lemon fizz predict this result?

There used to be a baking-powder product made with cream of tartar (also known as tartaric acid), baking soda, and cornstarch. Cream of tartar is an acid that can be packaged in a dry form and dissolves quickly in liquid. The cornstarch absorbs moisture in the powder mixture, so that the baking soda and cream of tartar are prevented from reacting with each other in the box. Batter mixed with cream of tartar baking powder had to be baked as soon as it was mixed. If it stood around for a while before baking, most of the gas escaped and the cake did not rise as much. You can test this idea with the cupcake recipe and some experimental procedures given in the next section.

Procedure 2

1 Half fill one glass with cold water and a second glass with hot water. Add $\frac{1}{2}$ teaspoon of double-acting baking powder to each glass. In which glass is the reaction stronger?

2 When no more bubbles are coming out in the first glass, heat the solution in a pan. Is there a second reaction?

Observations

A second type of baking powder was developed that could stand around and wait in batter before being baked. It contained an acid called sodium aluminum sulfate, which reacted with baking soda only when heated. So the carbon dioxide would be produced only when the cake was being baked.

There were two problems with baking powder containing sodium aluminum sulfate. First, it left a bitter aftertaste in the cake. Secondly, for certain recipes, the heat of the oven might set the structure of the cake before any gas was released, forming a very heavy product. For this reason, double-acting baking powder was developed. It contains two acid powders: a quick-acting acid powder, like cream of tartar, that starts releasing carbon dioxide as soon as it is mixed with a liquid, and sodium aluminum sulfate, to release more carbon dioxide when it is baked. Less of this acid is needed in such a powder, so there is less bitter aftertaste.

Procedure 3

1 Heat water until it is about 150°F (66°C). (Use a candy thermometer to measure temperature.) Half fill a glass tumbler with the hot water. Put the candy thermometer in the water.

2 When the temperature reading levels off and stays the same for

about five seconds, add a heaping teaspoonful of double-acting baking powder and stir.

Observations

Watch the thermometer as the reaction takes place. Does the solution get warmer or colder? By how many degrees? You can repeat this experiment using different amounts of baking powder.

What you have just witnessed is an example of a chemical reaction that takes up heat. Unlike combustion, in which heat is given off, the chemical reaction in which sodium aluminum sulfate breaks down and releases carbon dioxide requires heat to begin. The heat for this reaction is removed from the surrounding liquid, making it cooler.

Use the cupcake recipe below in the following experiments, which reveal how different baking powders act in batter.

Basic Cupcake Recipe

Materials & Equipment

+ 1 cup cake flour (not self-rising)
+ $\frac{1}{2}$ cup sugar
+ $\frac{1}{4}$ teaspoon salt
+ 1 egg

+ 1 teaspoon double-acting baking powder

- ✦ ¼ cup butter (½ stick), softened
- ✦ ¼ cup milk
- ✦ 1 teaspoon vanilla
- ✦ measuring cups and spoons
- ✦ waxed paper
- ✦ sifter
- ✦ two mixing bowls
- ✦ electric mixer
- ✦ spoon
- ✦ 12-cup muffin tin, greased or with paper liners

Basic Procedure

1 Preheat the oven to 350°F. Sift onto waxed paper and then measure the flour. Resift with the sugar, salt, and baking powder (or baking powder substitute, depending on the experiment) into a bowl. Set dry ingredients aside.

2 In a separate bowl, beat the softened butter with an electric mixer. Next beat in the egg, milk, and vanilla.

3 Add the liquid ingredients all at once to the dry ingredients. Stir carefully until all the flour is moistened, then beat just until the batter is smooth.

4 Pour the batter into 4 muffin cups. Bake for about 15 minutes. The cupcakes are done when the tops are brown and a toothpick stuck into a cupcake comes out clean.

Variation 1

Make 2 batches of cupcakes substituting $\frac{1}{2}$ teaspoon of baking soda and $\frac{1}{4}$ teaspoon of cream of tartar for the baking powder in each. Mix up the first batch and let it stand in its mixing bowl for at least an hour before you mix the second batch. Bake both batches at the same time.

Variation 2

Try making the cupcakes with different amounts of baking powder. Use $\frac{1}{2}$ teaspoon for one batch, 1 teaspoon for a second batch, and $1\frac{1}{2}$ teaspoons for a third batch.

Variation 3

If you want to try one large experiment, first mix a batter using $\frac{1}{2}$ teaspoon cream of tartar and $\frac{1}{4}$ teaspoon baking soda instead of the baking powder. Let this batter stand for about a half hour and then mix 2 more batters. In the second batch use the double-acting baking powder called for in the recipe. Then make a third batch the same as the first, using cream of tartar and baking soda. Bake all 3 batches together in a muffin tin with 12 cups. Since each batch makes 4 cupcakes, you can use one muffin tin for the entire experiment.

When you compare cupcakes, look for differences in height, crumb size, and taste.

Note: It's fun to watch a cake bake. If you have an oven with a window, leave the light on and look in during the baking process. If you don't have such a window, don't open the oven before it is time for the cupcakes to be done. If a blast of cold air hits a cake before it is finished setting, the hot gas in the cake suddenly contracts and the cake falls. Since the centers set last, a draft often produces a cake with a fallen center.

CARAMEL SYRUP:
SUGAR DECOMPOSES

Some compounds, like sugar, break down into simpler compounds and elements when heated. Sugar melts at 320°F (160°C) and starts to break down or decompose at 356°F (180°C). When sugar breaks down, water is one product and carbon is another. As more and more carbon forms, the liquid sugar becomes straw colored and eventually turns a dark brown. Sugar that has been partly broken down is known as caramel.

You can see the chemical breakdown of sugar when you make caramel. Be very careful in following the directions for this experiment, because you will be working with very hot material. You should have an adult help you with this experiment.

Materials & Equipment

+ ½ cup sugar
+ ½ cup water
+ a small, heavy frying pan
+ a wooden spoon

Procedure

1. Put the sugar in a small, heavy frying pan. Stirring constantly, cook the sugar over medium heat. It will soon melt and start turning brown. When the sugar is straw colored, remove the pan from the heat.

2. *Slowly and carefully* add the water. The caramel will be brittle and very hot. If you add water too quickly, it may spatter and burn you.

3. Return the pan to low heat and stir for about 10 minutes. Try to get all the caramel to dissolve. After 10 minutes, remove the pan from the heat and let the syrup cool.

Observations

When the syrup has cooled completely, taste it and compare the taste to sugar. Which is sweeter? You can serve this syrup over ice cream or use it to glaze the cupcakes from the last experiment.

For a second experiment, try heating ½ cup sugar until it is dark brown. Again, turn off the heat and add about ½ cup water. This time you will have to be even more careful, as the caramel is so hot there may be a violent reaction. A solution made of dark caramel is used to color gravies and stews. The sugar has been broken down so completely that no sweetness remains.

What change in the appearance of the sugar let you know that a chemical reaction was taking place? Can you think of any other color changes that are the result of a chemical reaction?

VITAMIN C FRUIT SALAD: OXIDATION OF FRUIT

Ever notice how certain fruits and vegetables turn brown when a cut surface is exposed to the air? This happens because there is a pigment in fruit that reacts with the oxygen in air (more on this reaction in Chapter 10). Oxygen is a very reactive element, which combines with many substances in a reaction called, fittingly, *oxidation*. Oxidation is a chemical reaction that always gives off energy. Combustion is oxidation of a fuel that is so rapid that a flame is produced. Rusting iron is slower oxidation that produces heat (but not so that you'd notice it under ordinary conditions). When an apple turns brown, oxidation is also fairly slow.

Apples, peaches, pears, and bananas are all easily oxidized. A fresh fruit salad can be protected from oxidation, however, by keeping it from the air or by treating it with vitamin C. Do the next experiment and see how.

Materials & Equipment

- ✦ water
- ✦ 1 chewable vitamin C tablet
- ✦ 1 apple
- ✦ 1 peach or 1 pear
- ✦ 1 banana
- ✦ a small deep bowl
- ✦ a sharp knife
- ✦ a slotted spoon
- ✦ 2 shallow soup bowls

Procedure

1 Put about a cup of water in the small, deep bowl and dissolve the vitamin C tablet in it.

2 Cut the apple in half. Peel and cut out the core of one half quickly. Slice this half into the bowl

of vitamin C solution. Make sure each slice is covered with the solution. Remove the apple slices with a slotted spoon and put them in one of the shallow bowls.

3 Peel, core, and then slice the other half of the apple directly into the other shallow bowl.

4 Repeat this procedure with the other fruits: Slice half into the vitamin C solution and leave slices from the other half untreated. Put all the vitamin C pieces in one bowl and the untreated pieces in the other. Arrange the fruit so that as much surface is exposed to the air as possible.

Let the two fruit salads stand for an hour or more. Watch to see where browning occurs.

Observations

Can you see a difference between the treated and untreated fruit? Why do you think lemon juice is put on apple slices as they are being prepared for apple pie? Do lemons contain vitamin C? Other fruits and vegetables that brown when exposed to air are eggplants, avocados, and raw potatoes. Can you design an experiment to see if vitamin C slows down their oxidation?

Oxidation of fruit is affected by temperature. You can test this by making two fruit salads. Leave one at room temperature and put the other in the refrigerator. Which salad browns first?

The term *oxidation* is used by chemists for any reaction in which substances combine in a manner similar to the way they combine with oxygen. The oxidation reaction of these fruits is sped up because of a certain protein in the fruit known as an *enzyme* (more on enzymes in Chapter 10). Before the fruit is cut, the enzyme and the compounds that will turn brown in the presence of oxygen are separated from each other. But when cells are injured as the fruit is cut, the enzyme and the compounds come in contact with each other and oxidation occurs. The enzyme is not present in melons and citrus fruits. They will eventually turn brown in air, but without the enzyme it takes days instead of minutes.

Fruits that oxidize easily will also react with copper and iron. Put a fruit salad in a copper bowl or an iron pan. Compare the browning of that salad with a fruit salad in a glass or china bowl. Cover these salads with plastic wrap to reduce oxidation with the air.

All the fruit salads in these experiments are good to eat, even if the fruit is discolored. Combine all the fruit when you have finished experimenting. Add a small can of apricots or some fruit syrup and chill before serving.

FRUIT AND TEA PUNCH: TESTING FOR IRON

For most people a test tube symbolizes chemistry. The beauty of the test tube is that it allows the chemist to combine small amounts of material in a vessel where it is easy to see if a chemical reaction takes place.

There are several changes that let you know when a reaction is taking place. In the experiments you have done up to now, you've seen reactions that produce a gas and reactions that produce a color change. Another way is to see a clear solution become cloudy as solid particles form. Such solid particles are called *precipitates*. You will be looking for a precipitate in the next experiment.

If you have a chemistry set with test tubes, use them for this experiment. If you don't, use small, clear, colorless juice glasses.

There are certain chemicals in tea that react with iron compounds in fruit juices to form a precipitate. This precipitate is very annoying if you are preparing a punch made with tea. All too often a crystal-clear iced tea punch becomes cloudy. Although the punch may taste fine, its muddy look is not what the party giver had in mind. Not all fruits contain iron, however. Learn which ones do in the next experiment and keep your iced tea punch sparkling clear.

Materials & Equipment

✦ 2 cups of strong tea
✦ an assortment of fruit juices, including canned and bottled juices, red juices, pineapple juice, and prune juice
✦ juice glasses or test tubes
✦ pen and paper

Procedure

1. Set out a row of small glasses or test tubes and put about an inch of tea in each glass. Label the glasses for each juice you are going to test.

2. You might also want to prepare a data sheet to record your observations. Here is an example of what a data sheet might look like:

FRUIT JUICE	TEST RESULT
orange	–
canned pineapple	–
cranberry	?
cherry Hi-C	?

3 Add about an inch of juice to each glass of tea. Watch for cloudiness. If a precipitate forms, put a plus sign (+) next to the name of the juice on your data sheet. If no precipitate forms and the mixture remains clear, put a minus sign (–). If you are not certain, put a ? on the data sheet and test the juice again. Some juices are cloudy to begin with. Make sure that a new precipitate forms by comparing the tea mixture with a plain sample of juice.

Observations

Which juices contain iron? Do canned juices contain more iron than bottled juices? According to a table of food composition, which tells the various vitamins, minerals, fats, proteins, etc., in food, the juices that contain the most iron are red juices, pineapple juice, and prune juice. Do your findings agree with this?

When you have finished the experiment, pour all the mixtures into a pitcher. Taste it to see if you might like to add more of any particular juice. Add any leftover tea. Pour over ice to serve.

Plants We Eat

All living things need a constant supply of energy in order to stay alive. The source of this energy is food combining with oxygen. The oxidation of food (sugar is an example) is the same basic overall reaction as that of fuel combining with oxygen to produce a fire. (There is, of course, a big difference that I'll tell you about in a minute.) Here's an equation that shows the similarity between the reactions:

sugar (fuel) + oxygen →
carbon dioxide + water + energy (fire)

When a fuel burns, the released energy is rapid and uncontrolled. In living things, there are many steps in the oxidation of food and the energy is released in a carefully controlled manner so that it can be used for the various activities of living. Scientists can measure the amount of energy that can be released from different kinds of food as heat energy. They put weighed amounts of food in a special instrument called a calorimeter. The food is burned with oxygen, and the heat energy given off by the reaction raises the temperature of the water outside the chamber where the food is burning. The change in temperature of the water is a measure of the amount of energy in the food. This heat is measured in calories. If you look in most general cookbooks, you can find a table that lists the calories in different foods. Fats have the most calories and proteins have the least.

We use the energy we get from food for moving and thinking and responding to the world. Energy from food goes into building new molecules of protein and carbohydrates in our bodies. Any leftover energy not used for these activities is used to build fat molecules.

The average growing kid needs between 2,600 and 3,000 calories a day. If you eat more than this and don't do enough to use them up, you will gain weight.

As one organism feeds on another, energy is passed along, forming a food chain linking all forms of life to each other. Meat eaters feed on plant eaters, some microorganisms feed on dead or living organisms, and plant eaters feed on plants. The question is: What organisms are at the bottom of the food chain? These living things must be able to get energy from some source other than feeding on other living things, and they must be able to convert this energy into a substance that is food for themselves. On our planet, the bottom of the food chain is plants.

Green plants produce their own food through a chemical reaction that is the reverse of the reaction in our bodies when we oxidize sugar:

carbon dioxide + water + energy →

sugar + oxygen

The outside source of energy for this reaction is sunlight. Carbon dioxide is present in air, and water is present in soil. The green pigment *chlorophyll* gives plants the ability to make sugar with these raw materials. This process of food manufacturing is called *photosynthesis*, which means "putting together with light."

Plants use the sugar made during photosynthesis to make proteins, other carbohydrates, and oils.

So when animals eat plants they get energy that originally came from the sun. The importance of green plants to all other forms of life on earth is clear. Without them, we could not survive.

The experiments in this chapter will show you some of the activities of plants that help keep them alive.

RAW VEGETABLE SALAD: HOW PLANTS TAKE IN WATER

The roots of a plant have several jobs. Most roots anchor a plant to the ground. Some roots, such as carrots, also store food made in the leaves. But their most important job is to absorb water from the soil.

Look at the tip of a fresh carrot that has not been trimmed or packaged. The main root becomes very slender at the tip, and there are many small roots sticking out from it. Look at these smaller roots with a magnifying glass. There are many tiny branches off each rootlet that increase the surface area of the root so more water can be absorbed. If you can't get an untrimmed carrot, put a fresh carrot, tip down, in a glass of water. It will develop new rootlets in a few days.

Water is absorbed into roots by a process called *osmosis*. In osmosis, water passes through a thin sheet of living material called a *cell membrane*. Cell membranes have holes in them that are larger than water molecules.

If the holes in cell membranes are bigger than water molecules, how come water flows *into* roots when it could just as easily flow *out*? Do the next experiment and discover the answer.

Materials & Equipment

- ✦ a large carrot
- ✦ water
- ✦ salt
- ✦ a vegetable peeler
- ✦ 2 bowls
- ✦ 2 spoons

Procedure

1 Peel the carrot. (Be sure to move the peeler away from your fingers.) Use the peeler to make strips of carrot.

2 Divide the strips between two bowls and add enough water to each bowl to completely

cover the strips. Put about a tablespoon of salt into one of the bowls and stir. The water should taste very salty.

3 Let the carrots soak for several hours. From time to time, take a strip from each bowl and bend it and taste it to see how crisp it is.

Observations

Which carrots are crisper? Which carrots have absorbed water and which have lost water?

The direction water flows in roots depends on the minerals dissolved in the water. When more minerals are inside the roots than in soil water, water flows into the roots, making them firm and crisp. When there are more minerals in the soil water than in roots' cells, water flows *out* of the roots, making them wilted and soft.

You can do many variations of this experiment with other vegetables. Thin slices of cucumber work especially well. Try different amounts of salt to see how fast wilting occurs. Find out if wilting occurs more quickly in warm (not hot) water than in cold water.

You can make a salad with all the vegetables from this experiment. Chill, then drain, the vegetables. Make a dressing of sour cream and fresh chopped dill or parsley, or try the vinaigrette from Chapter 3 (see pages 41–42).

STRIPED CELERY SNACK: HOW WATER MOVES UP STEMS

One of the important jobs of plant stems is to carry water from the roots to the leaves. You can see how this happens with a stalk of celery and some food coloring.

Materials & Equipment

+ celery stalks
+ water
+ food coloring
+ 2 glasses
+ vegetable peeler
+ a knife
+ a plastic sandwich bag

Procedure 1

1 Put a stalk of celery in half a glass of water colored with several drops of red food coloring.

2 When the water has moved all the way up the stem, use a vegetable peeler to shave away the outer surface of the celery.

Observations

Which parts of the stem have the most food coloring? The long strands that carry water are called the *xylem*. Xylem is made of hollow cells that form a

xylem

pipeline from roots to leaves. You can see where the xylem is in celery by cutting across the stalk.

Procedure 2

Repeat this experiment using 2 stalks of celery. One stalk should be quite leafy and the other should have no leaves.

Observations

In which stalk does the water reach the top of the stem first?

Procedure 3

For this experiment use two leafy stalks of celery. Put one glass with its celery stalk in the sunlight and keep the other in the shade, covering the celery with a small plastic bag.

Observations

In which stalk does the water rise more quickly? How do your findings support the theory that the speed with which water rises in plants is a result of how fast water evaporates from the leaves?

You can eat the celery when you have finished your experiments. It's good with some peanut butter or cream cheese spread down the middle.

Try putting other vegetables in colored water. See if you can find the xylem in white radishes, scallions, and carrots. Choose a dark-colored dye that will show up against the color of the vegetables.

SPINACH: COLOR CHANGES IN CHLOROPHYLL

Spinach is a treat for many food lovers. But if you don't love spinach, perhaps it's because it was over-cooked when you had it. When overcooked, spinach is a limp, unappetizing gray-green.

Fresh spinach, on the other hand, is a beautiful, rich green. When it is first put in boiling water, this green brightens as gases in the cells are forced out by heating. After this, the spinach becomes grayer and grayer. Cooking releases certain acids in spinach that change the color of chlorophyll.

The amount of acid that is released during cooking is very small. It would be possible to keep spinach a bright green if this acid could be removed as soon as it was released into the cooking water. A pinch of baking soda added to the cooking water will react with the acid and "neutralize" it. (Try this to see if it works.) Baking soda, however, makes vegetables mushy, so it is not often used.

When chemists want to prevent a solution from becoming too acid or basic, they use another kind of solution called a *buffer*. Buffers can absorb any acid or basic molecules and take them out of a solution as soon as they are released into it. Of course, many buffers used in laboratories are not suitable for eating. But one substance we do eat that can act as a buffer is milk.

Is it possible to preserve the color of spinach by cooking it in milk? Do the next experiment to find out.

Materials & Equipment

- ✦ milk
- ✦ water
- ✦ several fresh, washed spinach leaves
- ✦ a measuring cup
- ✦ 2 saucepans
- ✦ a slotted spoon
- ✦ a white plate

Procedure

1 Put 1 cup of milk in 1 saucepan and 1 cup of water in the other. Warm the liquids over low heat.

2 When they begin to simmer, drop a few leaves of spinach into each pan. Keep the temperature low so that the milk simmers but doesn't boil. Cook the spinach for 4 or 5 minutes. Turn off the heat and let the spinach stay in the hot liquids for another few minutes.

3 Remove the spinach with a slotted spoon to a white plate and compare the colors of the

cooked spinach leaves to each other and to a raw spinach leaf.

Observations

Have the colors changed after cooking? Which seems grayer, the spinach cooked in water or the spinach cooked in milk?

Choose either milk or water to cook the rest of the spinach. Season with salt, pepper, and butter to serve.

BOILED WINTER SQUASH: A STUDY OF CELLULOSE

The experiment you did to show how water gets into plants also showed how water is important for support. Without water, plants become wilted and limp. But in addition to water, plants contain a carbohydrate called *cellulose* that plays an important role in the supporting structure of a plant.

The soft protoplasm of each plant cell is surrounded on all sides by a cell wall made up mainly of cellulose. Cellulose is firmer than protoplasm, and the cell walls help to support a plant against the force of gravity.

Like starches, cellulose is made of chains of sugar

CELL WALL (CELLULOSE)

WATER VACUOLE

PROTOPLASM

molecules linked together. Cellulose would be a good source of food for us if we could digest it but, unfortunately, we can't. The sugar molecules in cellulose are linked together differently than the molecules in starch. Cellulose links make the chain rigid and make it useless to us as food, because our digestive tracts have no way of breaking these links. Some animals, like cows, have microorganisms in their stomachs that can break down the links in a cellulose chain. For this reason, they can live on hay and grass. But the cellulose in plants we eat leaves our bodies pretty much as it entered. It does, however, serve a useful function as fiber—also called roughage—which stimulates our digestive tracts.

The main reason we cook vegetables is to soften the cellulose so that it passes through our bodies more easily. The next experiment shows some of the conditions that change the rate at which cellulose softens during cooking.

Materials & Equipment

- ✦ a small butternut or other hard winter squash
- ✦ water
- ✦ 1 teaspoon vinegar
- ✦ $\frac{1}{2}$ teaspoon baking soda
- ✦ a vegetable peeler
- ✦ a large, sharp knife
- ✦ cutting board
- ✦ a spoon
- ✦ 3 saucepans
- ✦ measuring spoons
- ✦ a slotted spoon
- ✦ a fork
- ✦ a potato masher or electric mixer

Procedure

1 Peel the squash with the vegetable peeler, then cut it in half the long way. Be prepared; it will be hard to cut. Scrape out the seeds and pith with a spoon. Cut the squash into one-inch cubes, trying to keep them a similar size.

2 Divide the squash between 3 saucepans and add enough water to each to cover the squash. Add 1 teaspoon of vinegar to one pan and $\frac{1}{2}$ teaspoon of baking soda to another. The third pan containing only water is a control.

3 Cook all 3 pans over medium heat. Bring each pan to a boil and let it continue boiling while you make your observations.

4 Every few minutes remove a piece of squash from each pan with a slotted spoon. Test it for softness by trying to mash it with a fork.

Observations

Which squash becomes soft first? Does cooking squash in acid speed up the rate of softening cellulose?

When all the squash is cooked, drain it and then mash it with a potato masher or an electric mixer. The squash is good plain, but even better if you add 2 tablespoons butter, 2 tablespoons of brown sugar, and a dash of salt and pepper.

As you might expect, the length of cooking time for vegetables depends on the amount of cellulose in the plant. Leafy vegetables, such as spinach, do not contain much cellulose and need only be cooked a few minutes. Artichokes, on the other hand, are high in cellulose and must be cooked quite a while to get soft. Design an experiment to check this out.

CHOP SUEY:
HOW BEANS SPROUT

One of the main sources of food for people is seeds. Cereal grains, corn, rice, and beans are all seeds. Every seed is a remarkable package. It appears to be very simple. Yet it contains the cells that will become a plant and all the food needed for the baby plant to get a good start. Seeds are able to go through long periods of dryness and extreme cold and still burst with new life when conditions are right.

You can easily create the right conditions for sprouting seeds.

Materials & Equipment

- ✦ ¼ cup dried beans such as lentils, limas, kidneys, or blackeyes
- ✦ water
- ✦ a bowl
- ✦ a colander
- ✦ a clean, unglazed pot (a new flowerpot is good)
- ✦ a saucer to cover the pot

Procedure

1 Put the beans in the bowl and cover with water. Let them soak overnight. The starch in the beans absorbs the water and the beans will swell.

2 The next day, moisten the inside of a new flowerpot with water. Drain the beans in a colander and put them in the flowerpot. In order for

beans to sprout, they must be kept moist but not wet. Cover the pot with the saucer and put it in a closet.

3 Check the beans every day. If they appear dry or develop the smell of fermenting beans, wash them by running water over them in a colander and drain them well. Rinse out the flowerpot before you return the beans to it.

Observations

The first structure to grow from a seed is the root. This anchors the seedling to the ground and makes sure that there will be a continuous supply of water for the growing plant. Beans have two seedling leaves that contain stored food. (Do these contain chlorophyll when they first emerge?) When beans sprout in soil, these thick leaves are pushed up through the soil and become green. They make food until the thinner foliage leaves develop and take over the job. Then the seed leaves shrivel and die.

Additional Procedures

There are many experiments you can do to see how different conditions affect the sprouting of seeds. Put some soaked seeds in the refrigerator and compare them with seeds sprouting at room temperature. Find out if light and darkness affect sprouting. Take a few seeds just when the roots appear and put them between two pieces of moist folded paper towels held together by paper clips. Keep the towels moist and prop them up so the roots are pointed upward, away from the pull of gravity. Watch to see how these roots grow after several days.

Add the sprouts to canned or frozen chop suey and heat just until hot. They should be crisp and delicious.

POPCORN:
MEASURING MOISTURE IN SEEDS

No matter how dry seeds seem to be, all seeds contain a tiny bit of water that keeps the cells alive until conditions are favorable for sprouting. It is this tiny bit of water that makes popcorn popable.

When a kernel of popping corn is heated quickly, the water inside the kernel becomes a gas that exerts pressure strong enough to burst the tough seed coat. Once free of its container, the gas expands rapidly, causing the soft starch in the seed to puff up into millions of tiny rigid-walled bubbles.

What happens to the popability of popcorn

when you change the amount of moisture in the seed? Do the next experiment to find out.

Materials & Equipment

- ✦ fresh popping corn
- ✦ water
- ✦ 9 tablespoons vegetable oil
- ✦ measuring cups and spoons
- ✦ a cookie sheet
- ✦ a jar with a cover
- ✦ a hot air popper or a deep pot with a lid
- ✦ 3 identical 8-ounce glass tumblers
- ✦ a ruler

Procedure

1.

2. MOISTURE

1 Preheat the oven to 200°F. Put ½ cup of popping corn in a single layer on a cookie sheet and bake for 2 hours. (Does any corn pop during the heating? If not, why not?)

2 Put another ½ cup of popping corn in a jar. Add 1 tablespoon of water. Put the cover on the jar and shake it so that the water coats all the seeds. Let the jar stand overnight. Every few hours, give the jar a shake to redistribute the water. (You can let it stand without shaking while you sleep.)

3. MOISTURE/GAS EXPANDING DUE TO HEAT

4.

3 The next day pop the $\frac{1}{2}$ cup of dried corn, the $\frac{1}{2}$ cup of wet corn, and $\frac{1}{2}$ cup of un-treated corn in 3 separate batches. A hot-air pop-per works best, but if you don't have a popper, you can use a deep pot with a cover. Put about 3 table-spoons of vegetable oil on the bottom of the pot and add 2 kernels of popcorn from one batch. Heat the oil over high heat until the 2 kernels pop. Then add the rest of that batch of corn, cover, and shake over lower heat until popping stops. Remove the popcorn from the heat. Repeat for the other two batches.

4 Count 50 popped kernels from the first group into a glass and measure how high the pop-corn reaches. This is a measure of the volume of the popped corn. Measure 50 popped kernals from the other 2 batches in the same way and compare. Which corn has the largest volume? Which has the smallest?

Observations

How does the volume of the heated corn compare to the volume of the moistened corn and the un-treated corn? The amount of moisture in popcorn is crucial to the size of the finished product. Pop-corn manufacturers make it their business to know just how much water is needed. Popcorn is harvested when the moisture is 16–19 percent of the weight of a kernel. The optimal dryness is 13–14.5 percent. Popped corn is more than 25 percent larger than unpopped, and there are two basic shapes for popped corn—butterfly and mushroom. Popcorn pops when inside steam reaches 347°F (175°C) and the pressure is 9 times atmospheric pressure or 135 pounds per square inch. At this point the seed coat ruptures, and the internal starch rapidly expands into bubbles that solidify as they cool.

There are other seeds you can try to pop. Compare expensive popcorn with inexpensive brands. Try popping sweet corn seeds. Put a little oil in the bottom of a deep pot with a cover. Shake the seeds as you heat them. When I popped sweet corn, I got corn nuts. Another seed that pops is amaranth grain, which you can buy at health food stores. Pop them in a pot without oil. Use a magnifying glass to examine the popped amaranth.

Microwave popcorn also lends itself to some experiments . . . coming up in the next chapter.

CHAPTER 149

Microwave Cooking

There are thousands of professional food scientists who make a living working on science experiments you can eat. One of the biggest challenges to these scientists since this book was first published is the microwave oven.

Microwaves are a form of energy that occur in nature in sunlight as well as in the light from all other stars. Microwaves are one kind of *electromagnetic radiation*. Others are visible light, radio waves, X rays, gamma rays, and cosmic rays.

When microwaves come into contact with water molecules, they make the molecules twist their position. Microwave ovens produce a high concentration of microwave radiation, alternating its direction back and forth between 915 and 2,450 million times per second. Water molecules bombarded by microwaves twist back and forth that many times. They move! Increased motion of water molecules becomes heat energy that can cook food. Since the microwaves act directly on the water in food, and not on the container or the air in the oven, the food heats up while the oven itself stays cool. Cooking containers get hot as heat is transferred from the food to the container.

Microwaves in an oven are generated by a device called a *magnetron*, which uses a magnet to make electrons travel rapidly in a circular path. The circling electrons generate microwaves that pass through a wave guide to the top of the oven, where

STIRRER — MAGNETRON

the waves strike a rotating "stirrer" that looks something like a propeller. As the microwaves reflect off the stirrer, they are distributed in all directions into the space of the oven. The waves also bounce off the oven walls. Ideally, the microwaves should be evenly distributed throughout the oven so that food cooks evenly. But in reality, even with stirrers, all microwave ovens have hot spots. Putting food on a rotating carousel is one way to make sure it cooks evenly. You can make a map of the hot spots in your microwave oven with the next experiment.

HONEY CAKE: A MAP OF MICROWAVE HOT SPOTS

A mixture of honey and flour will caramelize to show the places where the microwaves are focused.

Materials & Equipment

- ✦ I cup cake flour
- ✦ I teaspoon baking soda
- ✦ I egg
- ✦ I cup honey
- ✦ measuring cups and spoons
- ✦ mixing bowl
- ✦ a big spoon
- ✦ 9" x 13" glass baking dish

Procedure 1

1 Measure the flour and baking soda into the bowl. Stir in the egg, then the honey to make a smooth mixture.

2 Pour the batter into the baking dish and smooth out the surface so that there is a thin layer that completely covers the bottom.

3 If your microwave has a revolving tray, remove it and then microwave on high for 7 minutes.

Observations

Notice the pattern of browning on the top of the cake. This shows where the microwaves are focused in the oven to form hotter areas. The brownness is due to the caramelizing of the honey. Is the browning on top only, or does it go through the thickness of the cake? What does the browning tell you about the way the inside of the cake is heated compared to the outside? If your microwave has a revolving tray, try cooking another honey cake using the tray. How effective is this method for counteracting the hot spots in your oven?

I cannot recommend this cake for its taste. Microwaving seems to develop the gluten in wheat flour, and it also causes a gummy material to form on the bottom of the cake. You might want to experiment to see if you can improve the recipe by adding butter and substituting another kind of flour for the wheat flour.

Procedure 2

Cover the bottom of a glass baking dish with egg white and watch to see which areas coagulate first. The egg white is edible, but it's even less tasty than the honey cake.

Procedure 3

Microwave heat-sensitive fax paper for about 7 minutes. There's no way "nuked" fax paper can be a science experiment you can eat, but it does give you a map of your microwave's hot spots.

BOILING MICROWAVED WATER WITHOUT HEAT

In an ordinary oven, heat penetrates food from the outside in. Microwaves can penetrate about an inch into whatever you're heating. All the water molecules respond wherever they are struck, so if you boil water in a cup with a 2" diameter, the inside molecules are heated at the same time as the outside molecules (except for the hot spots). This accounts for the speed of microwave heating, the main advantage of the oven.

Water boils when the molecules move fast enough to escape from the surface into the air. When you boil water in a pot, the heat source is at the bottom, and the molecules at the bottom move faster than those at the top. In early stages of heating, the molecules lose some of this motion as they encounter cooler molecules on their rise to the top. Boiling is when bubbles of water vapor collect on the bottom of the pot and rise to the surface.

You can create boiling in microwave-heated water by adding some sugar.

Materials & Equipment

+ 1 cup water
+ $\frac{1}{2}$ teaspoon sugar
+ Pyrex measuring cup
+ measuring spoons

Procedure

1 Fill a Pyrex measuring cup with 1 cup of water and microwave it on high for 2 minutes and 30 seconds.

2 Remove the cup from the oven. Add ½ teaspoon of sugar. See a rush of bubbles come to the surface about a second after you add the sugar.

Observations

When you boil water by microwave, the entire container is evenly heated. Molecules capable of escaping can be right in the middle of the liquid with cooler molecules around the edges, depending on where the hot spots of your oven are located. The sugar crystals act as points of disturbance that bubbles of water vapor form around. The bubbles quickly rise to the surface.

You can also boil water that contains ice. The trick is to put very little water in a Pyrex measuring cup with a lot of ice cubes. Water molecules are free to move when struck by microwaves but frozen water molecules are not. Until the ice is surrounded by enough hot water to liquefy them, they remain solid.

You won't save time trying to microwave frozen soup. In fact, liquid soup can boil away before a solid block of frozen soup melts. Defrosting by microwave consists of alternating a blast of microwaves with a period of no microwaves. The heat picked up by liquid water molecules is transferred to liquefy adjacent frozen molecules during the resting period.

MICROWAVING AWAY STALENESS

As bread ages, it gets stale. The moisture in the bread evaporates, and the bread dries out. Also as time passes, the starch in bread recrystallizes, causing it to become hard or stale. Temperature is one variable that affects staling. Bread will get stale faster at lower temperatures that are above freezing than at room temperature. So putting bread in the refrigerator can hasten its staling, not preserve it. Freezing almost completely stops staling. Can you design an experiment to test this idea?

Stale starch crystals melt at 140°F (60°C). Reheating stale bread seems like a good solution, but even more moisture will be lost, making the bread dryer. But you can freshen stale bread in a microwave: Sprinkle it with water, wrap it in a paper towel, and heat it 5–10 seconds on high.

Microwaving causes water molecules to migrate through food and condense on the surface. This tends to make the surfaces of baked goods gummy instead of crisp. Paper towels wrapped around food absorb some of the surface moisture and keep baked goods from becoming soggy. Microwave ovens destroy a crisp crust. But don't take my word for it; try it and see for yourself. The reason cakes and breads baked in microwaves don't brown is because water at their surfaces makes them too cool to brown.

You can also freshen bread in a regular oven if you sprinkle it with water, wrap it in foil, and heat it for 3–4 minutes.

MICROWAVE POPCORN

The heating ability of microwaves was discovered accidentally by Dr. Percy Spencer, a researcher on shortwave electromagnetic energy for the Raytheon Company. He was visiting a laboratory that made magnetrons for radar tracking devices. He noticed that the microwaves from a magnetron melted a piece of candy in his pocket. He sent out for a bag of popcorn, which popped when he put it near the magnetron. Although many radar engineers were aware of the heating properties of microwaves, Spencer was the first to apply them to cooking food. Raytheon went on to build the first microwave ovens in 1946. And the rest, as they say, is history.

One of the most successful products designed for the microwave oven is popcorn. The key to microwaved popcorn is not in the corn but in the bag. Do the following experiments to learn more about popcorn and its amazing microwavable bag.

Materials & Equipment

- ✦ a package of microwave popcorn
- ✦ ½ cup ordinary popping corn
- ✦ scissors
- ✦ waxed paper
- ✦ measuring cup
- ✦ 2 large glass bowls
- ✦ plastic wrap
- ✦ a small, sharp knife
- ✦ pot holders

Procedure

1 Cut open the end of a microwave popcorn bag. Empty the contents onto a piece of waxed paper. Notice that the kernels are embedded in a solid, fatty material.

2 Put about ½ cup of embedded kernels in the bottom of a glass bowl. Seal the top with plastic wrap. Make a small slit in the middle of the plastic wrap with a knife.

3 Put the ordinary popping corn in the other glass bowl. Cover this bowl with plastic wrap as well and make a vent.

4 Microwave each bowl of corn separately on high for 4 minutes. Remove the bowls with pot holders. Carefully pull off the plastic wrap. **Warning**: There is a lot of steam trapped in the bowls. Loosen the wrap on the side of the bowl farthest from you and pull it back slowly. This way your hands and arms will not be exposed to the steam.

Observations

In each sample, see how many unpopped kernels (UPKs) there are. There are about 200 kernels in $\frac{1}{2}$ cup of popcorn, so you can calculate the percentage of UPKs with the following formula:

(Number of UPKs ÷ 200) x 100 =
the percent of UPKs

The solid fatty material that the microwave popcorn comes in converts microwave energy into heat energy and is in direct contact with the kernels. Since the kernels are not agitated as they are in an air popper or when you shake a pot over a flame, the fatty material makes sure that the kernels are all heated fairly evenly. But microwave popcorn still has a higher percentage of UPKs than popcorn popped in oil. (Can you design an experiment to check out this idea?)

The popcorn that is popped dry still pops, but there is usually an even higher percentage of UPKs, and there is also a higher percentage of kernels that are not completely popped.

Food engineers went to work: How could the number of UPKs be reduced? They discovered that the key was not the popcorn but the design of the bag. For more kernels to pop, you need to concentrate the heat. You are instructed to place the bag in the oven with a particular side down. Cut the bag close to the center panel that is supposed to rest on the oven floor. Tear it toward the center. Notice that the bag is made of three layers. The outer layer is a grease-resistant paper. The inner layer is a grease-proof paper. The middle layer is a polyester film embedded with a light layer of aluminum. The film absorbs microwaves and

becomes hot. An interesting aside: The Stealth bomber is coated with a ceramic embedded with aluminum that absorbs the microwaves of radar and allows the plane to avoid being tracked.

Popcorn also needs space. The problem the engineers faced was how to design a package that could be compact on the supermarket shelf yet be large enough to give the popcorn room to pop. The answer is in the expandable, pleated bag. If the volume of a container is restricted, the popcorn will not pop as large. Can you design an experiment to test this idea?

Microbes

ver clean out the refrigerator and discover that some once-appetizing foods are now mushy, fuzzy, or foul smelling? Now imagine what our ancestors, who had no refrigerators, had to deal with. Your senses find rotting food unpleasant for good reason: It can make you sick.

Cooking was one way our ancestors tried to delay spoilage. Strong spices and herbs were used to mask the flavor of tainted meat and fish. It is not surprising that the strongest spices, like pepper, chili, and curry, were first used in warm climates, where food spoils more quickly than in colder parts of the world.

But not all the changes in food left to stand were unpleasant. Milk could be made into cheese, grape juice could become wine, flour and water paste developed bubbles and became bread when baked. These pleasant changes became ways of preserving food also. Cheese and wine could be eaten months after they were prepared. Dry grain could be stored without rotting to be ground into flour at some later time. In days where there were no such things as canning, freezing, or refrigerating food, cheese, bread, and wine were a protection against famine. They were among the most important foods of early civilizations.

The change in grape juice as it became wine was so well known that it had its own name, *fermentation*, meaning "to boil." As grape juice ferments, tiny bubbles form that are similar to the bubbles in boiling liquids, except that the grape juice is not hot. Although people have known how to make wine for centuries, it wasn't until the middle of the nineteenth century, when something went wrong with the wine industry of France, that we began to understand what caused grape juice to ferment.

The problem was that some wine went sour as it aged. Since the spoiled wine was prepared in exactly the same way as wine that was good, the wine makers couldn't understand how the spoiling occurred. In desperation, they called in a great scientist, Louis Pasteur (1822–1895), to try to solve their problem.

Pasteur studied the wine in good vats and in spoiled vats. He found that both fermentation and wine spoilage were products of living things, *microbes*, that could be seen only with a microscope. The microbe that fermented grape juice into wine used sugar from the grapes as food and produced alcohol and carbon dioxide as waste products. The microbes that spoiled the wine used alcohol formed by the first microbes as food. It was the wastes of these second microbes that gave the wine a bad taste.

To solve the wine makers' problem Pasteur made the following suggestion: Kill the microbes by heating the wine gently to denature the protein in the microbes but not hot enough to boil the wine. This heating process, called *pasteurization*, is a standard procedure today for killing harmful microbes in dairy products, beer, and wine.

Microbes are everywhere—in air, in water, in soil, in our bodies. The study of microbes has touched on all aspects of human life, including agriculture, medicine, chemical products for industry, and biotechnical engineering as well as food preparation and preservation. The experiments in this chapter will show you how microbes act in some of the foods we eat.

SALLY LUNN BREAD: A STUDY OF YEAST ACTIVITY

Yeasts are one-celled plants that are distant cousins of mushrooms. Like mushrooms and other plants that do not contain chlorophyll, yeasts cannot make their own food and must get it from their surroundings. When conditions are not favorable, yeasts become inactive, only to spring to life when conditions are right.

The products of fermentation, alcohol and carbon dioxide, are of utmost importance to the wine maker and the baker. The wine maker is interested in alcohol production and the baker is interested in carbon dioxide, for it is this gas that makes bread rise.

The next experiment is designed to show what food yeasts need for growth. Other essential conditions for growth—temperature and moisture—will be made as favorable as possible.

Materials & Equipment

- ✦ I package of dry yeast
- ✦ water
- ✦ I tablespoon sugar
- ✦ I tablespoon corn syrup
- ✦ I tablespoon cornstarch

- ✦ measuring cups and spoons
- ✦ a candy thermometer
- ✦ 3 6-ounce glasses
- ✦ 3 spoons
- ✦ a large pot

Procedure

1 Dissolve the yeast in ½ cup of 110°F water. Divide the yeast mixture equally between the 3 glasses.

2 Put 1 tablespoon of sugar in the first glass, 1 tablespoon of corn syrup in the next glass, and 1 tablespoon of cornstarch in the third glass. Stir each glass with a different spoon.

3 Set up a warm-water bath for the yeast in the large pot. Put enough 110°F water in the pot to

come about halfway up the sides of the glasses containing the yeast mixture, as shown in the illustration.

Be sure not to let any of the water from the bath get into the glasses. The bath water will cool slowly, but the temperature will remain warm long enough to generate active fermentation.

Measure fermentation by the size of the bubbles in the foam and the rate at which they form.

Observations

The material a microbe uses as food is called a *substrate*. Which substrate in your experiment starts being fermented first? Which substrate has the steadiest rate of fermentation? Can you smell the alcohol produced by fermentation?

Glucose is the principle food of yeast used for baking. When yeast comes into contact with glucose, fermentation begins immediately. Glucose is present in corn syrup. Yeast can also get glucose from sucrose (table sugar) and starch, but it takes longer to get going, as sucrose and starch have to be broken down into simpler sugars before fermentation can occur. How do your findings support this idea?

Materials & Equipment

+ ½ cup milk
+ 1 stick (½ cup) butter

+ all the mixtures from the preceding experiment

+ about 3½ cups flour
+ 1 teaspoon salt
+ 3 eggs
+ a medium-sized saucepan
+ a candy thermometer
+ a large bowl
+ an electric mixer
+ a damp, clean dish towel
+ an 8" x 4" x 2" loaf pan
+ a sharp knife
+ a wire rack

Procedure

1 Put the milk and butter in a saucepan and heat until the milk is about 85°F. Don't let the milk get too hot, or you will kill the yeast.

2 Pour all 3 glasses from your experiment into a large bowl and add the milk-and-butter mixture.

3 Add about a cup of the flour and the salt to the liquids. Mix at low speed with an electric mixer. When all the flour is moistened, beat the batter for about 2 minutes at a medium speed to develop the gluten.

4 Beat in the eggs and add another cup of flour. Finally add enough of the remaining flour to make a stiff batter that can still be stirred.

5 Cover the bowl with a moist, clean dish towel and place in a warm spot to rise.

While the batter is rising, grease the loaf pan and sprinkle a few tablespoons of flour on the pan.

Shake it so that the flour evenly coats all sides of the pan, and dump out any extra flour.

6 Let the batter rise until it doubles in size—about an hour. Then punch it down with your fist. What gives the batter its stretchy consistency? Examine the air pockets in the batter. Are they evenly distributed? Are there larger air pockets near the source of heat?

7 Beat the batter for about 30 seconds. Put the batter in the loaf pan, cover with the dish towel, and let it rise again until it has doubled in size (about an hour). Preheat the oven to 325°F.

8 Bake the bread at 325°F for about 50 minutes. It is done when the sides draw slightly away from the sides of the pan. Run a sharp knife around the bread as soon as you take it from the oven. Remove the bread from the pan and let it cool on a wire rack. Sally Lunn bread is best served while still warm.

PRETZELS:
INHIBITING YEAST ACTION

When you add other chemicals to the yeast environment, you can affect fermentation. The next experiment shows how.

Materials & Equipment

- ✦ I package of dry yeast
- ✦ water
- ✦ ½ teaspoon sugar
- ✦ ¼ teaspoon salt
- ✦ a candy thermometer

- ✦ measuring cups and spoons
- ✦ 3 small glasses
- ✦ 3 spoons
- ✦ a large pot

Procedure

1 Dissolve the yeast in I cup of 110°F water. Divide the yeast solution between the 3 glasses.

2 Put ¼ teaspoon sugar in the first glass and ¼ teaspoon salt plus ¼ teaspoon sugar in the second glass. Leave the third glass untreated as a control. Stir each glass with a different spoon.

3 Make a warm-water bath as you did for the previous experiment. Put the 3 glasses in the water bath and watch for fermentation activity.

Observations

Which glass has the most activity? Which glass has the least? Does salt inhibit yeast activity? How can you tell?

Use this experiment to make pretzels.

Materials & Equipment

- yeast mixtures from your experiment
- about 4½ cups flour
- vegetable oil
- 1 egg yolk, beaten
- 1 tablespoon water
- coarse (kosher) salt
- 2 large bowls
- a big spoon
- a clean, damp dish towel
- a cookie sheet
- a small bowl
- a whisk or fork
- a pastry brush

Procedure

1 Pour the contents of your experiment into a large bowl. Add between 4 and 4½ cups flour. Mix to form a stiff dough.

2 Knead the dough on a floured surface for about 8 minutes. Kneading develops the gluten, which is the only protein that supports pretzels. (Sally Lunn bread has milk and eggs to help do this job.) To knead, turn the dough out onto a

floured surface and rub some flour on your hands to keep them from sticking to the dough. Fold over, toward you, the side of the dough farthest from you. Push the fold into the rest of the dough with the heel of your hand. Give the dough a quarter turn and repeat the motion. Dough that has been properly kneaded is no longer sticky but smooth and elastic.

3 Oil a large bowl and put in the kneaded dough, turning it so the surface becomes slightly oiled and will not dry out. Cover the dough with a clean, damp towel. Let it rise in a warm place until it doubles in size.

4 While the dough is rising, grease the cookie sheet and make the egg mixture: Separate an egg. In a small bowl or custard cup beat the yolk together with 1 tablespoon of water using a whisk or a fork.

5 When the dough is finished rising, punch it down with your fist. Break off balls of dough and roll them between your hands into long ropes. Then shape them into pretzels and put them on the cookie sheet. You can make many different shapes.

6 Use a pastry brush to paint each pretzel with the egg yolk mixture. Sprinkle the pretzels with coarse salt.

7 Preheat the oven to 475°F. Let the pretzels rise again in a warm place until they have almost doubled in size. Then bake them for about 10 minutes or until the pretzels are firm and golden brown.

A COMPARISON OF YOGURT CULTURES

Bacteria are one-celled microbes that are smaller than yeast. Bacteria, like yeast, must also get food from their surroundings, and they can use many substances as food. Some even live on such unappetizing materials as rubber and petroleum. The bacteria you'll be experimenting with live on milk.

Milk is a mixture of many substances—water, proteins, fats, and a sugar, found only in milk, known as *lactose*. Certain bacteria feed on lactose and give off *lactic acid* as a waste product.

As lactic-acid bacteria grow, more and more lactic acid collects, giving the milk a sour taste, typical of acids. What is even more striking than the change in taste is the change in texture. Lactic acid causes milk proteins to become denatured, making the milk thicker and thicker. Such cultured milk, called yogurt, has a nutty, sour taste and a custardy texture.

Frozen yogurt has become a popular dessert. But the first frozen yogurts were simply frozen versions of traditional yogurt, and they did not sell. People did not like sour ice cream. The successful versions on the market today use different strains of bacteria in the culture. Culture your own yogurt at home using two different starter cultures to see what the difference really is.

It is simple to make yogurt at home. The recipe that follows is certain to produce good results because you will be creating ideal conditions for the growth of lactic-acid bacteria.

Materials & Equipment

+ $\frac{1}{2}$ gallon skim milk
+ $\frac{1}{2}$ cup of commercially prepared plain yogurt
+ I cup melted vanilla frozen yogurt
+ a saucepan
+ a candy thermometer
+ measuring cups
+ 2 medium-sized bowls
+ 2 spoons
+ 2 clean I$\frac{1}{2}$-quart glass jars with covers
+ labels
+ a pen
+ 2 dish towels
+ I insulated picnic cooler

Procedure

1 Warm the milk in the pan over low heat until a skin forms (160°F). This kills any bacteria that may cause the milk to spoil before the yogurt forms. Let the milk cool until it is 110°F.

2 Mix ½ cup of yogurt and 1 cup of the warm milk in a bowl. Next, mix 1 cup of melted frozen yogurt with 1 cup of warm milk in another bowl. Divide the remaining warm milk equally between the 2 glass jars.

3 Stir each of the starter cultures into a different jar of milk. Label the jars so you know which contains the plain yogurt starter culture and which contains the frozen yogurt starter culture.

4 Wrap each jar in a dish towel and place in the cooler. Cover the cooler and check your yogurt after about 6 hours. The yogurt is finished when it moves away from the side of the container in one piece if you tilt it. Refrigerate the finished yogurt to stop the growth of the bacteria.

Observations

Which culture finished first? Which was more sour? How does the consistency compare? Look at the labels on the original containers of both yogurts. Which type has more ingredients? The plain yogurt uses a strain of bacteria called *Lactobacillus acidophilus*. Frozen yogurts don't usually identify the microbes they use, but it is normally a combination of *Streptococcus thermophilus* and *Lactobacillus bulgaricus* in secret proportions.

The recipe produced good results because you created ideal conditions for the growth of lactic-acid bacteria. Try making yogurt at different temperatures. Compare yogurt made with fresh whole milk, condensed milk, and powdered milk. Find out what happens when you add sugar to the milk. Use different brands of commercially prepared yogurt as starter cultures. Try using acidophilus powders or capsules from a health food store as starter cultures. See how many generations of yogurt you can produce from the yogurt you make. Use red-cabbage indicator to measure changes in acidity as the culture grows.

Your yogurt may be eaten plain or mixed with fresh fruit, fruit preserves, honey, maple syrup, or a small amount of defrosted concentrated orange juice.

Enzymes

In 1897 Eduard Buechner, a German chemist, ground up some yeast cells and made an extract from them. He put this extract in grape juice and found, to his astonishment, that the grape juice still fermented. For the first time, glucose became alcohol and carbon dioxide without using living cells. The substance in Buechner's extract that caused fermentation was called *enzyme*, from the Greek roots *en* and *zyme* meaning "leavened."

Today we think of enzymes as the molecules that control the countless numbers of chemical reactions in living organisms. The role of enzymes becomes impressive when you take a close look at a few of the reactions that take place in a living thing. The oxidation of food, for example, does not burn in your body the way it burns in a calorimeter. If it did, a piece of chocolate cake containing 400 calories would raise the body temperature of a 100-pound person to about 117°F, high enough to cause death. In your body, food combines with many different substances in a chain of reactions in which a little energy is released with each step. Controlled release of energy during the oxidation of food allows this energy to be used for the work that the body does in all its activities, including movement, digestion, repair of injured tissues, sensing the environment, and so on. Without enzymes, life is not possible.

RENNET CUSTARD: A STUDY OF ENZYME ACTION

One of the first steps in the digestion of milk is denaturing milk protein, or curdling it, so it becomes more solid. If milk remained a liquid, it would quickly pass through the stomach before it could be digested. But curdled milk moves slowly enough for digestion to take place.

A great many things will denature milk protein,

including heat and acids. In the stomachs of mammals, milk protein is denatured by an enzyme called *rennin* (or, commercially, *rennet*).

Rennet used to be prepared commercially from the linings of calves' stomachs. But today you can buy vegetable-based rennet tablets in some health food stores. They are used for preparing cottage cheese and thickening milk desserts. The next experiment will show you some of the properties of enzymes by varying the conditions necessary for the enzyme to work.

Materials & Equipment

- ✦ 3 teaspoons water
- ✦ vegetable-based liquid rennet
- ✦ 1½ cups whole milk
- ✦ 6 teaspoons sugar
- ✦ vanilla
- ✦ measuring cups and spoons
- ✦ 3 6-ounce clear custard cups
- ✦ masking tape
- ✦ a pen or marker
- ✦ a spoon
- ✦ a saucepan
- ✦ a candy thermometer

Procedure

1 Put 1 teaspoon of water in each of the 3 cups. Add a drop of rennet to each and swirl to mix. Label each cup, using masking tape. They should read: "cold," "110°F," and "160°F."

2 Put $\frac{1}{2}$ cup cold milk in a measuring cup. Add 2 teaspoons sugar and a dash (less than $\frac{1}{4}$ teaspoon) of vanilla and stir well. Pour the mixture into the cup labeled "cold" and stir well.

3 Mix another $\frac{1}{2}$ cup of milk with sugar and vanilla. Warm this in a saucepan until its temperature is 110°F. Pour into the cup labeled "110°F" and stir well.

4 Make another milk mixture and heat this one to 160°F. Pour into the remaining cup and stir well. Let the mixtures stand, without disturbing them, until they set (if they do).

Observations

In which cup does the custard become firm most quickly? In which does it fail to set? How does this support the idea that enzymes are proteins? (Hint: What happens to proteins when they are heated to a high temperature?) What does this tell you about the amount of an enzyme needed to cause a reaction? Try the experiment with two drops of rennet and see if it makes a difference.

Do an experiment to see if rennet will work on other proteins. Substitute soybean milk, skim milk, non-fat dry milk, or evaporated milk. Suppose you denature the milk some other way, like boiling it. Let the boiled milk cool to 110°F before adding it to the rennet. How do your findings support the idea that rennin, like many other enzymes, controls only one reaction—in this case, denaturing milk protein?

CUT APPLES: KIWI STOPS THE BROWNING

The browning-of-fruit reaction studied in Vitamin C Fruit Salad (see Chapter 6, pages 121–25) is more complicated than simple oxidation. An enzyme called *polyphenol oxidase* is involved. This enzyme causes certain compounds in cells to react with oxygen and become brown or gray. The reaction is similar to human skin turning brown in the sun. When the cells are intact, the enzyme and the compounds in the tissues (the phenols) are not in contact. When you cut an apple, the enzyme is released to act on the phenols and the browning reaction starts.

Is there any way to stop or slow down enzymatic browning? Do the next experiment and find out.

Materials & Equipment

- ✦ a kiwifruit
- ✦ an apple
- ✦ a knife
- ✦ a new sponge
- ✦ scissors

Procedure

1 Peel the brown skin off the kiwi and slice the fruit.

2 Cut out a piece of sponge about the same size as a slice of kiwi.

3 Cut the apple in half. Place a slice of kiwi on the cut surface of one half of the apple. Place the piece of sponge on the cut surface of the other half of the apple. Wait at least 1 hour, or until the exposed surface of the apple is brown. Lift the sponge and the piece of kiwi.

Observations

What color is the apple under the kiwi and under the sponge? The sponge was the control so that you could see what happens when the surface is shielded from the air. Is shielding from air sufficient to slow down the browning reaction? There obviously is some substance in the kiwi that interferes with the browning reaction. In lemons that substance is vitamin C, also called ascorbic acid. Kiwis are another source of this compound. You might want to compare how kiwis, lemons, and a solution of vitamin C slow down enzymatic browning in apples. Design an experiment to do this.

JELL-O WITH PINEAPPLE: HOW HEAT AFFECTS AN ENZYME

If you read the instructions on a box of Jell-O, you are warned never to add fresh or frozen pineapple to the dessert. This warning is a perfect opening for a science experiment. Fresh pineapple contains an enzyme called bromelain that breaks down proteins. Gelatin desserts are protein, and the bromelain in fresh pineapple would break down the protein so the dessert wouldn't gel. Since the enzymes themselves are also protein, it makes sense that heat can denature the enzyme and make it inactive. Do the next experiment to see the effect of heat on enzyme action.

Materials & Equipment

- ✦ a fresh, ripe pineapple
- ✦ a package of Jell-O
- ✦ water
- ✦ a large, sharp knife
- ✦ 6 clear plastic cups
- ✦ a marker
- ✦ a plate
- ✦ a small saucepan
- ✦ a bowl
- ✦ measuring cups and spoons

Procedure

1 Since pineapples are difficult to cut, get an adult to help you. Cut the pineapple into quarters. Taking one quarter, cut away the rind and the hard, inner core. Then cut the fruit into bite-sized pieces. Make them all the same size.

2 You are going to heat the pieces of pineapple different lengths of time in the microwave. Raw pineapple will be the control. So mark one of the plastic cups "raw" and put 2 pieces of fresh pineapple into that cup. Mark the rest of the cups as follows: "10 seconds," "30 seconds," "1 minute," "2 minutes," and "boiled."

3 Put 8 pieces of pineapple on a plate in the microwave oven. Microwave on high for 10 seconds. Quickly remove 2 pieces and put them in the cup marked "10 seconds." Immediately microwave the remaining pineapple on high for 20 seconds. Remove 2 pieces and put them in the cup marked "30 seconds." Microwave the remaining pineapple for 30 seconds and then remove 2 pieces and put them in the cup marked "1 minute." Microwave the last 2 pieces for another minute. Remove them and put them in the cup marked "2 minutes."

4 Next put 2 pieces of pineapple in a small saucepan. Cover with water and boil them for 5 minutes. Drain off the water, and place these pieces in the last cup, marked "boiled."

5 Mix the Jell-O according to the directions on the package. Spoon 4 tablespoons of liquid Jell-O into each cup, then put them in the refrigerator to cool.

Observations

Which cups gelled? Do your findings support the idea that a high temperature alone is not enough to "kill" an enzyme? Is the length of time the enzyme is exposed to a high heat also a factor?

Other fruits also contain protein-splitting enzymes. Design an experiment using Jell-O to see which fruits they are.

BAKED STEAK: ACIDS, BASES, AND ENZYME ACTION

Papain is an enzyme that is commercially prepared from papayas, a tropical fruit. It is one of a number of enzymes found in plants and animals that break down proteins. For this reason, papain is sold as a meat tenderizer.

The purpose of the next experiment is to answer two questions: Is meat treated with papain more tender than untreated meat? Does an acid or a base have an effect on the tenderizing activity of papain?

Of course, to answer these questions we have to have a way of measuring meat tenderness. Here's where science gets creative. I tried cutting the meat with a knife and piercing it with a fork and estimating the force I needed. But this kind of measurement is very subjective and inaccurate. So I finally came up with feeding my experiment to an unsuspecting friend, one piece of meat at a time, and counting the number of chews before swallowing. The tenderer the meat, the fewer the chews.

Needless to say, counting chews is not the most precise method of measuring tenderness. Two pieces of meat, prepared in exactly the same manner, might require different numbers of chews depending on the size of the pieces, whether or not there was gristle, how it tasted, how dry the chewer's mouth was, whether or not the chewer expected it to be tender, and how hungry the chewer was.

Since there are so many known possibilities of error, the procedure for this experiment is the most elaborate one in this book. You will be taking precautions wherever possible to reduce the sources of error.

Materials & Equipment

- ³/₄ pound round steak. (When you buy the steak, look for the most evenly red piece with very little fat and gristle and a uniform thickness.)
- water
- ³/₄ teaspoon unseasoned meat tenderizer
- vinegar
- baking soda
- a sharp knife
- a cutting board
- a fork
- 6 bowls
- index cards
- pencil and paper
- 5 juice glasses
- measuring spoons
- 5 spoons
- scissors
- a broiling pan
- 6 plates
- a pot with a cover
- barrier for table
- A hungry friend who doesn't know anything about your experiment. Tell your friend you will call when you are ready.

Procedure

1 Trim any fat and gristle from the meat and cut the trimmed meat into ³/₄-inch cubes. Try to keep the size of the cubes as uniform as possible. Pierce each piece of meat twice with a fork. (This is to allow the solutions you will be putting on the meat to penetrate inside.) Mix up all the cubes of meat in a pile.

2 Set the 6 bowls in a row. Deal out the cubes of meat, as you would deal cards, into the 6 bowls to form 6 equal groups of meat cubes. Try and get the same number in each group. If you have any extra pieces, put them in the last (control) group. Set an index card above each bowl and number the groups 1 through 6.

3 Put juice glasses in front of groups 1 through 5 and put 2 tablespoons of water in each glass. Put 2 tablespoons of water on the meat in group 6.

Put ¼ teaspoon of meat tenderizer in the glasses in front of groups 1, 2, and 3.

¼ Teaspoon
Meat Tenderizer

¼ Teaspoon
Meat Tenderizer
½ Teaspoon
Vinegar

¼ Teaspoon
Meat Tenderizer
½ Teaspoon
Baking Soda

½ Teaspoon
Vinegar

½ Teaspoon
Baking Soda

2 TABLESPOONS
Water

Put ½ teaspoon of vinegar in the solutions for groups 2 and 4.

Put ½ teaspoon baking soda in the glasses for groups 3 and 5.

So, the solutions you've created for each group are:

Group 1: Meat tenderizer and water

Group 2: Meat tenderizer, acid, water

Group 3: Meat tenderizer, base, water

Group 4: Acid, water

Group 5: Base, water

Group 6: Water

Stir each solution with a different spoon and pour over its group of meat cubes. Be sure to thoroughly moisten all the meat in each group.

4 Preheat the oven to 400°F. Let the meat stand in the solutions while the oven is preheating and you complete the next step.

5 The order in which each piece of meat is chewed can affect your results. The best way to reduce this source of error is to present the pieces of meat in a completely random order. Here's one way to come up with a random list of numbers:

a Cut index cards into as many small squares as the *total number* of pieces of meat in your experiment. If you have 6 groups of 10 pieces each, you will need 60 small squares.

b Put the numeral "1" on as many squares of card as you have pieces of meat in group 1. If you have 10 pieces, 10 squares of index card should be marked "1." Do the same for groups 2, 3, 4, 5, and 6.

c Put all the numbered squares in a bowl. Cover the bowl and shake it to mix up all the squares. Draw out one square at a time, without looking, and mark down the number on a piece of paper. The order might look something like this:

4, 4, 6, 6, 6, 2, 1, 1, 3, 5, 6, 4, etc.

6 After you have made out your table of random numbers, drain the solutions from each bowl and put the drained meat on the broiling pan in separate groups. Keep the groups in the right order so you know which is which. Arrange the meat in a single layer with the pieces spaced fairly evenly so all the pieces will be heated the same amount. Bake for 15 minutes.

7 While the meat is baking, prepare a sheet of paper to record your data:

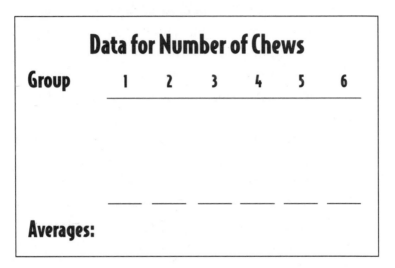

Data for Number of Chews

Group	1	2	3	4	5	6

Averages:

Test the meat for doneness by pressing with a fork. It should be springy and firm. Meat that is rare will be softer, as all the protein has not been set by heat.

8 Put each group of cubes on a plate and label it using your numbered index cards again. Set up a table with some kind of barrier so your friend cannot see where each piece comes from. Get your data sheet and pencil, your table of random numbers and call your friend.

9 Show your friend where to sit. Say: "I'm going to give you pieces of baked steak to eat. I am testing the meat for tenderness. Please count the number of chews you need for each piece before you swallow it. Chew as naturally as possible."

Your table of random numbers tells you the order of choosing pieces of meat. If the first three numerals were 4, 4, 6, you would give your friend a piece from Group 4, another piece from Group 4, and a piece from Group 6, in that order. Check off each number on your table as your friend chews the meat.

Record the number of chews for each piece in the proper column on your data sheet. When you have the data for all the pieces of meat, take the average for each group.

Observations

Was meat treated with tenderizer more tender than untreated meat? (Compare the averages for Group 1 and Group 6.) Did acid or base alone affect meat tenderness? (Compare Groups 4 and 5 with Group 6.) Did acid have an effect on the action of the enzyme? (Compare Groups 1 and 2.) Did a base have an effect on enzyme action? (Compare Groups 1 and 3.)

If you are not certain of your results, compare

them with the data on the next page that I obtained when I did the experiment. Your numbers may be very different, but you probably will come to the same conclusions.

You can use the procedure for this experiment to test many other substances. See if you get similar results with another acid, such as vitamin C. Try the experiment on other kinds of meat. Find out if the enzyme has any other effect on meat, like juiciness. Can you think of a way to modify the procedure so that you can measure juiciness? You might find using another kind of meat, like hamburger, useful for studying the enzyme's effect on juiciness. You might also do an experiment to see if you can denature the enzyme by heating it. Boil an enzyme solution before you put it on the meat and compare its activity with an unheated enzyme in solution.

Data for Number of Chews

Group	1	2	3	4	5	6
	26	42	25	54	44	45
	35	33	28	53	22	29
	29	25	20	48	27	54
	32	35	18	30	47	37
						60
Averages:	30.5	33.75	22.75	46.25	35.0	45.0

Cooking Terms and Instructions

basting: To moisten food while it cooks, so that the surface doesn't dry out and flavor is added, coat it with its own juices or a prepared marinade. A pastry brush is helpful, but you can also use a spoon.

beating egg whites: Start with egg whites that are at room temperature. It is best to use an electric mixer for beating egg whites. (If you don't have one, use an egg beater or a wire whisk. You might want to have a friend handy to help when your arm gets tired.) Beat the whites on low speed until they become foamy, then increase the speed gradually to high and beat until the whites become stiff. They should have a glossy surface and will stand in peaks when you lift the beater slowly from the bowl. Don't overbeat egg whites or they will start to dry out.

boiling: When a liquid boils, bubbles are constantly rising to the surface and breaking.

creaming: Creaming is used to mix a shortening like butter with other ingredients such as sugar until well blended. It is easiest to cream butter with an electric mixer, and the mixture will be fluffier and lighter in color if you do. If you don't have an electric mixer, you can do it by hand with a large spoon (a wooden spoon works well) and a lot of muscle. Either way you should start with softened butter. To cream by hand, press down on the butter with the back of the spoon, drawing the spoon towards you across the bottom of the bowl. Turn the bowl as you go and periodically scrape around the sides of the bowl to collect the ingredients in the middle again. Continue creaming until the mixture is thoroughly combined and smooth.

cutting in: Cutting in is done to distribute solid fat in flour by using a pastry blender or two knives until flour-coated fat particles are the size you want. If you have a pastry blender, roll the blades along the bottom of the bowl, then lift it up, turn the bowl and slice down again. You'll need to stop and scrape off the blender and bring all the ingredients into the center every few turns. If you're using two knives, take a knife in each hand. Start with your hands close together over the center of the bowl then move them apart, drawing the two blades across each other, scraping the bottom of the bowl as you go.

dropping by spoonfuls: Take a spoonful of batter for cookies or biscuits and push it off onto your baking sheet with another spoon or your fingers. Leave a couple of inches between drops to give them room to spread out as they bake.

folding: Folding is a way to combine delicate ingredients such as whipped cream or beaten egg whites with other foods without losing too much of the volume and the air bubbles. Add the whipped ingredient to the heavier ingredient and, using a rubber spatula, cut down into the mixture, slide across the bottom of the bowl, and bring some of the mixture up and over the surface. Give the bowl a quarter turn and repeat this circular motion. Continue to fold just until the two ingredients are combined. If you fold too much, you'll lose more air than necessary, and your cake won't rise as high.

kneading dough: Flour your hands liberally, then turn the dough out onto a lightly floured surface and shape it into a ball. Pull the far end of the dough toward you, folding it over. Then, using the heels of your hands, push it away with a rolling motion. Give the dough a quarter turn and continue folding and pushing the dough, adding flour as necessary to keep the dough from sticking. Get yourself into a rhythm and use your whole body, not just your arms, when you knead. You'll need to knead for about ten minutes to make the dough smooth and elastic.

measuring dry ingredients: Scoop up dry ingredients in your measuring cup, or spoon them lightly into the cup. Level off with a knife or other straight edge. Use this scoop-and-sweep method with your measuring spoons as well.

measuring liquids: Use a glass measuring cup with a spout for measuring liquids. Pour the liquid into the cup and check the measure at eye level. Liquids measured in measuring spoons should fill the spoon but not overflow.

preparing baking pans: For cakes, muffins, and cupcakes: Rub the inner surface of a baking dish with butter or vegetable fat. Then add a tablespoon or so of flour and swirl it around in the pan to coat all the surfaces. Dump out any extra flour. For breads, cookies, or biscuits: Just grease the inside of the pan or the surface of the baking sheet. This should ensure that your cakes, breads, and cookies will not stick to the pan.

separating eggs: Have two bowls ready, one for the white and one for the yolk. Gently crack the egg close to the middle against the edge of a bowl, or by tapping it with a knife. Carefully pull apart the shell with your thumbs and finger- tips. Tip one half of the shell to catch the yolk and let the egg white slip into a bowl. Pass the egg yolk from shell to shell until all the white has run into the bowl, then drop the egg yolk into a second bowl. Don't let any egg yolk mix with the whites. For egg whites to be beaten to their absolute peaks, they cannot be mixed with any fat. If you are separating several eggs, it is safer to let each white drop into a new bowl; that way if the yolk of one egg breaks, it won't ruin the whole bowl of whites.

1.

2.

3.

4.

5.

simmering: A simmering liquid is below the boiling point. Bubbles form slowly and collapse just below the surface.

whipping cream: You can whip cream with an electric mixer, an eggbeater, or a wire whisk. Cream whips faster when cold, so if you are beating cream by hand, it might help to place the bowl of cream over a bowl of ice cubes. Beat the cream at high speed until soft peaks form when you raise the beater straight up.

Equivalent Measures

pinch = less than $\frac{1}{4}$ teaspoon

dash = 2 or 3 drops

1 tablespoon = 3 teaspoons = $\frac{1}{2}$ ounce

1 ounce = 2 tablespoons

1 cup = 16 tablespoons = 8 ounces = $\frac{1}{2}$ pint (liquid)

1 pint = 2 cups = 16 ounces (liquid)

1 quart = 2 pints = 4 cups = 32 ounces

1 gallon = 4 quarts = 8 pints = 16 cups = 128 ounces

1 pound = 16 ounces

1 cup broth = 1 bouillon cube dissolved in 1 cup water

1 quarter-pound stick of butter = $\frac{1}{2}$ cup = 8 tablespoons

1 envelope of gelatin = 1 tablespoon

Science Glossary

acid: Any substance that can react with a base to form a salt. In water solutions an acid tastes sour, as in lemon juice or vinegar, but tasting is not a good method for testing for acids since many acids are dangerous. Sulfuric acid and nitric acid can burn the skin and eat away at metals. Citric acid in oranges and acetic acid in vinegar are harmless, and ascorbic acid (vitamin C) is needed by the body.

alchemist: A chemist who lived during the Middle Ages whose aim was to change other metals into gold.

alkali: Any soluble substance that can neutralize acids to form salts. Also called a base.

amino acids: Molecules made up of carbon, hydrogen, oxygen, nitrogen, and sometimes sulfur that link together into chains to form proteins. When protein is digested, it is broken down into its amino acids, and then the amino acids reconnect to make up the kind of protein needed by the digester.

atom: The smallest particle of an element that still has the chemical properties of that element. Atoms of one element can combine with atoms of one or more other elements to produce compounds.

bacteria: Microscopic one-celled organisms that have no chlorophyll. Bacteria are found almost everywhere on earth, including in and on the human body. Some bacteria are harmful and cause diseases, but others are beneficial, such as the bacteria that turn milk into cheese.

base: Any compound that can react with an acid to neutralize it and form a salt. Base solutions are bitter and can also conduct electricity. Baking soda when dissolved in water is a base. Also called alkali.

bromelain: An enzyme found in fresh pineapple that breaks down proteins.

buffer: A substance that can absorb acid or basic molecules and take them out of solution.

carbohydrate: A substance made up of carbon, hydrogen, and oxygen with two hydrogen atoms and one oxygen atom for every atom of carbon. Sugar and starch are both carbohydrates.

cell: The smallest unit of a living thing. Cells are made up of a substance called protoplasm surrounded by a thin membrane.

cell membrane: The outer skin of a cell.

cellulose: A carbohydrate contained in the cell walls of plants that helps to support their structure.

chemical reaction: Any change that alters the chemical properties of a substance, or that forms a new substance.

chlorophyll: The green pigment in plants that gives them the ability to make food for themselves through photosynthesis.

cholesterol: A white, waxy substance found in animal fat, blood, and nerve tissue. If too much cholesterol is present in the blood vessels that nourish your heart, it can cause heart disease.

clarify: To make clear or free from impurities.

coagulation: The process by which a liquid becomes a soft semisolid. Coagulation is one way a protein is denatured.

coalesce: To grow together; to merge.

collagen: A solid protein that will not dissolve in water. Collagen is found in cartilage, tendons, ligaments, and bones.

colloid: A homogeneous mixture made up of two phases, the solvent and the solute, in which the particles of the solute are larger than single molecules but are small enough to remain suspended in the mixture permanently. A colloid is between a solution and a suspension.

compound: A pure substance made up of fixed amounts of two or more different elements. A compound differs from a mixture because the substances forming the compound lose their individual characteristics, and the compound takes on its own, often quite different, characteristics.

continuous: Going on or extending without a break. Describes the solvent phase of a solution or suspension, in which all the particles of the solvent are in contact with each other.

control: The part of an experiment that is used to check or compare results.

crystal: A solid bit of pure matter in which the atoms or molecules are arranged in a definite pattern so that the solid has a regular geometric shape with many sides or faces. Examples are salt and sugar.

decant: To pour off gently, leaving the sediment behind. Decanting is one method used to separate two parts of a suspension.

denature: To change the nature of a protein by adding heat, acid, base, etc., so that the original properties are greatly changed or eliminated.

density: A measure of the mass of an object in proportion to its volume. For example, a block of lead will weigh much more than an equal-sized block of wood. That means that lead is denser than wood.

diffusion: An intermingling of the molecules of liquids or gases. The process by which solute particles move through a solvent to form a solution.

discontinuous: Broken up by interruptions or gaps. Describes the solute phase of a solution or suspension in which the particles are not in contact with each other, but are separated by the solvent.

electromagnetic radiation: Waves of energy that radiate through space, including light waves, radio waves, X rays, and microwaves.

element: The simplest form of pure matter. There are ninety-two naturally occuring elements on the earth and eleven man-made elements.

emulsifying agent: A substance that will keep two immiscible liquids from separating, creating an emulsion.

emulsion: A suspension of two immiscible liquids that does not separate on standing.

enzyme: A complex protein found in living things that controls chemical reactions without being changed itself.

fermentation: A chemical change in sugars brought about by the enzymes of living organisms such as yeast. The transformation of grape juice to wine is a good example.

flocculation: The process of drawing impurities out of a substance by collecting them in bunches.

fructose: A simple sugar found in fruits.

gelatin: A jellylike, soluble protein derived from collagen by heating it with water. When gelatin cools, it forms a clear solid.

gelatinization: The process by which a substance swells when it is heated with water.

glucose: A simple sugar found in fruits, green plants, and blood.

gluten: A mixture of proteins found in wheat and other grains. Gluten gives dough a tough, elastic quality.

homogeneous: Composed of similar or identical parts. In the study of fluids, describes a solution or a colloid in which the solute is evenly mixed into the solvent.

hygroscopic: Describes a substance that absorbs moisture from the air.

immiscible: Describes a liquid that cannot be mixed or blended with another liquid. An immiscible liquid will not form a solution.

indicator: A substance that changes its color or some other property when combined with a solution in which an acid or base is present. For example, litmus paper is an indicator that turns blue when dipped in a base, and pink when dipped in acid.

lactic acid: A waste product of bacteria that feed off lactose.

lactose: A simple sugar found in milk.

magnetron: A device that uses a magnet to make electrons move rapidly in a circular path. Found in microwave ovens.

matter: Anything that has weight and takes up space. Matter can usually be classified as a solid, a liquid, or a gas and is made up of atoms.

microbe: A microscopic living thing such as a bacterium. Microbes are often associated with disease or with fermentation.

microwave: A type of energy that causes the water molecules in a substance to move.

molecule: The smallest particle of a substance that can exist and still retain the characteristics of the substance. The molecule of an element consists of one atom or two or more similar atoms, while the molecule of a compound consists of two or more different atoms.

optically active: Describes a substance that has the ability to rotate polarized light.

optics: The science of the nature and properties of light and vision.

osmosis: The movement of molecules of a solvent through a membrane that separates two solutions. The process by which water is absorbed into roots.

oxidation: The chemical reaction of a substance with oxygen.

pasteurization: A method of killing harmful microbes in dairy products, wine, and beer by heating them to denature the protein in the microbes.

photosynthesis: The process by which green plants make sugar from water and air in the presence of chlorophyll, using light energy.

pigment: A natural substance that gives color to the tissues of plants or animals.

polarized light: Light with light rays all vibrating in the same direction. Normal light contains rays vibrating in all directions.

polarizer: A lens, say of a pair of sunglasses, that filters light so that when ordinary light passes through, only light that is traveling in a single direction emerges from the lens.

precipitate: Solid particles that form in a liquid.

protein: A complex compound made up of amino acids. Proteins are found in all animal or plant matter and are essential to the diet of animals.

protoplasm: The living material of all cells.

puree: A suspension of food particles in a liquid: for example, pea soup or tomato sauce.

rennin: An enzyme, found in the stomachs of mammals, which will denature milk protein. This enzyme is commercially distributed under the name **rennet**.

saturated solution: A solution that has absorbed as much of a solute as possible at a given temperature.

serial dilution: A systematic way of varying the amount of water in a solution.

simple sugar: A sugar that contains only 5 or 6 carbon atoms per molecule.

sol: The liquid stage of a colloid, such as gelatin, dissolved in water. When cooled, it sets into the gel form.

solute: The discontinuous phase of a solution.

solution: A homogeneous mixture with two phases, the solvent and the solute, in which the particles of the solute are the size of single molecules and disperse into the solvent permanently so that the mixture remains homogeneous or evenly mixed.

solvent: A substance that dissolves another substance. The continuous phase of a solution.

starch: A complex carbohydrate found in potatoes, rice, corn, wheat, and other food. A starch molecule is made of long chains of simple sugar molecules.

substrate: The material a microbe uses for food.

sucrose: Table sugar. Sucrose is a two-molecule chain with one molecule of glucose and one molecule of fructose.

supersaturated solution: A clear solution that contains more solute than would normally dissolve at a certain temperature.

suspension: A mixture with two phases, the solvent and the solute, in which the particles of the solute are made up of countless molecules and combine temporarily in a solvent when stirred, but do not dissolve. The particles will eventually separate from the solvent and either sink or float, depending on their relative density.

Tyndall effect: A phenomenon in which particles of a certain size reflect light. You can see the Tyndall effect in a beam of sunlight in a dusty room. Dust particles are big enough to reflect light, while air molecules are too small.

xylem: A stiff, long strand found in plants such as celery, that carries water from the roots of the plant to the leaves.

Index

Page numbers in *italics* refer to illustrations.